COMPLE ASCENS
INDEX

By

Light Technology Research

THE EASY-TO-READ ENCYCLOPEDIA
of the SPIRITUAL PATH
✦ Volume XIV — Index ✦

Light Technology Publishing

Cover design by
Fay Richards

ISBN 1-891824-30-9

Published by
Light Technology Publishing
P.O. Box 3540
Flagstaff, AZ 86003
(800) 450-0985

Printed by
Sedona Color Graphics
2020 Contractors Road
Sedona, AZ 86336

THE ENCYCLOPEDIA OF THE SPIRITUAL PATH

DR. JOSHUA DAVID STONE

Dr. Stone has a Ph.D. in Transpersonal Psychology and is a licensed marriage, family and child counselor in Los Angeles, California. On a spiritual level, he anchors the Melchizedek Synthesis Light Academy & Ashram.

The Encyclopedia of the Spiritual Path consists of thirteen books and an index in this ongoing series on the subject of **ascension, self-realization** and **a further deepening of the ascended-master teachings.**

These books collectively explore the **deepest levels** and understanding of ascension through the personal, planetary and cosmic levels, offering the reader tools to work with that span the spectrum of all of the bodies and ultimately bring them into the subtle realms of cosmic ascension.

These tools are practical gems for the **purification, healing, cleansing, acceleration** and **ascension process** that covers the individual incarnated soul and extends into the vast monadic and cosmic realms.

Volumes in the series
The Easy-to-Read Encyclopedia of the Spiritual Path
by Joshua David Stone, Ph.D.
published by Light Technology

1 THE COMPLETE ASCENSION MANUAL
How to Achieve Ascension in This Lifetime

2 SOUL PSYCHOLOGY
Keys to Ascension

3 BEYOND ASCENSION
How to Complete the Seven Levels of Initiation

4 HIDDEN MYSTERIES
ETs, Ancient Mystery Schools and Ascension

5 THE ASCENDED MASTERS LIGHT THE WAY
Beacons of Ascension

6 COSMIC ASCENSION
Your Cosmic Map Home

7 A BEGINNER'S GUIDE TO THE PATH OF ASCENSION

8 GOLDEN KEYS TO ASCENSION AND HEALING
Revelations of Sai Baba and the Ascended Masters

9 MANUAL FOR PLANETARY LEADERSHIP

10 YOUR ASCENSION MISSION
Embracing Your Puzzle Piece

11 REVELATIONS OF A MELCHIZEDEK INITIATE

12 HOW TO TEACH ASCENSION CLASSES

13 ASCENSION AND ROMANTIC RELATIONSHIPS

14 COMPLETE ASCENSION INDEX
Index to Dr. Joshua Stone's Ascension Series

Editor's Note

In the index listings, the volume number of the book in the series is denoted by uppercase Roman numerals. Boldface entries indicate a chart, graph or illustration on that page.

A

Aaron (brother of Moses), I:228

abduction, IV:6–7, 9, 73–74, 78, 97, VII:134–36. *See also* extraterrestrials: negative extraterrestrials
 ~ and crossbred pregnancies, IV:7, 73–75, 97–98
 ~ and genetic experimentation, IV:7, 73–74, 97

Abhedananda, Swami, I:174

abortion, IX:126, 137–38, XIII:77–78. *See also* death, physical; miscarriage
 ~ and Christianity, IV:274
 ~ late-term, XIII:78–79
 ~ and the soul, IX:96, XIII:77–78

Abraham (prophet), I:228, IV:277–81, 286, 288, V:156
 ~ as an incarnation of El Morya, I:171, 237, IV:277, 287,
  V:175, VI:148
 ~ and Jesus, I:171
 ~ and Judaism, IV:287
 ~ and the Kabbalistic tree of life, IV:297
 ~ and Melchizedek (of Salem), I:171, 227, 230, 235

abstinence. *See* celibacy

abundance, III:87, 165, IV:207, V:115, VI:244, VIII:14, 18, 77,
81–85, 105, X:96, 216–19
 ~ and Atlantis, X:216
 ~ fear of, X:216–17
 ~ lack of, X:218

abuse, VII:154–55, XIII:29, 159
 ~ child, IX:128, 149–50, XII:59–60, XIII:43
 ~ emotional, XIII:22, 24–25
 ~ physical, X:134, XIII:22, 25, 94
 ~ psychic, XIII:22, 94
 ~ spousal, IX:149–50, XII:59–60

Abyssinia, IV:173

acupuncture, IX:56, X:69, 89, 243. *See also* healing
 ~ etheric, III:49, VIII:32

Adama (ascended master), XI:28

Adam and Eve, I:2–3, X:215. *See also* Garden of Eden
~ Adam as an incarnation of Jesus, I:169, IV:284, VI:147
Adamic race (humans), IV:51, 54
Adam Kadmon (body type), I:8, III:223, IV:2, 37, 55, 102, VII:146, X:205
~ higher, III:218, 225, VI:25–26, VIII:59, XI:154, 195
adepts, **I:199,** I:200, **IV:130.** *See also* initiation: fifth
adi plane, **I:184**
adi plane, cosmic, **I:184**
Adonai (God), IV:278
Adonis, I:179–81, 208, 212, **VI:111**
adultery, IX:126–27, XIII:24, 29, 94, 96, 117–23, 133, 143–44, 149, 172
~ affirmations for stopping, XIII:120–21
~ in Atlantis, I:9
~ and communication, XIII:118–20
advetta, X:76
Aesculapius (temple of), V:173
The Affirmation of the Disciple, XII:5, 8–9, 77, 87, 91. *See also* prayers
affirmations, I:266, 268, 271, IV:162, 205, 262, 317–18, V:25, VII:30, 43, 49, 51, 105, VIII:70–73, 77, 81–84, 92, 104–5, 111, 119, IX:51, X:49, XIII:73–75, 146. *See also* prayers; visualization
~ and activating the chakras, III:19
~ for ascension, III:215–16
~ of Baba Muktananda, V:90–91
~ and building the light quotient, III:24
~ and core fear matrix removal, III:73
~ for family healing, VII:155–56
~ for healing, VI:117, IX:83
~ I Am affirmations, IV:318–19, XII:111–12
~ language of, VIII:70
~ of the Mahatma energy, I:216
~ for self-integration, VII:159–62
~ for stopping adultery, XIII:120–21
~ and world service, VIII:20
affirmative action, IX:45, 251–52
Africa, III:131, IV:60, VI:185, XI:207
~ blocked grid point in, IV:61
~ entrance to the inner Earth in, IV:25
~ underground ascension seat in, I:279, III:30
African-Americans, IX:241
~ and AIDS, IV:8, XIII:131
~ and the educational system, IX:116

~ and the judicial system, IX:156, 158–59, 161

Africa, West
     ~ and the "black root race," I:3

Agam Purusha (ruler of the Agam Lok dimension), **IV:196**

Agartha, IV:19–28. *See also* hollow Earth
     ~ entrances to, IV:20–23, 25
     ~ landscape of, IV:20–21, 23, 27
     ~ population of, IV:22–23, 25–26
     ~ scientific evidence of, IV:20
     ~ technology of, IV:22–23, 26
     ~ and underground tunnels, IV:23–26

Agartha Network, IV:26

Agastyar, I:159–60

Agni (Hindu god of fire), IV:219, V:11

Aha! The Realization Book, IV:205–6. *See also* McClure, Janet

ahimsa (nonviolence), V:15, 17. *See also* Gandhi, Mahatma; harmlessness; nonviolence

Ahriman (the devil), V:152–54

Ahura Mazda, V:151–54

AIDS, IV:8–9, 89, IX:87, 117, XIII:129–32
     ~ and AZT, IV:9, IX:87
     ~ cure for, I:243, IV:9
     ~ as germ-warfare experiment, IV:8–9, IX:163
     ~ history of, IV:8

aikido, VI:50

air spirits, **IV:135**. *See also* devas; elementals: sylphs (nature spirits of air); nature spirits

aka cords, IV:160–62, 164–65, VI:170. *See also* antakarana (rainbow bridge); Huna teachings

Akashic Records, I:188, III:201, IV:31, 167, 179, 291, IX:10

Akhenaton, III:56, V:133–34. *See also* Egypt
     ~ as an incarnation of Zoroaster, V:133–34
     ~ and the Ra, IV:93

akousmatikoi. *See* Pythagorean Mystery School

Alabram, IV:95. *See also* extraterrestrials

Alakh Purusha (ruler of the Alakh Lok dimension), **IV:196**

Alameda, California, V:37

Alaya Purusha (ruler of the Alaya Lok dimension), **IV:196**

alchemy, IV:188, V:123, 126–27, 241, VIII:79, X:240–43

alcohol, IV:3, V:170
     ~ and Baha'i, IV:328
     ~ and disease, IX:59
     ~ and Islam, V:158

alcoholics, I:93, 98, IV:30

Aleutian Islands, IV:75

Alexandre, Raney, IX:11

Al-Ghazzali, Abu-Hamid Mohammed, V:160

Alhim, III:221

Alice in Wonderland, IV:131

aliens. *See* extraterrestrials

Aliens Among Us, IV:70, 81. *See also* Montgomery, Ruth

Allah, V:155–61, 166, VII:148
~ and Sufism, IV:323–24

Allah consciousness, IX:53

Allah Gobi (Manu), I:189, **I:199, III:238, VI:3, 112,** VII:19, IX:9
~ and the first ray, I:189, 201, X:27
~ and Wesak, VI:151, XII:78

All That Is, I:220, VII:31, 101, VIII:ix, XIII:57

Alpha Centauri, IV:83

Alpha Centaurians, IV:83. *See also* extraterrestrials

Alps, the. *See* Swiss Alps

Altai-Himalaya, Heart of Asia and Himalaya, I:174. *See also* Roerich, Nicholas

Altair, IV:38–39, 99

Alzheimer's disease, IX:60. *See also* disease

Amaterasu-omi Kami (Shinto sun god), IV:325

Amazon jungle, IV:91

Amenhotep, III:56

America, **I:5, VI:78**
~ and the "red root race," I:3

American Health, IV:112

American Medical Association (AMA)
~ and psychotronics, IV:13

American Revolution, I:244. *See also* war

Amethyst (archangel), **I:199,** III:199, X:44
~ and the seventh ray, **I:204, IV:124, VII:115,** X:95

Amilius, the Light, I:1
~ as an incarnation of Jesus, I:2–3, 169, VI:147

Amitabha Buddha, V:100, **V:101**

Amos (prophet), IV:285, 288

amrita (divine nectar), III:55

Amritanandamayi Ma (Ammachi), VIII:166

amulets, VIII:147

ananda (absolute bliss), V:20

Anandamayi Ma (Joy-Permeated Mother), V:47–49
    ~ quotations from, V:52–53
    ~ teachings of, V:50–52
Anandamayi Ma, the Mother Bliss Incarnate, V:52
Ancient of Days, I:255, III:228
    ~ and the first ray, **VI:179**
    ~ and the keys of Enoch, IV:314
The Ancient Wisdom: An Outline of Theosophical Teachings, IX:264.
    See also Besant, Annie
Andes Mountains, XI:207
    ~ and the "brown root race," I:3
Andraes, Valentine, V:240, 243
Andrew (disciple of Jesus), IV:288
androids, IV:36
Andromeda, IV:37, 87, 89, 95
Andromeda Council, IV:39
Andromedans, IV:89–90. *See also* extraterrestrials
angelic kingdom, III:153, IV:110, 120–21, **IV:130,** IV:287, VI:6,
    VII:110, 115, 120, VIII:129–30, IX:115, 133, 240, X:6, 97, 235,
    XIII:69. *See also* angels; archangels; cherubim (heavenly counsel-
    ors); devas; elohim; guardian angels; sanobim; seraphim (heavenly
    counselors)
    ~ and the arts, III:148, **IV:128,** IX:52, X:24, 95
    ~ and color, IV:207
    ~ and Commander Ashtar, IV:56
    ~ divine mission of, X:94–95
    ~ and elementals, IV:135
    ~ and the Essenes, IV:293–95
    ~ evolution of, I:191, III:181, IV:121–23, **IV:130,** IV:133,
        VII:32, 65, 83, 109, 118, 120–21, X:23, 34, 96–97
    ~ hierarchy of, IV:119, 121–23, **IV:123,** IV:124–28, 130,
        VII:110–11, 114, 117–18, 122, XII:107
    ~ incarnation of, IV:122–23
    ~ and the Kabbalistic tree of life, **IV:303**–5
    ~ and music, III:148
    ~ and the rays, I:195, X:35, 37, 44
    ~ and Sanat Kumara, I:182
    ~ and Solara, I:233
    ~ and sound, IX:260
    ~ telepathic rapport with, XIII:102
    ~ three spheres of, IV:123
    ~ three waves of angelic contact, IV:122
angel of the presence, I:57–58, 66
    ~ as a remedy for the dweller on the threshold, **I:58**
angels, I:215, 226, III:199, IV:119–20, 123, **IV:123, 128,** IV:140,

VII:20, 83–84, 109–11, 113–14, 116–19, VIII:124, 129–30, X:35, 42, 55, 97, 117, XI:26, 32. *See also* angelic kingdom; archangels; devas; elohim; guardian angels
~ angels of birth and death, IV:124
~ of art, IV:123, **IV:128,** VIII:129, X:37
~ ascension angels, III:199, 225, VIII:40, 129
~ of beauty, **IV:128,** VII:117
~ of building, I:189, **IV:128,** X:97
~ and building the light quotient, III:25, 31
~ of healing, IV:123, VI:45, 118–20, 231, 237, VII:82, 114–15, 117–18, 120, VIII:32, 129, IX:35, 61, X:95, 141, XII:12, 60, 124, XIII:173
~ initiations of, VII:109
~ of joy, **IV:128**
~ and the Kabbalistic tree of life, **IV:304**–5
~ of leadership, VIII:129
~ of music, IV:123, **IV:128,** VIII:129
~ of nature, IV:123, **IV:128**
~ and the Path the Solar Logos Himself Is On, III:181
~ platinum angels, XI:255
~ of poetry, VIII:129
~ progress angels, IV:126
~ recording angels, I:188, V:160, VII:65
~ and Wesak, X:152
anger, I:124, IV:225, V:73, 75–76, 102, 110, VI:101, VIII:33, X:237, XIII:137. *See also* emotions: negative
~ and the death penalty, IX:98
~ and negative elementals, IV:138
~ in relationships, XIII:22–23, 29, 95, 170
~ transforming (positive anger), V:253–54, VIII:22, IX:2, X:134, XIII:137
Angra Mainyu (Lie Demon), V:151
animal kingdom, I:105, **I:199,** III:119, **III:238,** IV:119, 122, **IV:130,** IV:147–52, **VI:3,** X:42, 97, 214, 235, 239, XII:132, XIII:69
~ clearing implants and negative elementals from, VIII:34
~ cruelty toward, VI:178, IX:110, 126, 146–47
~ and devas, IV:131, 139–40
~ domesticated, VII:124–27
~ as emotional buffers for humans, IV:148, VII:124–25, XIII:69–70
~ emotions of, VII:124–25, 127, XIII:69
~ evolution of, I:101, 186, IV:147–48, 150, V:111, VII:111, 124–27, X:213, XIII:69–70
~ and the fur trade, IX:167, 273
~ human service to, I:2–3, 270, IV:140, 151, X:212–13, 244
~ and hunting, IX:99, 102, 124–25

~ in the inner Earth, IV:20–21, 27
~ instincts of, **I:67**
~ meditations for, XII:68–69
~ mutilation of, I:7, IV:6, 74–75
~ and Native Americans, IV:151, VII:150, IX:99, 167, XIII:70
~ psychology of, VII:126–27
~ sacrifice of, V:16, 49, 163, 177
~ and scientific research, IX:61
~ and the seventh ray, VI:186
~ and telepathy, IX:125, X:239
~ wild animals, VII:123–24
~ wisdom of, VIII:94–95

Animi Purusha (ruler of the Animi Lok dimension), **IV:196**

Anka, Darryl, IV:103

ankhs, III:121, IV:169, XI:31
~ and initiation, IV:185–90

The Annals of Spring and Autumn, Ch'um Ch'iu, V:119. *See also* Confucius

Annu, IV:23, 25, 169. *See also* Agartha; Anunnaki; hollow Earth

Anointed Christ Overself body, III:219, VI:25, 51, 90, 138–39, 206, VIII:51, XI:151, 154, 194–95
~ anchoring of, III:218, 220, **VI:62,** VIII:59, XI:266, 268

antakarana (rainbow bridge), I:25, 54, 77, 110, 113, 288, III:9, 19, IV:162, VI:170, VIII:44, X:215. *See also* aka cords
~ and ascension, I:44–45, 48–49, 51
~ building of, I:43–51, 53, 56, 212, 271, III:47–48, 91, 174–75, VI:57, VIII:39, XII:100
~ contraction of, VI:59
~ cosmic, III:48, 91–93, 174–75
~ group, X:225
~ invocation for, III:48, 92
~ meditations for, I:43, 49–50
~ spiritual impressions from, I:113, VI:188, VII:31
~ widening and clearing of, I:285, III:47–48, 91–92, VI:57–58, 174, VIII:39–40

Antares, IV:87

antichrist, the, I:241, IX:99–100

Anunnaki, IV:23, 169, 171. *See also* Agartha; Annu; hollow Earth; Sirius

apartheid, III:141, XI:116. *See also* South Africa

Apex (planet), IV:97. *See also* Zeta Reticulum

Apollonius of Tyana, I:170, IV:198, V:173–77
~ as an incarnation of Jesus, I:169, IV:198, V:142, 173–75, VI:147
~ initiations of, V:173, 175

Apostles' Creed, V:184. *See also* prayers

apports, IV:164–65

Aquarian Age, I:139, 240, IV:54, 192, 281, VI:181, VIII:127, IX:114, 132, 143, 169, 274, X:68, 80, 164, 217, 225, 227, 232–33, 246, XIII:86
> ~ and Ashtanga yoga, IV:257
> ~ and group consciousness, IX:221, 240, 257, X:31
> ~ healers of, X:243
> ~ and mass ascension, VI:6, 122, IX:133
> ~ and the seventh ray, X:25, 83, 120, 228
> ~ and the sixth ray, I:195, VI:180, X:40

The Aquarian Conspiracy: Personal and Social Transformation in the 1980's, IX:131

The Aquarian Gospel of Jesus the Christ, I:169, 173, IV:184, VIII:134. *See also* Levi

Aquarius. *See also* astrology
> ~ and color healing, **IV:212**

Araaraat, IV:171, 173–74

Ararat, Mount, IV:283

Arart, IV:171

archangels, **I:199,** I:203–4, 233, IV:121–23, **IV:123,** IV:124, **IV:124,** VI:6, **VI:111,** VI:113, VII:84, 110, 114–16, 120, VIII:129, IX:115, 133, X:55, 97, 212, XI:54, XIII:55, 65. *See also* angelic kingdom; angels; guardian angels; individual archangels
> ~ ashrams of, VIII:127
> ~ divine mission of, VII:109, 114–15, X:94–95
> ~ and the Kabbalistic tree of life, IV:124, **IV:303**–4
> ~ and the rays, I:204, **IV:121, 123**–24, **VII:115,** VII:117, X:45, 94–95
> ~ seven mighty, **I:199,** I:204, III:198–99, 243
> ~ telepathic rapport with, XIII:102
> ~ twelve mighty, III:190, 222, 232, **III:238,** III:250, **VI:3**
> ~ and Wesak, X:152

"archetypal race." *See* root races: Polarian ("archetypal race")

archetypes, I:67–68, **I:69,** VI:79, 83, 86, VIII:161–62, IX:6, 185–86
> ~ angry-victim, IX:182
> ~ attunement to, VIII:107
> ~ Buddha, VI:239
> ~ Buddha/Christ, VI:194–95, VIII:107
> ~ and channeling, VI:228
> ~ Christ, VI:239, IX:9
> ~ Christ/Buddha/Melchizedek, VI:195, 240
> ~ clearing of, VI:87, 125, 239, XII:121
> ~ destroyer, **I:69**

~ an exercise in psychological archetypal personages, XI:260–62

~ fool, I:68, **I:69**

~ high priest/priestess, IX:6

~ inner-child, IX:6 (*See also* inner child)

~ innocent, **I:69**

~ integration of, I:68, VI:57, 59–60, 67, 87, VIII:107, IX:4

~ king or queen lineage, IX:182

~ magician, **I:69**

~ martyr, I:68, **I:69**

~ Melchizedek, VI:239

~ negative, VI:101

~ patriarch, **I:69**

~ of romantic relationships, XIII:10–19

~ ruler, **I:69**

~ salesperson, VIII:172, IX:23–24

~ seducer, **I:69**

~ seeker, **I:69**

~ servant, **I:69**

~ Spiritual Warrior, VI:141, 223, VIII:20–22, IX:1–2, 19, 100, X:70

~ top-dog/underdog syndrome, VIII:16, X:48, 113–14, 173, 245

~ warrior, **I:69**

~ wisdom, VI:141

~ wise one, I:68, **I:69,** IX:16, 186, 205

Arctic Circle

~ blocked grid point in, IV:61

Arcturians, III:15–17, **III:238,** III:243, IV:63–68, 85, **VI:3,** VI:52, 77, 224, 230, 240, VII:131–32, VIII:147, 180, IX:105, XI:131, XII:109. *See also* extraterrestrials; Lord of Arcturus

~ advanced light technologies of, III:26, 37, 75–84, 122, IV:66–67, VI:119, 213–14, 231, VII:132, VIII:28–30, 34, XI:28, 90, XII:109, XIII:174

~ appearance of, III:78, IV:64

~ ascension of, XI:142–43

~ ascension seat of, III:32, 34, VI:32, 115

~ and the Atomic Accelerator, VI:37, XI:224

~ bases of, IV:66, VII:132

~ and building the light quotient, III:25, 27–28, 30, 37, 43, 76–77, 82–83, 85–86, 108, VI:113, 115, 122, 195, 213, 231, 235, VII:132, VIII:30

~ and cancer, VI:125–26

~ and the cosmic computer, III:205

~ electronic plating system of, III:80–81, 83, VI:213, VIII:30, XI:93

~ Golden Cylinder of, VI:213, 231, 241, VIII:28–29, 34, IX:58, XII:12, 66–67, XIII:174

~ grid integration technology of, III:80
~ and healing, III:38, 79, 98, VI:45, 118–21, 231, VII:132, VIII:28–29, IX:58, 83–84
~ heart operation of, XI:236–37
~ and the Information Exchange Chamber, III:79
~ joy machine of, III:78–79, 204, VI:213, VIII:30
~ light information packets from, III:83
~ and the Light Synthesis Chamber, I:279, III:30, 32, 43, 77–78, VI:212–13, 231, VIII:41, XI:93, 236–39
~ Mechanism Chamber of, I:283, III:79, 86, 97, VI:119, 213, VIII:29
~ and the prana wind-clearing technology, III:79–80, VI:120, 212–14, 231, VIII:29, XI:50–51, 53, 67
~ protection by, III:122, VII:132
~ society of, IV:64–65, IX:52
~ spacecraft of, III:25, 27, 43, IV:64, 66–67, VI:212–13, 231, VII:132, VIII:28, XI:28, 205, 224, 239
~ teachings of, IV:63–64, VII:132
~ telepathic rapport with, VII:132, XIII:102
~ and Wesak, X:153

Arcturus, I:215, 242, III:75, 82, 119, 175, **IV:33,** IV:58, 63–68, 314, VI:71, 77, 80, XI:28

arhat, I:25, **I:199,** I:200, V:97, 108. *See also* initiation: fourth (crucifixion)

Arianni, IV:27. *See also* Agartha

Aries. *See also* astrology
~ and color healing, **IV:212**
~ and the first ray, I:119, **XI:176**
~ full moon in, VI:149, VIII:139
~ and Mars, **XI:176**

Aries, Age of, IV:280

Aristaeus, V:145

Aristotle, V:148

Arjuna, I:137, IV:219, 230, V:71, VIII:21, IX:99, 116, X:51. *See also Bhagavad-Gita;* Hinduism; Krishna (avatar)
~ as an incarnation of Gautama Buddha, IV:223–24, VI:148, 154, XI:225, XII:80
~ and Kriya yoga, I:160

Ark of the Covenant, I:37, 245, III:56, IV:168–69, 171, XI:31

arks of the covenant, I:38, 245–46, IV:23, 169–70, 189, XI:31

Armageddon, IV:275, VII:86

Armstrong, Neil, IV:8

Arnobius, V:176

aromatherapy, VIII:80, IX:83. *See also* healing

Arthur, King, V:239

arts, the, I:3, VII:96–98, VIII:98, IX:51–52, X:57. *See also* dance;
film industry; music
> ~ and angels, III:148, **IV:128,** IX:52, X:24, 95
> ~ and channeling, III:127, VII:11, 79, VIII:105, IX:51–52
> ~ and dimensional shifting, III:148
> ~ and the fourth ray, X:18–19, 23–24, 35–37, 39, 56, 93
> ~ and healing, X:37
> ~ and the negative ego, X:37
> ~ and the seventh ray, VI:187
> ~ tools for handling for the lightworker, IX:34

Arundale, George, V:230

Aryan Age, III:55
> ~ and the antakarana, I:44
> ~ and the dweller on the threshold, I:66
> ~ and the rays, VI:182, 189–90

Asapha
> ~ as an incarnation of Jesus, I:169–70, VI:147

ascended masters, I:17–18, 22, 27, 30, 32, 35, 38–39, 45, 51, 100,
108, 198, **I:199,** I:200, 226, 265, 278, III:5, 57, 245, IV:31, 55,
64–65, 67, 259, 318, VI:61–62, 86, 107, 133, 140, 143, 149,
215–16, 219–20, 224, 227, 237, 244, VII:15–20, 22–23, 33–34,
50, 56, 90, 116, 145, VIII:93, 122–28, 134, IX:112–13, 133, 146,
176, 240, X:2, 9, 17, 76, 79–80, 107, 116, 120–21, 128, 136, 203,
209–11, 232, 234–36, 245, XI:15–17, 28–30, 44, 48, 68, 112, 269,
XII:10, 122, XIII:57, 137, 173. *See also* cosmic masters; galactic
masters; universal masters; individual masters
> ~ advanced abilities of, I:28, 33, 186, IV:69, 193, VI:11–12,
> 59, 61, 122–23, 134, 161, 208–9, VII:17, 35, 54, VIII:18, 51,
> 116, 129, IX:128–29, XI:12–13, 130, 187
> ~ anchoring the energies and lightbodies of, XI:139–40, 258
> ~ ashrams of, I:110–13, VIII:126–27, IX:178, 200
> ~ attunement to, X:75–76, 139–43
> ~ auras of, VI:170–71, VII:36, X:237
> ~ benediction from, VIII:187–92
> ~ bodies of, I:25, 32, III:193, VI:22, 93, VII:84, XI:99,
> XIII:67–68
> ~ and building the light quotient, III:25
> ~ communicating with, I:213, VI:113–15, 202–3, VII:32, 45,
> VIII:123–25, IX:177–78, X:7, 76, 238
> ~ cosmic, I:141, X:55, 159, 212, 235–36
> ~ cosmology of, **VI:111**–12, VI:113
> ~ divine mission of, I:144–45, X:27–46, 239
> ~ glamour of, IX:262–64
> ~ and healing, III:39, VI:118–20, VII:20, 82, VIII:31, IX:61

~ inner-plane, VI:108, 202, 233, VII:16, VIII:129, 131, vii, viii,
　　ix, IX:143, X:8, 179, 182, 188, 205, 212, 235–39, 244, XI:77
~ kindergarten masters, I:275–76, III:4, 32, VI:87, 220, VII:18,
　　33, XI:15–16, 72–73, 77–78, 132, 173
~ light quotient level of, VI:44
~ merging with, III:257–58, VII:24, VIII:122, X:117,
　　XIII:66–68, 101–3
~ personality of, X:207–8
~ on the physical plane, I:32–33, 78, 200, 275–76, III:197,
　　IV:314, VII:17, IX:132, X:28, 108–9, 118, 237, XI:15–16,
　　72, 76–78, 186
~ repeating the names of, I:259, VII:107
~ sensing the presence of, VII:83–84
~ sexual union with, XIII:67–68
~ and spiritual etiquette, X:235
~ teachings of, I:21–22, VII:7, 9, 148
~ telepathic rapport with, VII:16, 77, XIII:102–3
~ and Wesak, X:152–53, XI:174–75

The Ascending Times, IX:213

ascension, I:27–28, 30, 34, 64, 160, 197, 200, 212, 215, 277, 283,
　　III:3–5, 19, 40, 116, 118, 126, 132, 140, 142, 146, 167, 177, 197,
　　206, 237, **III:238,** III:239–40, 244–45, IV:69, 259, V:108, 127,
　　129, VI:2, **VI:3,** VI:7, 14, 36, 57, 60, 63, **VI:63,** VI:64–65, 85,
　　88, **VI:89,** VI:92, 99–100, 103, 107, 109–10, 113, 120–21, 123,
　　141, 161, 163, 193–94, 208, 232, VII:1, 4–6, 9, 11, 13, 16, 25,
　　32–34, 37, 86, 89–93, 119, 135, 137–40, 164, VIII:30, 44, 51, 92,
　　129, 133, IX:96–97, 117, 136, 188, 218, 266–67, X:1, 4, 13, 34,
　　52, 91, 93, 108, 118, 120, 133, 222, 245, XI:3, 15–17, 21, 40,
　　42–44, 143, 153, 160–62, 173, 186–87, 191, 232–33, XII:126,
　　132–33, XIII:11, 106. *See also* initiation: sixth (ascension)
~ affirmations for, III:215–16
~ and the antakarana, I:44–45, 48–49, 51
~ of Arcturians, XI:142–43
~ of Brian Grattan, V:133
~ and the chakras, I:30, 34, 38, III:7, 9, 14
~ and channeling, III:127
~ and competition, IX:267, XIII:31–33
~ core ascension group, XI:44–45
~ delayed, I:30
~ as *descension*, III:126, VI:58–59, VII:32, 89, 98–99, 141,
　　VIII:40, 154, IX:39, 112, X:119, 163, XIII:4, 6, 48
~ of Djwhal Khul, I:187, VI:6
~ and the dream state, XI:157–71
~ of Earth, III:12, 119, 196, 201, VI:77, 223, VII:16, IX:8–9,
　　133, X:221, XI:173
~ of El Morya, VI:6
~ and evolution, I:17, 31, 198

~ glamour of, VI:134, VIII:18, X:107–24, XII:129

~ and the Huna prayers, III:156

~ integrated, VI:249, VII:90–91, 141, X:2–8, 15–16, 155, 178, 222, XI:21, 35, 266–67, XII:124

~ of Jesus, I:25, III:10, VI:6

~ Kabbalistic techniques for, III:217–36, IV:300, 303

~ and karma, III:5, VI:92, 216, VII:11, XI:21, 44, 129, 248–49, 266

~ of Kuthumi, VI:6

~ light quotient for, I:32–33, 36, 277, III:6, 8, 24, 76, **III:238,** VI:3, **VI:3,** VI:216, XI:16, 43

~ mass, I:6, 29, 32–35, 146, 240, III:6, 14, 64, 131, 196, 249, 266, VI:6, 12–13, 29, 55, 122, 209, 222, 224, VII:18, VIII:92, 133–34, 181, IX:9, 114, 133, 201, 266, X:34, 69, 92, 155, 164, 182, 202, 225, 235, 245–46, XI:4, 16, 43, 49–50, 64, 76, 115–16, 142, 173, 175, 177, 214, 219, 269

~ meaning of, III:194–96

~ and meditation, I:39, III:204–5, VII:23–24, XI:25–34

~ misconceptions about, VI:61, 132–34, 214–23, VIII:128, XI:12–13

~ and the ninth and tenth rays, I:126

~ nonintegrated, XII:125

~ a personal experience of, XI:9–13, 63–84

~ preparation for, I:33–34, 38–39

~ psychology of, VII:39–56, 139

~ and romantic relationships, XIII:11, 49

~ of Saint Germain, V:239–40, VI:6

~ of Sanat Kumara, I:178

~ and service work, III:205, IX:199, 234, XI:186, 190–91

~ short path of, I:29, IV:303

~ and spiritual leadership, IX:178, 235–36

~ techniques for, I:28–29, 34, 36–40, 207, 213, 254, 263–74, 279–85, III:37–68, 94–95, 97–108, 120–33, 187–92, 198–201, 205–6, IV:303, VI:237–46, VIII:80–82, XI:25–40, 43–45, 66–67

~ of Venus, VI:77

~ of the Virgin Mary, I:175

~ of Vywamus, I:178

ascension-activation meditations, III:56, 59, 187–89, 202–4, 207–15, VI:194, VIII:99–100, 181, XI:25, 235. *See also* ascension meditation treatment; meditation

~ for the core fear matrix removal program, III:201–2

~ cosmic ascension activations in the Temple of God, XI:296–99

~ in the Golden Chamber of Melchizedek, XI:289–92, 302–5

~ Mount Shasta meditation, XI:180–82

~ personal growth meditations, XII:31–56

~ special ascension activation, XI:281–84
~ Spiritual Artery-Connection Activation, VI:135
~ the Ultimate Ascension Meditation, III:135–37, 255, XI:77
~ world service meditations, III:67–68, 129, XII:56–76

ascension buddy system, III:17, 40–41, 250, VI:21, VIII:105, 135, IX:186–88, XI:10, 220–22, 235, XIII:32, 67, 93, 105

ascension classes
~ class outlines for, XII:93–135
~ opening and closing your classes, XII:1–12, 15, 25, 27
~ structure of, XII:25–29

ascension column, I:284–85, III:9, 19, 47–48, 59, 92–93, 189, VI:57, VIII:39, 102, XII:2
~ clearing of, VI:58
~ contraction of, VI:59

ascension, cosmic, I:213, III:93, 237, 245, 253, VI:1–30, 42, 56, 80, 83–84, 87, 109, 117, 161, 194, 200–201, 207, 216, 232, 237, 242, 244–46, VII:35, VIII:42, 47, 116, 126, 129, 133, IX:136, 188, X:148, XI:17, 32, 186–87, 191–92, 214, 222, 233, 252, XII:106, 122, 131–32, XIII:55
~ of Melchizedek (Universal Logos), VI:9
~ techniques for, III:245–47, 249–50, 253–61, VI:115–17, 124–25, 127, 130, 135–36, 193–203, 210–14, 230–36, 244, VIII:40, 46

ascension, galactic, VI:2, 87, 161, IX:188, XI:17

ascension, group-monadic, VI:87

ascension healing module, I:284, III:45, 49

ascension lineage, III:131–33, VI:9, 135, VIII:102, 122, IX:192–93, X:7–8, 74–76, 107, 140–43, 151, XI:4–5

Ascension Manifestation Council, XI:61–62

ascension meditation treatment, I:37, 39, 274, 287–94, III:28, 64–66, XI:29, XII:45–52. *See also* ascension-activation meditations; meditation

ascension, monadic, **VI:62,** VI:63–65, XII:130

ascension, multiuniversal, VI:2, 161, IX:188, XI:17

ascension poetry, IX:52

ascension and resurrection flame, III:198, XII:2

ascension rosary, XI:206. *See also* New Age Rosary; prayers; Rosary

ascension seats, I:30, 36, 279–80, 282, III:19, 21, 25, 30–32, 34, 37, 43–44, 46–47, 56, 61–62, 85, 94, 107–8, 129, 147, 187, 189–91, 258, VI:31–34, 36–37, 113, 115, 231–32, 236, VIII:38, 41–42, 99, 179, 183, X:34, XI:27–28, 59–60, 77, 100, 199–200, 203, 231–34, 246, 253–55, 262, XII:11, 98, 123. *See also* individual masters and place names
~ advanced, VIII:65–66

~ African underground ascension seat, I:279, III:30
~ anchoring of, III:258, VI:37, VIII:102
~ Arcturian ascension seat, III:32, 34, VI:32, 115
~ Ashtar Command ascension seat, I:36, 279, III:25, 30, 32, 43, 189–90, VI:32, XI:27
~ Atomic Accelerator, I:279–80, III:43, 46–47, 94, VI:32, 37, VIII:42, XI:205, 224–25
~ Buddha's sacred garden ascension seat, III:191
~ El Morya's sacred glen ascension seat, III:191
~ the Father's ascension seat, VI:31, 35, XI:262
~ Galactic Core ascension seat, III:44, 147, 187, 258, VI:32, 43, 115, XI:100
~ Godhead ascension seat, VI:31, 34–35, VIII:65–66, XI:199, 203, 231–34, 246, 253–55
~ Golden Chamber of Melchizedek, I:279, 281, III:32, 44–46, 62–63, 85–86, 91, 128–29, 135, 148, 187, 198–99, 201, 255, 258–59, VI:31, 34, **VI:41**, VI:43, 54, 115, 124, 193, 195, 204, 235, VIII:41, 99, 102, 183, XI:74, 131, 199, XII:11
~ Great Central Sun ascension seat, VI:31, VIII:65
~ Great Pyramid ascension seat, I:279, VI:32, VIII:41
~ Great White Lodge ascension seat, VI:32–33, 115
~ and healing, VI:120
~ hollow Earth ascension seat, VI:32
~ Jupiter ascension seat, VI:36
~ Lenduce's ascension seat, VI:32
~ Luxor ascension seat, I:30, 279, III:25, 30, 32, 43, VI:32–33, X:34, XI:27, 29, 31
~ Mahatma's ascension seat, XI:199
~ Mars ascension seat, VI:36
~ Melchizedek's ascension seat in the center of the Earth, III:44
~ Mercury ascension seat, VI:36
~ merging of, III:135, 192
~ Metatron's ascension seat, VI:115
~ Archangel Michael's ascension seat, VI:115
~ Moon ascension seat, VI:36
~ the Mother's ascension seat, VI:31, 35, VIII:179, XI:262
~ Neptune ascension seat, VI:36
~ New Jerusalem ascension seat, III:131
~ the Pleiades ascension seat, VI:32
~ Pluto ascension seat, VI:36
~ Quan Yin's sacred garden ascension seat, III:191
~ Saint Germain's Lemurian ascension seat, III:30
~ Sananda's ascension seat, VI:32
~ Sanat Kumara's ascension seat, III:32, 44, 62
~ Saturn ascension seat, VI:36
~ Shamballa ascension seat, I:279, III:21, 30, 32, 44, 46, 85, 135, 187, VI:32, 43–44

~ Mount Shasta ascension seat, I:279, III:25, 32, 43–44, 94,
VI:32–33, VIII:41, XI:26–27
~ Solar Core ascension seat, III:32, 44, 258, VI:32, 43, 115,
XI:59
~ Source ascension seat, VI:35, 37
~ Telos ascension seat, I:279, III:25, 30, 32, 43, 47, VI:32,
XI:27–28
~ ten lost cosmic rays ascension seat, VI:115
~ Universal Core ascension seat, III:258
~ Uranus ascension seat, VI:36
~ Venus ascension seat, VI:32
ascension seats, cosmic, VI:31–35, XI:60
ascension seats, galactic, III:32, VI:32–33, 37, 45, VIII:102, XI:59
ascension seats, multiuniversal, VI:31, 34, 37, 42, 75, VIII:65, XI:59
~ of the multiuniverses of this cosmic day, XI:199–201, 203,
230–31
ascension seats, solar, VI:32, 37, VIII:102, XI:59
ascension seats, Source-level, XI:60
ascension seats, universal, III:32, VI:31, 34, 37, 45, VIII:102,
XI:59–60
ascension, solar, VI:2, 87, 117, 161, VIII:102, XI:17
ascension, solar-system, IX:188
ascension, ultimate monadic, VI:85–89, **VI:89,** VI:90
ascension, universal, VI:2, 87, 161, IX:188, XI:17
ascension walks, I:281–82, III:34, XI:67
asceticism, IV:222, V:15–16, 93
ashrams, I:110–13, III:119, 244, V:52, VI:35, 124, 144, 168, **VI:204,**
VI:236, VII:144, VIII:102, 126–27, IX:178–81, 192–93, 200, 220,
XI:70–71. *See also* individual ascended masters: ashrams of
~ cosmic, **VI:204**
~ and dimensions, **VI:204**
~ and discipleship, VI:168–71
~ inner-plane, VI:135, VII:143, VIII:127, IX:9–10, 115,
219–20, X:71, 202
~ multiuniversal-level, **VI:204,** VIII:127
Ashtar: A Tribute, IV:56, 61. *See also* Tuella
Ashtar Command, I:32, 215, 275, III:43, 84, IV:55–61, 67, 93–94,
112, VI:224, VII:131–32, 135, VIII:130, 180, IX:105, 142,
XI:205–6, XII:118. *See also* Commander Ashtar; extraterrestrials
~ ascension seat of, I:36, 279, III:25, 30, 32, 43, 189–90,
VI:32, XI:27
~ and the Atomic Accelerator, VI:37
~ and building the light quotient, III:28
~ and crystal technology, I:242

~ motherships of, III:25, 30, 189–90, IV:55, 57, 59, VI:32, XI:205
~ and negative extraterrestrials, IV:58
~ and Seattle, XI:205
~ telepathic rapport with, XIII:102
~ and Wesak, X:153

Ashtar (planet), IV:55. *See also* Ashtar Command; Commander Ashtar

Asia, East
~ and the "yellow root race," I:3

Asia Minor, **I:5**, I:230, **VI:78**

Ask Your Angels, IV:122

Assagioli, Robert, I:106, VIII:159

Association for the Integration of the Whole Person, VIII:159

Association of Worlds, IV:36–37, 107

Assyrian art, I:3

Astara mystery school, I:82, 166–67, 245, IV:192, VII:23, 148, VIII:164, IX:93, X:74. *See also* Chaney, Earlyne

astral body, I:53, 91, 97, 109, **III:238**, III:239, IV:199, V:129, 223, **VI:3**, VI:203, **VI:205**, VII:1–3, 21, 138, IX:55, 127, XI:150. *See also* emotional body; four-body system
~ anchoring of, VI:194, XI:154
~ and the antakarana, I:45
~ and the astral plane, VII:10
~ between lives, I:89–90, 93
~ clearing of, III:201, VI:45, 240
~ death of, I:75, 97, 180, XIII:62
~ and the etheric nervous system, III:21
~ and the fourth dimension, **VI:205**
~ glamour of, IX:75
~ and implants, IV:105
~ mastery of, I:23, 64, 197, III:1–2, VII:25, IX:4
~ and physical death, I:75, 81, 84–85
~ and the rays, I:117, VI:189
~ and the second initiation, I:23, 64, III:1, **VI:17**, VII:25–26
~ and the sleep state, VI:71
~ and the soul, I:108

astral body, cosmic, **III:238**, III:259, **VI:3, 24, 205**, VI:206, XI:155

astral energy, III:171

astral plane, I:16, 97, **I:184, 197**, III:139, 170, 172, IV:139, 186, 193, **IV:195**, IV:199, **IV:267, VI:8**, VI:56, 167, 181, 186, 207, VII:4, 8–10, 12, 62, 162, IX:114, X:200, XIII:61–62. *See also* emotional plane
~ between lives, I:84, 87–90, 92–93, 97–101
~ and the Cosmic Night, VI:67

~ and glamour, I:57, **I:58**
~ higher, I:87, 97, VII:10
~ incarnation of masters on, VII:16
~ and the Kabbalistic tree of life, **IV:307**
~ lower, I:87, 89, 101, IV:198, VII:8
~ mastery of, I:197, **III:139**
~ middle, I:87–88
~ and negative thought forms, VII:104
~ and physical death, I:75–77, 84
~ rift in, IX:159
~ and the second initiation, **III:4, 139, VI:17, XI:127**
~ sexual expression on, XIII:61–62
~ and the sixth ray, **I:132,** VI:180, 188
~ and the supersenses, **I:71**
~ universities on, VII:9

The Astral Plane, V:226. *See also* Leadbeater, C.W.

astral plane, cosmic, I:17, **I:184,** I:198, **I:199,** III:167, 171, 181, **III:238,** III:240, **VI:3, 8, 24,** VI:206
~ and the Path of Earth Service, III:169–70

astral projection, III:41

astral ray. *See also* rays, seven: configuration of
~ of humanity, **VI:184**

astral rebirth, V:46

astral travel, I:154, IV:165, 193–95, 199, V:223, XI:29. *See also* ascended masters: advanced abilities of; soul travel

astrology, I:68, 129, 133, 139, 145, 188, IV:287, V:19, 123, 127, VI:40, 79, 156, 187, VII:65, 156–57, VIII:61, 125, 161–62, 168, IX:4, 253, X:11, 15, 26. *See also* individual signs
~ and building the light quotient, III:29
~ and channeling, VI:228
~ of cities, VI:185
~ clearing of, VI:125, 241–42
~ and color, **XI:176**–77
~ and color healing, **IV:212**
~ cosmic, I:245, VI:79
~ and the Essene Brotherhood, IV:291
~ grand alignment, I:245
~ and Hinduism, IV:220–21
~ houses of, III:246, VI:242
~ integration of, VI:57, 59
~ and the Kabbalistic tree of life, **IV:302**
~ and Mantra yoga, IV:245
~ and meditation, I:283
~ and physical birth, XIII:71–72
~ and the planets, I:96–97, **XI:176**–77
~ and the rays, I:191, **XI:176**–77

~ and reincarnation, VI:70

~ and Zoroastrianism, V:154

astronomy, V:140

Ataien, IV:101–2. *See also* extraterrestrials

Athena, VIII:178

Atkisson, Alan, III:110–11

Atlantic Ocean, I:7

Atlantis, **I:5,** I:7, 134, 169, 214, 237, 241, IV:25–26, 38, 169,
    171–72, 175, 213, **VI:78,** X:216, 225. *See also* Earth, history of:
    Atlantean times; Poseidia; root races: Atlantean; souls: Atlantean
        ~ advanced technologies of, I:8, 244–45
        ~ and Agartha, IV:26
        ~ Alta (city), IV:172
        ~ and the Anunnaki and the Annu, IV:23, 169
        ~ and the consciousness cord, I:44
        ~ and Egypt, I:9, IV:167–68
        ~ and extraterrestrials, I:8–9, 231, IV:1, 168
        ~ and glamour, I:58, **I:59**
        ~ great crystal of, I:9–10, III:149, IV:1, 169, VI:127–28
        ~ and the Great Flood, I:9, IV:23, 25, 168–69, 283
        ~ and healing, I:242, IX:83
        ~ and illusion, I:63
        ~ and the Kantarians, IV:70
        ~ and the Law of One, I:8–9, IV:41, 167, 172, 283, VI:178
        ~ and the Order of Melchizedek, XI:1
        ~ and the rays, VI:178, 182, 189
        ~ records of, I:142, IV:170, X:226
        ~ and the "red root race," I:3
        ~ sinking of, I:9–10, IV:2, 23, 70, 167–68, 283, X:216–17
        ~ and the Sons of Belial, I:8–9, IV:23, 41, 59–60, 169, 172–73,
            VI:178

Atlanto, I:208–9, **VI:111**

Atma, I:155, IV:226, 300, V:112, VI:8, 159–60

Atman (self), IV:217, 219, 233, 235, V:12–13, 20–22, 48, 50–51, 60,
    66, 82, VII:6, VIII:190, 192, xiii. *See also* Eternal Self

atmic body, III:239, VI:203, **VI:205,** XI:150
        ~ anchoring of, VIII:59, XI:154
        ~ death of, I:97, 180
        ~ and the fifth initiation, IV:270, **VI:17**
        ~ and the fourth dimension, **VI:205**
        ~ and physical death, I:75, 84
        ~ and the sleep state, VI:71

atmic body, cosmic, **III:238,** III:259, **VI:3, 24, 205,** VI:206,
    XI:155

atmic plane, I:16, 25, **I:184, 197,** III:139, IV:269, **VI:8,** VI:207, VII:12–13, 31, XIII:64. *See also* spiritual plane
  ~ anchoring of, **III:139**
  ~ between lives, I:87–89, 92, 97
  ~ and the fifth initiation, **III:4, 139, VI:17, XI:127**
  ~ and the Kabbalistic tree of life, **IV:303, 307**
  ~ sexual expression on, XIII:64–65
  ~ and the supersenses, I:70, **I:71**
  ~ and the third ray, **I:132**
atmic plane, cosmic, I:17, **I:184,** I:198, **I:199,** III:167, 181, **III:238,** III:240, **VI:3, 8, 24,** VI:206
Atomic Accelerator, I:279–80, III:43, 46–47, 94, VI:32, 37, VIII:42, XI:205, 224–25. *See also* ascension seats
atomic body, III:245–46
atomic bombs. *See* nuclear weapons
Atomic Doorway, III:64
attachment, I:60, 89, 267–68, III:2, 103, IV:183, 225, 228, 235, V:22, 26, 31, 50, 61, 75, 96, 164, 168, 170, 250, VI:190, VIII:10, 25, 72, 85, 138, IX:5, X:208, XI:36, XIII:112, 136, 150–52, 156–58, 169. *See also* detachment
At the Feet of the Master, V:232. *See also* Krishnamurti
attunement, I:63, 197, 206, 213–14, 221, 224, III:241, IV:102, 256, 281, V:116, VI:58, 155, 170, 172, VII:60, 67, 69, VIII:44, 97, IX:34, 124, X:3, 49, 182, XII:10–11, 15, 19. *See also* merging
  ~ to archetypes, VIII:107
  ~ to ascended masters, X:75–76, 139–43
  ~ astral, I:58, VI:188
  ~ emotional, **I:5,** I:58, IV:240, **VI:78**
  ~ galactic, III:240
  ~ to the Galactic Core, I:207
  ~ to God, III:87, IV:143, VII:132, 136, X:20, 47–48, 80, 90, 105, 154, 179, 226, XIII:160
  ~ to the higher self, X:72
  ~ to the I Am Presence, X:16, 18
  ~ lack of, IV:3
  ~ mental, **I:5,** I:58, 63, **VI:78,** VI:188
  ~ to the monad, I:56, VI:4, X:72, 133
  ~ to the oversoul, X:133
  ~ to the personality, **I:5, VI:78**
  ~ physical, **I:5,** I:7, 58, 60, **VI:78**
  ~ to self, X:105
  ~ of the seven root races, I:4, **I:5,** I:58
  ~ and the sixth ray, VI:188
  ~ solar, III:240
  ~ to the soul, **I:5,** I:56, III:53, VI:4, **VI:78,** VI:172, X:70–72

~ to Source, I:234
~ spiritual, I:6, IX:275
~ universal, III:240

aumakua (higher self), XIII:89, 151. *See also* soul

"The Aura of Divinity" (video), I:150, VIII:xxvi

auras, I:22, 28, 53, 216, 251, 274, III:54, V:246, VI:170, 200, VII:3, 21, 23, 59, 88, 138, VIII:143, 147, X:7, 15, XI:129, 132, XIII:103
~ appearance of, XIII:7
~ of ascended masters, VI:170–71, VII:36, X:237
~ clearing of, I:53–54, III:34, VI:120, VII:112, VIII:34
~ and drugs, VIII:143, IX:118
~ of Earth, VI:126
~ and the etheric body/plane, VII:2, 7
~ holes in, VI:126
~ and negative thought forms, I:34, VII:102, 104–5
~ of a Planetary Logos, I:179
~ and professions on Arcturus, IV:64
~ and relationships, XIII:1, 3, 7
~ of Telos' residents, IV:24

Aurelian, Emperor, V:175

Auriel (archangel)
~ and the Kabbalistic tree of life, **IV:303**

Aurobindo, Sri, I:153
~ and Integral yoga, IV:250–51

Aurora (archangel), **I:199,** III:199
~ and the sixth ray, **I:204, IV:124, VII:115,** X:95

aurora borealis, IV:23, 25

Australia, VI:185

Austria
~ and the rays, **VI:183**

Autobiography of a Yogi, I:162–63, V:39, 47, 55–56, VI:162, VIII:165, XII:110, XIII:132. *See also* Yogananda, Paramahansa

automatic writing, V:202

autosuggestion, VIII:69, IX:55

Avalokitesvara (Avalokita), V:98–100, **V:101,** V:102, 105, 113, VIII:168. *See also* Quan Yin (Bodhisattva of Compassion); Tara

Avatar of Synthesis, I:141–42

avatars, I:6, 147–49, 153, 236, III:131, 182, 241–42, IV:218, V:8, 19, 77, VI:17, 44, 161, 207, 216, 248, VII:18, VIII:188, xiv, xvii, xviii, IX:114. *See also* individual avatars
~ galactic, I:216, III:193–94, VI:208, XI:17
~ the Kalki Avatar, I:137, IV:220
~ sixteen signs of, I:153, III:130

Averran, I:209–10, 274, **VI:112**

Avesta, V:151. *See also* Zoroastrianism
   ~ excerpts from, V:154
Avidya (ignorance), IV:261
axiatonal alignment, I:36, 274, III:44, 54–55, VI:231, XII:2, 10, 56
axiatonal alignment, cosmic, III:250
ayurveda, V:65. *See also* healing
Azrael (angel of death), V:160
AZT, IV:9, IX:87
Aztec Indians, IV:26. *See also* Native Americans
Aztec, New Mexico, IV:4

B

Babaji and the Eighteen Siddha Yogis, I:165. *See also* Govindan, Marshall

Babaji and the 18 Siddha Kriya Yoga Tradition, VI:162

Babaji, the Yogi Christ, I:159, 164–65, 237, V:40, 42, 44, **VI:112,** VI:162, 248, VIII:161, IX:115, XII:114–15, XIII:132
    ~ his Seat of Immortal Bliss, III:130–31, VIII:41, XI:105
    ~ and Kriya yoga, I:160–64, 166, IV:249, V:44
    ~ as Nagaraj, I:159
    ~ physical body of, I:159
    ~ and the Self-Realization Fellowship, I:159–61
    ~ teachings of, I:160–62, 164

Baba, the Breath of Sai, VIII:xxv

Bach, Johann Sabastian, VII:97

Bacon, Francis, V:239–41, 243
    ~ as an incarnation of Saint Germain, V:239–41, 243, VI:148

Baghela, King Vir Singh, V:164

Baha'i, IV:327–29

The Baha'i Faith, IV:329

Bahaullah, IV:327

Bailey, Alice A., I:11, 13, 16, 21, 25, 41, 47, 50, 57, 61, 63–65, 67, 70, 105, 108, 129, 131–33, 135, 139, 142, 144, 169–70, 177, 197, 205, 213, 242–43, 260, 275, 277, III:4, 8, 11, 20, 91, 103, 139, 168, 180–85, IV:253–54, 258, 267, 270–71, 281, 300, 317, 319, V:107, VI:6, 13, 17, 49, 68, 72–73, 81–83, 132, 149, 152–55, 165, 167, 170–71, 175, 177, 179, 182, 184, 186–87, 190, 199–200, 205, 226, 228–29, VII:16, 32, 34, 107, 148, VIII:95–96, 159, 163–64, 168, xxv, IX:53, 220, 245, 260, 264, X:16, 31, 44, 59, 68, 82, 148, 151, 207, XI:19–20, 24, 36–37, 39, 65, 82, 108, 174–75, 191, XII:2–5, 8, 79–80, 88, XIII:31, 55
    ~ initiation system of, I:276, III:7

Baker, James, IV:9

Ballard, Guy, VIII:163

Banaras, India. *See* Benares, India

bandhas, IV:240

~ and Kriya yoga, I:163
~ and Kundalini yoga, IV:246
Bangladesh, V:48
Bank of England, IX:168
banns of noninterference, VI:130–31, VIII:97, IX:194
baptism
~ and the Essene Brotherhood, IV:291
bardo experience, I:31, 73, 75, 77, 79, 81–82, 87, 91, III:8, IV:180, 189, V:108, IX:8, 118, XII:100, 129. *See also* (prebirth) bardo experience; death, physical
~ first phase, I:79–80, 83
~ of plants, IV:145
~ second phase, I:80, 83–84
~ third phase (Valley of Judgment), I:80, 88–89
(prebirth) bardo experience, I:91–92, XIII:82–83. *See also* bardo experience; birth, physical
Bartholomew (disciple of Jesus)
~ and Mohammed, I:175, VI:148
bases, extraterrestrial, IX:105, 162
~ on Earth, IV:6–8, 17, 43, 66, 74–75, VI:127, VII:132
~ on Mars, IV:53
~ on the Moon, IV:8, 53, 66, 74, XI:227
~ in New Mexico, IV:6–7, VI:127
~ on Venus, IV:53
bases, human, IX:162
~ on Mars, IV:17–18, 47
~ on the Moon, IV:8
Bassano, Mary, IV:214
Beasley, Ronald, I:244, IV:251, VIII:89, XI:209
Beasts, Men and Gods, IV:26
Beelzebub. *See* Satan
Beethoven, Ludwig van, III:148, VII:97, X:36
Behaving as if the God in All Life Mattered, IV:142, VII:119. *See also* Wright, Machaelle Small
Behold a Pale Horse, IV:16, 18
Benares, India, IV:222, V:40
Benedictine Monastery of Monte Cassino, IV:292
Berlin Wall, I:240, XI:116
Bermuda Triangle, I:10, III:149, VI:127–29
~ entrances to the inner Earth in, IV:25
Bernard, Raymond, IV:21–23, 28, V:144
Besant, Annie, I:132, 139, V:209–11, 219–20, 224, 227–31, 233–35, IX:264. *See also* Theosophical Society; Theosophy

B

~ and the externalization of the Spiritual Hierarchy, I:142

Beta Andromeda, IV:89. *See also* Andromeda

Better Homes and Gardens, IV:111

Betts, Charles T., IV:14

Beyond Tomorrow, IV:24. *See also* Chaney, Earlyne

Bhagavad-Gita, I:122, 147, 155, 236–37, 249, 267, 270–71, IV:200, 218–19, 224–30, 243, 253, 258, V:9, 17, 20, 69, 71, 74–75, 78, 211, VIII:16, 92, 160, 166, IX:182, XI:36, XII:119. *See also* Arjuna; Hinduism; Krishna (avatar); Mahabharata
    ~ and Kriya yoga, I:163–64
    ~ quotations from, I:73, 75–76, 79, 137, IV:223, 230, 242, V:75, VI:117, VII:6, 154, VIII:21, IX:99, 116, X:51, 247, XIII:85, 89
    ~ and soul travel, IV:200
    ~ and the three gunas, IV:228–30
    ~ Vyassa as an incarnation of Gautama Buddha, I:237, IV:219, 223, V:20, VI:148
    ~ wisdom teachings of, IV:224–27

Bhagavan Sri Ramana, A Pictorial Biography, V:57–59

Bhagavatpada, Govinda, V:19

bhajans, XII:29. *See also* devotional songs; music
    ~ and Sankirtan yoga, IV:249

Bhakta (a devotional yogi), V:24

bhakti (devotion), XIII:101, 110

Bible, I:2–3, 171–74, 251, IV:273, 275, V:25, 66, VI:228, VII:110, 113, VIII:160, XI:176, 230, XII:89. *See also* Christianity
    ~ and the antichrist, I:241
    ~ and the ego, IV:271–75
    ~ and the elohim, I:202, IV:120, 278
    ~ King James translation of, V:243
    ~ New Testament, IV:253, VII:97
    ~ Old Testament, I:170–71, IV:273, 281, VII:147
    ~ prophecies of, I:215, 240, IV:275, VII:86, 147
    ~ Psalms, V:134
    ~ quotations from, I:253, III:7, 23, 71, IV:262, 265, 277–80, 282, VI:13–14, 55, 59, 85, 122, 141, VII:4, 101, VIII:133, IX:4, 25, 124, 160, 209, XIII:35, 66, 89, 160
    ~ and reincarnation, I:73, 174, IV:273, VII:6
    ~ Revelations, III:11, XI:84
    ~ and the Second Council of Constantinople, I:73, 174, IV:273
    ~ and the story of Job, IX:81
    ~ and the story of Noah's ark, I:9, IV:168, 283, V:156
    ~ and the story of Samson, V:245

Bielek, Al, IV:15

Bieler, Henry, VIII:142

bilocation, I:28, 33, 282, III:16, 41–44, 81, IV:197, VI:33, VII:17, 35, VIII:41, 107, 183, XI:30, 57. *See also* ascended masters: advanced abilities of

biorhythms, XIII:167–68

Biosophy, V:139–40. *See also* Pythagoras

biostratus, III:221, VIII:57

birth control, IV:274

birth, physical, I:74, 91–92, 94, 147–48, V:110, VII:47, IX:96, XIII:81–83
    ~ and astrology, XIII:71–72
    ~ compared to death, I:83
    ~ induction, XIII:71–72
    ~ and the soul, I:107
    ~ water births, XIII:81

Black League, IV:41

black magic, I:250, VI:181, VIII:80

Black Sea, I:3

Blake, William, VII:97

Blavatsky, Madam, I:139, 275, III:95, IV:38, V:201–11, 214–16, 219–21, 225, 243, VI:49, 72, 229, VII:16, VIII:164, XI:19, 61–62, 101, XII:117. *See also* Theosophical Society; Theosophy
    ~ and the externalization of the Spiritual Hierarchy, I:142
    ~ psychic abilities of, V:201–4, 206–7, 209–10, 214, 216–18

Block, Sherman, IX:69

Blofeld, John, **V:101**

Blue Lodge. *See* Sirius

Blue Pearl, the, V:87–88

bodhichitta (mind of enlightenment), V:110, 112–13

bodhi mind (the bodhisattva mind), V:110

bodhisattva, III:11, IV:129, V:95, 105, 108–10, 113, VI:224, 244–45, VII:34, IX:113, 235
    ~ vow of, V:112–13, VIII:23, 160, IX:218, 234, 237, XI:42

Bodhisattva of Compassion: The Mystical Tradition of Quan Yin, **V:101**

Bodhi Tree Bookstore, I:150

body elemental, V:234

Body of Knowledge, III:217

Boganathar, I:159

Bolivia, IV:91

Bombay, India, V:2

Bonds, Barry, IX:123

The Book of Changes, I-Ching, V:119. *See also* Confucius

"The Book of Enoch," IV:288, 291. *See also* Enoch (ascended master)

The Book of History, Shu-Ching, V:119. *See also* Confucius

B

"Book of Knowledge," IV:56

The Book of Knowledge: The Keys of Enoch, I:39, 203, 227–28, 249, 274, III:25, 61–62, 217–21, 224–25, 230–36, 253, IV:63, 120, 125, 197, 278, 288, 291, 311, 313–15, VI:6, 25–26, 43, 51, 71, 227, VII:113, VIII:55, 59–60, 63, 65, 103, 165, XI:30, 95, 100, 126, 143, 145, 149–51, 154, 182, 189, 192, 194–96, 241, 266. *See also* Enoch (ascended master); Hurtak, J.J.; keys of Enoch

The Book of Knowledge: The Keys of Enoch, XII:114

The Book of Mormon, V:197, 199

The Book of Music, Ueh-Ching, V:119. *See also* Confucius

The Book of Poetry, Shih-Ching, V:119. *See also* Confucius

A Book of Prophecy, I:260–61, V:183, XII:7. *See also* Chaney, Earlyne

The Book of Rites, Li-Chi, V:119. *See also* Confucius

Boötes constellation, IV:63

Bosnia, IX:99, 107–8, 161, XII:57. *See also* war

Bradshaw, John, III:73, IX:230

Brahma (God), I:142, 153, 256, 270, IV:205, 217–19, 221–22, 226, 233–37, 250, 257, V:8–9, 12, 20–22, 28, 30–31, 50, 60, 66–67, 70, 90, 168–70, VI:68, 77, 82, VII:6, 148, VIII:190, 192, xiii, xx, XII:21, 119
~ inbreath and outbreath of, I:11–12, 162, 219–26, III:144, VI:6, 67, 73, 75–76, 79–81, 84, IX:114, 133, X:36, XII:115
~ life of, I:10–11, **I:11**, VI:68, **VI:68,** VI:73, 81–82
~ Maha Kalpa, I:10

Brahmand (land of Brahm), V:170

brain, human, VI:56, 58
~ and the chakra system, III:21
~ and contact with the soul, I:108
~ illumination of, I:270, III:49, VIII:46, 59, IX:122
~ left, X:39
~ right, X:39

Bramacharya, vow of, I:270, V:70, VIII:24

Branch Davidians. *See* Koresh, David

Brazil, IV:23, 26, VI:184
~ and the feminine principle, VI:184
~ and the rays, VI:183, **VI:183**
~ rods of power in, I:206
~ vortexes of, III:149

breathing, IV:175, 205, 258–59. *See also* pranayama
~ and building the light quotient, III:24
~ with color, IV:209–10

~ Kriya technique of, I:163–65, V:56
~ and meditation, I:255, XII:20
~ in the process of replacing food with light, XI:131–32
~ So Ham, I:156, 255, 271, IV:197, V:87, VIII:101, XII:20
~ techniques of the Huna, IV:162
~ in yoga, IV:240, 246, 264–65

Brennan, Barbara, VIII:168

Brigham, William Tufts, IV:157–58

Brinkley, David, IX:77

Brompton cocktail, I:83. *See also* death, physical

The Brotherhood of Angels and Men, IV:128. *See also* Hodson, Geoffrey

Brotherhood of Light, IV:313–14
~ and the Ashtar Command, IV:55

Brotherhood of the All. *See* ascended masters

brownies, IV:122, **IV:128,** IV:131, **IV:135,** IV:136, 141. *See also* devas; elementals: gnomes (nature spirits of earth); nature spirits

Bryant, Susan, XI:213

Bryiere, Rosalyn, VIII:168

Buddha consciousness, VII:140, VIII:76, 154, IX:38, 53, 131, 166, X:4, 44, 48–49, 51, 66, 69, 85, 111–12, 136, 176, 202, 229, 234, 238. *See also* Buddha mind; Buddha, the; consciousness

Buddha, Gautama, I:137, 141, 143–44, 190, IV:51, 153, 288, 327, V:15, 93–98, 100, 102–3, 109, 203, 229, VI:6, **VI:112,** VI:114, 131, 149, 194–95, 207, 219, 229–30, 237, 242, 248, VII:16, xvii, VIII:46, 49, 57, 62, 75, 97, 107, 122, 131, 177–78, IX:84, 93, 112, 114–15, 179, 194, 235–37, X:2, 114, 117, XI:31, 71, 226, 242, 257, XII:104, 115. *See also* Buddha, the; Buddhism
~ ascension of, I:134
~ ashram of, **VI:204,** VI:225, VIII:127, IX:200, 220
~ and the Eightfold Path, IV:264, V:96, X:215
~ and the Festival of Humanity, VI:155, XII:87
~ and the Four Noble Truths, I:60, V:94–96, VIII:10, 160
~ and initiation, VI:144, 163, 214–15, 220
~ light rods of, VIII:181, XI:259
~ and the Middle Way, III:109, IV:303, V:15, 93, 96, 110, 130, VIII:14, XI:255
~ other lives of, I:169, 236–37, IV:168, 198, 219, 223–24, V:20, 123, 128, 135, 141, 147, 151, 175, VI:145, 148, 154, 243, XI:225, XII:80
~ and the paths to higher evolution, I:41, III:169, 177
~ as the Planetary Logos, VI:86, 125, 220, 243, VII:19, 116, 133, 149, VIII:50, 127, 181, IX:7–9, 115, X:115, 152, XI:18, 30–31, 168, 225–26, 242, XII:84
~ sacred garden ascension seat of, III:191

B

~ sayings of, I:267, IV:224, V:102, 105, 128, VII:29, 160, VIII:25, XI:36–37, 268, XIII:136

~ and the second ray, I:120

~ and the Shamballa ascension seat, VI:32, 43

~ teachings of, V:96–97

~ and Wesak, I:278, III:29, V:93, 95–96, VI:28, 125, 150–54, VII:116, 149, VIII:138, IX:7, 93, 200, X:152–53, XI:30, 174–75, 226, XII:77–81, 84

~ white ray of, VIII:50

Buddha Maitreya, I:137, IV:281, V:95, 100, 113. *See also* Maitreya (Planetary Christ)

Buddha mind, III:23, IX:169, X:7, 54, 115, 185. *See also* Buddha consciousness; Buddha, the

Buddhas of Activity (Pratyeka Buddhas), I:185–87, 192, 194, **I:199,** I:201, III:173–75, **III:238, VI:3,** VI:188

Buddha, the, I:27, 155, 211, V:96, 98, 100, 111, VI:181, 240, VII:15, VIII:178, IX:8–9, 80, 164, XII:11

~ and Wesak, VI:150–54, VIII:138, XI:174–75, XII:78–80

Buddhic body, III:239, VI:203, **VI:205,** VII:73, XI:150. *See also* causal body

~ anchoring of, VIII:59, XI:154

~ death of, I:97, 180

~ and the fourth dimension, **VI:205**

~ and the fourth initiation, IV:270, **VI:17**

~ and physical death, I:75, 84

~ and the sleep state, VI:71

Buddhic body, cosmic, **III:238,** III:259, **VI:3, 24, 205,** VI:206, XI:155

Buddhic plane, I:16–17, 24, **I:132, 184, 197,** III:139, **IV:267,** IV:269, **VI:8,** VI:207, VII:5, 11–12, 21, 30, 63–64, 73, 84, XIII:63–64. *See also* causal plane

~ anchoring of, **III:139**

~ and the fourth initiation, **III:4, 139, VI:17, XI:127**

~ and the Kabbalistic tree of life, **IV:303, 307**

~ between lives, I:87–89, 92, 97

~ sexual expression on, XIII:64

~ and the supersenses, I:70, **I:71**

Buddhic plane, cosmic, I:17, **I:184,** I:198, **I:199,** III:167, 169–70, 181, **III:238,** III:240, **VI:3, 8, 24,** VI:206

Buddhi (intuition), IV:300, VI:175, VIII:160. *See also* intuition

Buddhism, I:156, 237, III:103, IV:140, 256, 281, V:16, 96–97, 99–100, 102, 105, 108–9, 225, VII:63, VIII:160, X:166, XI:2, 42. *See also* Buddha, Gautama; *Dhammapada;* Tibetan Buddhism

~ and Agartha, IV:19–20, 25

~ and the coming of Buddha Maitreya, I:137, IV:281, V:95, 100

~ and the Four Noble Truths, I:60, V:94–96, VIII:10, 160
~ and Jesus, IV:274
~ mantras of, I:258, XII:23
~ mythology of, V:100
~ reform of, I:144, IV:283
~ trinity of, V:100
~ and Yantra yoga, IV:247
Buddhist Catechism, V:217. *See also* Olcott, Henry S.
Bulagoras, V:145
Burbank, Luther, I:160
Bureau of Chemistry (FDA), IX:59
burial. *See* death, physical: burial
Burns, Sandy, XI:213
Burton, Robert, V:240
Bush, George, IV:9–10, 16
business world, VII:28, 93–94, IX:50–51, X:18, 57, 70
~ and integrity, IX:34
~ and service work, IX:50
~ and the third ray, X:34
~ tools for handling for lightworkers, VIII:171–73, IX:33–34, 50–51, 195, 208–9, 213–16, 224–25, XIII:34
Byrd, Admiral Richard E., IV:20–21, 24–25, 27–28
Byrd, Harley, IV:28

C

Cabala, IV:309, 311. *See also* McClure, Janet

Caddy, Eileen, III:119, IV:132

Caddy, Peter, III:119, IV:132–33

Cagliostro, V:242

Calcutta, India, V:34, 42
~ and Mother Teresa, V:191–92

California, IV:6, V:37, 46, IX:48. *See also* Los Angeles, California
~ and the medfly, IV:12, IX:87
~ and nuclear energy, IX:104
~ and Saint Germain's ascension seat, III:30

Calvin, John, I:124

Cambodia, IV:23

Cambridge History Book, Volume II, V:134

Camelot, X:226, 240–41

Canaan, I:230

Canada
~ blocked grid point in, IV:61

Cancer. *See also* astrology
~ and color healing, **IV:212**
~ and the Moon, **XI:177**
~ and New York City, **VI:185**
~ and the sixth ray, **XI:177**
~ and Tokyo, Japan, **VI:185**

cancer, I:77–78, 250, IV:13, VI:240, VIII:33, 35, 88–89, IX:56, 86–87, 118, 146, 154. *See also* disease
~ removal activation for, VI:125–26

Canfield, Jack, XIII:22

Canis Major, IV:69

Canis Minoris, IV:79

Capitol Drugs, III:34

Capricorn. *See also* astrology
~ and color healing, **IV:212**

Carey, Ken, I:220, 222, 225, IV:122, VIII:166

Carlyle, Thomas, I:118

Carmel, Mount
~ school of the prophets, I:171–73, IV:288, 290

Carpathian Mountains
~ and the "white root race," I:3

Carrey, Jim, VIII:90

Carson, Johnny, XI:164

Carter, Jimmy, IX:231

Caspari, Elisabeth, I:174

caste system, IV:220–21, 282, V:15–16, 27, 38, 50, 72, 88, 166. *See also* Hinduism; India

Catholic Church, IV:274, 292, V:181–82, 191, 230, IX:137–38, 148, 240. *See also* Christianity

Caucasus Mountains, IV:171

causal body, IV:130, V:87, VI:18, VII:73, 84. *See also* Buddhic body; soul body
~ building of, I:200
~ and the dreamless deep-sleep state of consciousness, **V:21**
~ and the fourth initiation, I:24, 44, 74, 105, 108, 110, 170, 200, III:2, VII:30
~ and the path of probation, I:21
~ of a Solar Logos, **I:184**
~ and the third initiation, I:23

causal plane, **IV:195,** VII:5, 11, 30, 84, IX:264, XIII:63–64. *See also* Buddhic plane
~ and intuition, VII:73
~ and the Mahatma energy, I:215
~ sexual expression on, XIII:64
~ and the supersenses, I:70

Cayce, Edgar, I:1, 169, 174–75, 209, 214, 227, 231, 234–36, 251, IV:138, 148, 175, 177, 184, 192, 277, 284, 288–91, V:125, 129, 245–47, 253, VI:7, 132, 226, 228–29, VII:69, VIII:74, 78, 146, 167, IX:53, 123, X:172, XI:222, XII:117
~ and Egypt, IV:167, 171–74
~ mantras of, I:257, XII:22
~ other lives of, IV:171–74, V:245
~ predictions by, I:9–10, 215, 240, III:99, VI:217
~ quotations from, I:239, 269, III:75, 135, 155–56, IV:63, 174, VI:70, VII:3, 10, VIII:77, 84, 97, 115, XII:13
~ as Ra-Ta, IV:171–74, V:245
~ return of, I:245

The Celestine Prophecy
~ nine insights of, III:110–11

celibacy, XIII:46–47, 96–97, 126, 132–33

Centauri, IV:38, 99

centaurs, I:2

Center for Disease Control (CDC), IX:62–63

Central America, IV:169

central canal, I:51–53, 56. *See also* chakras: chakra column
 ~ widening and clearing of, I:51–55, III:47 (*See also* meditation: corkscrew meditation; meditation: spiritual whirlwind meditation; meditation: triangulation meditation)

Cervantes, V:240

Cessna, IV:81–82. *See also* extraterrestrials

chakras, I:30, 37, 81, III:13, **III:13,** III:14, 20–21, 48, 122, 192–93, 219, 227, **III:238,** IV:2, **IV:208,** V:49, VI:1, **VI:3,** VI:50–51, 206–7, 213–14, 241, VII:8, VIII:42–44, 104, 147, IX:5, X:40, 89, XI:47, 187, XII:101, 105, XIII:4
 ~ activating, III:19, 21–22, 97, VIII:42–43
 ~ Ajna, I:130, **I:130, XI:127**
 ~ alignment of, I:112, III:255–56, XII:12
 ~ alpha and omega, III:56
 ~ anchoring of, III:15–19, 237, IV:211, VI:49, 63, 87, VIII:42–43, XI:23–24, 31, 47–49, 54, 66, 154–55, 185–87, 209
 ~ and ascension, I:30, 34, 38, III:9, VI:216
 ~ ascension chakra, III:17, VIII:42
 ~ and the bodies, VI:205–6
 ~ chakra column (sushumna), I:50–52, 83, 285, III:19, 52, 63, VI:57–59, VIII:42 (*See also* central canal)
 ~ chakra zips, VIII:146
 ~ chamber recalibration, III:20
 ~ and color, IV:205, **IV:211**
 ~ and color healing, **IV:208,** IV:211
 ~ crown (seventh), I:30, 40, 45, 54, 81–83, 92, 130, **I:130,** I:257–58, 267, 271, 280, III:13–14, 17, **III:20,** III:51–52, IV:184, 198, 201, 203, **IV:208,** VI:170, VII:8, 151, VIII:42, 57, **XI:127,** XII:21, 23
 ~ and the dimensions, III:193, VI:205–6
 ~ of Earth, III:131, 149
 ~ Earth star, VII:8
 ~ of the Great Pyramid, IV:171
 ~ heart (fourth), **I:5,** I:43, 45, 52, **I:52,** I:81, 130, 256, 258, 277, III:9, **III:20, IV:208, VI:78,** VI:181, VII:8, 83, 151, X:41, 87, **XI:127,** XI:176, XII:21, 23, XIII:99
 ~ implants in, IV:105
 ~ and initiation, I:277, III:9, VI:205–6, XI:23–24, **XI:127**
 ~ and the Kabbalistic tree of life, IV:305
 ~ knee, **I:52,** I:53, VII:8
 ~ and Kriya yoga, I:163

chakras, (cont.)
    ~ and Kundalini Yoga, IV:246
    ~ and light quotient, VI:18, 205–6
    ~ mantras for, I:256–58, XII:21, 23
    ~ and maya, I:65–66
    ~ meditations for, III:19, 202, 211–15
    ~ and music, IV:39
    ~ petals of, III:20, **III:20,** III:21, VIII:42
    ~ during physical death, I:81–82
    ~ and the rays, I:118, 121, 130
    ~ root (first), **I:5,** I:26, 52, **I:52,** I:53, 130, 256, 258, 285,
        III:20, IV:208, **VI:78,** VII:8, 151, **XI:127,** XII:21, 23
    ~ and the root races, I:4, **I:5,** VI:72, 77, **VI:78**
    ~ sacral (second), **I:5, 52,** I:53, 83, 130, 256, 258, **III:20,**
        IV:208, VI:78, VII:8, 151, IX:122, 138, **XI:127,** XII:21,
        23, XIII:98–99
    ~ seven chambers in, III:17–18, **III:18,** III:19–21
    ~ solar plexus (third), **I:5,** I:45, 52, **I:52,** I:53, 65, 81, 83, 121,
        130, 256, 258, **III:20,** IV:158, **IV:208, VI:78,** VI:181,
        VII:8, 73, 151, **XI:127,** XII:21, 23
    ~ in the soles of the feet, **I:52,** I:53, 285, VII:8
    ~ soul star, VII:8
    ~ and soul travel, IV:198–99, 201, 203
    ~ third-dimensional chakra grid, III:13–14, 193, **III:238,**
        IV:211, **VI:3,** VI:10, XI:23, 47
    ~ third-eye (sixth), **I:5,** I:24, 30, 34, 43, 45, 52, **I:52,** I:81, 83,
        257–58, III:17, **III:20,** III:52, 231, IV:196, 198–99,
        IV:208, VI:78, VI:174, VII:8, 82, 84, 151, VIII:57–58,
        IX:138, **XI:127,** XI:176, XII:21, 23 (*See also* pineal gland)
    ~ throat (fifth), **I:5,** I:22, 30, 52, **I:52,** I:81, 130, 256, 258,
        III:9, 17, **III:20,** III:52, **IV:208, VI:78,** VII:8, 151,
        XI:127, XI:176, XII:21, 23
    ~ thymus, III:198
    ~ tuning of, IV:213
    ~ unified, I:285
    ~ universal chakra, VIII:43
    ~ universal pattern of, III:102
    ~ zeal point, III:191
chakras, cosmic, III:181, **VI:3,** VI:12, 16, 20, 24, XI:210
chakras, galactic, **VI:3,** VI:12, 53, 194, 206
    ~ anchoring of, VI:53, **VI:62**
chakras, higher, I:30, 269, 271, III:13, **III:13,** III:14–15, 20, 28, 48,
    237, **III:238, VI:3,** VI:10, 194, 206–7, 230, XI:31, 47, 187,
    210–11
    ~ alignment of, III:255–56
    ~ anchoring of, III:7, 14–19, 51–52, 199, 237, 239, 257,

C

IV:211, VI:5, 10–11, 13, **VI:62,** VI:87, 95, 122, 246,
  VIII:42–43, 50–51, XI:23–24, 31, 47–49, 54, 57, 59, 61, 66,
  154–55, 185–87, 209, 211, 252, 265, 268
~ and ascension, III:7, 14
~ and the bodies, VI:205–6
~ chamber recalibration, III:20
~ clearing of, VI:241
~ and color, IV:211, **IV:212**
~ and color healing, IV:211
~ eighth-dimensional chakra grid, **III:13,** III:17, 193, 237,
  III:238, VI:3, VI:10, 19, XI:54, 136
~ fifteenth, I:30, VI:10
~ fifth-dimensional chakra grid, I:30, 37, III:7, **III:13,**
  III:14–15, 193, **III:238, VI:3,** VI:10, XI:23, 31, 47, 61
~ fiftieth, VI:11
~ forty-eighth, VI:11
~ forty-ninth, VI:11
~ fourteenth, I:30, VI:10
~ fourth-dimensional chakra grid, I:30, III:7, **III:13,** III:14–15,
  193, **III:238, VI:3,** VI:10, XI:23, 47
~ and initiation, III:13–14, XI:23–24, **XI:127**
~ ninth-dimensional chakra grid, **III:13,** III:17, 193, 237,
  III:238, VI:3, VI:10, 19, XI:54, 136
~ seven chambers in, III:19–20
~ seventh-dimensional chakra grid, III:7, 10, **III:13,** III:14, 52,
  193, **III:238, VI:3,** VI:10, XI:47–48, 54, 59, 83
~ sixteenth, I:30, III:7, 14, VI:10, VIII:42, XI:186
~ sixth-dimensional chakra grid, III:7, **III:13,** III:14, 16–17,
  52, 193, **III:238, VI:3,** VI:10, XI:47–49, 61
~ tenth, XI:159
~ thirty-fifth (third-eye), **III:14,** III:52
~ thirty-fourth (throat), **III:14,** III:52
~ thirty-sixth (crown), III:13–14, **III:14,** III:52, XI:186
~ thirty-third (heart), III:14, **III:14**
~ three-hundred-thirtieth, VI:14
~ twenty-second, III:15, XI:186
~ two-hundredth, VI:14
chakras, multiuniversal, **VI:3,** VI:12, 205
chakras, solar, **VI:3,** VI:12, 51–52, 194, 206, XI:210–11
  ~ anchoring of, VI:52, **VI:62,** VI:117
chakras, universal, **VI:3,** VI:12, 54, 161, 194, 205
  ~ anchoring of, VI:54, **VI:62**
Championing Your Inner Child, III:73. *See also* Bradshaw, John
Chamuel (archangel), **I:199,** III:199
        ~ and grounding, XI:26
        ~ and the third ray, **I:204, IV:121, 123, VII:115,** X:35, 95

Chandra (Hindu Moon god), IV:219

Chaney, Earlyne, I:134, 166–67, 230, 237, 260–61, IV:24–25, 167,
169–71, 174, 177, V:181, 183–84, 187, 211, VI:7, VII:23, 133,
VIII:134, 164–65, XI:6, XII:7. *See also* Astara mystery school
~ channelings about the hollow Earth, IV:23–24
~ and initiation in the Great Pyramid, I:231, 236, IV:174–76,
181, 184–92
~ as Nefre-Tah-Khet, IV:174–76
~ prophecies of, I:245–46

Chaney, Robert, I:166, VII:23. *See also* Astara mystery school

channeled dancing, III:192

channeling, I:90, 265, III:60, 170, 192, IV:287, V:205, VI:57, 114,
132, 226–29, VII:77–81, 132, VIII:105–6, 128, IX:55, 58, 83,
X:22, 55–57, 172, XI:66, XII:98–99
~ of the arts, III:127, VII:11, 79, VIII:105, IX:51–52
~ and ascension, III:127
~ of color, IV:210
~ and communication, IX:177
~ as described by Madam Blavatsky, V:205
~ glamour of, X:121–23
~ of healing energy, III:107–8
~ and the negative ego, VI:132, 226, 228, VII:78, 80,
IX:140–43
~ and personal power, VIII:7
~ of sound, III:192

chanting, I:249, 253, 270–71, III:224, V:90, VII:107. *See also*
mantras; words of power
~ of bhajans/sankirtan, IV:249
~ and building the light quotient, III:24
~ and healing, I:251, 253, IV:172, VII:105–6, 108
~ and Kriya yoga, I:163
~ and physical death, I:82
~ repetition of the name of God, I:49, 82, 99, 155, 249–53, 265,
III:24, IV:218, 262, V:9, 12, 25, 27, 29–32, 51, 61, 74, 159,
161, 166, 168–71, VIII:96, XI:37, XII:19–23
~ repetition of the names of the masters, I:259, VII:107
~ tempo of, I:253

Chaplet of Divine Mercy. *See* Kowalska, Sister Faustina

charisma, IX:22, 140

Charity (archangel), **I:199,** III:199
~ and the third ray, **I:204, IV:123, VII:115,** X:35, 95

Charlton, Hilda, XIII:99

chela, VI:165–72. *See also* disciples

Chenrezi, V:105. *See also* Avalokitesvara (Avalokita); Dalai Lama;
Quan Yin (Bodhisattva of Compassion); Tara

Chernobyl, IX:104

cherubim (heavenly counselors), III:199, **IV:123,** IV:124–25. *See also* angelic kingdom; angels

cherubs, IV:138

Chicago, Illinois, V:36

Chidvilasananda, Gurumayi, V:86

Children of One, IV:172

China, IV:26, 173, V:100, IX:7
~ art of, X:93
~ and the first ray, **VI:182**
~ invasion of Tibet, V:105–7
~ and the masculine principle, VI:184
~ and nuclear weapon testing, VI:126
~ rods of power in, I:206
~ and the third ray, **VI:182**
~ and the U.S. trade agreement, IX:164–65

Chinese, V:130, VII:134
~ writings of the inner Earth, IV:25

chiropractic treatment, X:89, 243. *See also* healing

chit (absolute knowledge), V:20

Chogyam, Hgakpa, V:107

Chopra, Deepak, IX:58

Christ consciousness, I:22, 138, 141, 143–44, 146, 221–22, 224–26, 290, III:204, IV:150, 256, 260, 301, 310, VI:40, 59, 139, 172, 240, VII:49, 62, 90, 96, 140, VIII:21–22, 76, 79, 81, 114, 118, 132, 134, 154, IX:38, 46, 51, 53, 70, 80, 124, 131, 166, 193–94, X:4, **X:13,** X:49, 51, 66, 69, 85, 112, 176, 202, 223, 229, 234, 238, XI:36, 198, 216, 267, 269, XII:94–95, XIII:113–14, 150, 180. *See also* Christ mind; Christ, the; consciousness
~ and the color indigo, IV:206
~ and the fourth ray, VI:190
~ and Jesus, I:195
~ *vs. the negative ego,* I:267, III:23, 69, 71, 88, VI:103, 138, 190, 218, 244, VII:27, 42, 75, 150, VIII:4, 13, IX:18, 64, 67, 69, 122, 259, 271, 278, X:44, 48, 70, 111, 128, 136, XI:35, XII:11, XIII:155
~ and the rays, I:127–28, VI:187
~ and repetition of the name of God, I:253
~ in social issues, IX:45, 62, 84

Christianity, I:40, 144, 171, 236, IV:275, 278, 280, 288, V:25, 112, VII:146–47, VIII:160, IX:239, XI:2
~ and Djwhal Khul, I:237
~ fundamentalist, I:123, VI:129–30, 138, IX:53, 96, 109, 137, XII:108
~ holy places of, V:156

~ and Jesus, I:73, 144, 241, IV:271–75, 281, 283, 287, VI:180, IX:137–38

~ and Judaism, IV:277

~ mantras of, I:258, XII:22–23

~ and the negative ego, IV:271–75, 281–82, IX:137

~ and the Order of Melchizedek, I:230, IV:277

~ and the Pythagorean mystery school, I:237

~ reform of, IV:283

~ and reincarnation, VII:6

~ and the second coming of Christ, I:137–38, 220

~ and the sixth ray, I:123, 194, VI:180

~ trinity of (Father, Son and Holy Spirit), IV:161

Christine (archangel), **I:199,** III:199

~ and the second ray, **I:204, IV:123, VII:115,** X:94

Christmas, I:283, IX:91, 166, XII:77, 89

Christ mind, I:267, III:69, 71, VI:51, 103, 244, VII:161, VIII:4–5, 8, 13, 117, IX:169, X:7, 48, 54, 115, 185. *See also* Christ consciousness; Christ, the

Christ, the, I:17, 21, 27, 45, 60, 138, 155, 190, 192, 196, 220–21, 267, 273, III:102, 201, 260, IV:57, 184, 223, 272, 274, V:112, 236, VI:138, 141, 219, 240, 244, VII:15, 19, VIII:77, 178, IX:8–9, 80, 116, 121, 141, 164, X:32, 52, 116–17, 236, XII:11, XIII:101. *See also* Cosmic Christ; Maitreya (Planetary Christ); Planetary Christ; Sathya Sai Baba (Cosmic Christ)

~ ashram of, I:144, X:202

~ and healing, X:141

~ mantle of, III:246

~ and protection from negative thoughts, VII:111

~ and the rays, I:190, 201, **VI:179,** VI:181, 187, 190–91

~ second coming of, I:56, 137–46, 220, 225, 233, VI:174, 190–91, X:30–32

~ and Wesak, V:95–96, VI:153–54, VIII:138, XI:174–75, XII:78–80

Churchill, Winston, I:118

Church of Jesus Christ of Latter Day Saints, V:199. *See also* Mormon religion

CIA, IX:45, 71, 100–101, 130

~ and drugs, IV:9, 17, IX:166

~ and extraterrestrials, IV:4

~ origin of, IV:4

~ and the secret government, IV:3–4, 15

cities, underground, I:279, IV:26, 169, VII:133–34. *See also* Agartha; Agartha Network; individual underground cities

Civil War, I:244. *See also* war

clairaudience, I:33, **I:71,** III:104, 107, **IV:267,** VI:113, VII:79, 83, VIII:105, X:57, 121. *See also* psychic powers

clairsentience, I:33, III:104, 107, X:121. *See also* psychic powers

clairvoyance, I:33, **I:71,** III:104, 107, **IV:267**–68, VI:113, 131, 143, VII:2, 84, IX:58, X:57, 121. *See also* psychic powers

Clark, Marsha, IX:67

Clinton, Hillary, IX:147, XIII:85
   ~ and the health-care system, IX:81

Clinton, William Jefferson, IV:16, VI:90, IX:97, 112, 147–48
   ~ and the environment, IV:152
   ~ and the health-care system, IX:81
   ~ initiations of, IX:81, 113
   ~ sayings of, IX:162

cloning, IX:165–66. *See also* extraterrestrials
   ~ by Grays, IV:73–74
   ~ and healing, IX:165
   ~ and Zeta Reticulum, IV:97

Close Encounters of the Third Kind, IV:5–6, XI:231

CNN, XI:41

Coat of Many Colors, III:222, VIII:60, XI:194

cocaine. *See* drugs

Cochran, Johnnie, IX:67

cocreation, VII:3, 57, 64
   ~ and the arts, VII:97–98
   ~ and prayer, VII:107

cocreator gods, **I:199,** I:203

cocreator level, I:180, **I:199,** I:202, III:145–46, IV:207

codependency, IX:92, 150, XIII:13, 88, 142, 157, 169, 178

Cold War, V:181, IX:106. *See also* Russia; Soviet Union

color, III:172, VI:43, VIII:80, 96
   ~ and astrology, **IV:212, XI:176**–77
   ~ and building the light quotient, III:24
   ~ and the chakras, IV:205, **IV:208,** IV:211, **IV:211**
   ~ and dimensions, **IV:195**–96, IV:197
   ~ and healing, I:246, III:107, IV:172, 205–7, **IV:208,** IV:209–12, **IV:212,** IV:213–15, VIII:32–34, IX:83, X:36–37, 39, XII:107
   ~ and the Kabbalistic tree of life, **IV:304, 308**–9
   ~ and music, IV:205, 208, 213–15, X:36
   ~ and the Path of Training for Planetary Logos, III:173
   ~ and the planets, **IV:212, XI:176**–77
   ~ and the rays, I:134–35, 268, **X:12**–13, **XI:176**–77
   ~ and soul travel, **IV:195**–96
   ~ spiritual meanings of, IV:205–7, **IV:208**

~ and world service, III:68

Color and Music in the New Age, IV:214

Columbia, IV:61

Columbus, Christopher, I:118
~ as an incarnation of Saint Germain, I:245, V:239, 242, VI:148, VIII:163
~ as a walk-in, IV:31

Commander Ashtar, I:36, 279, III:43, 190, IV:55–61, VI:32, **VI:112,** VII:131, VIII:130, XI:27, 205–6. *See also* Ashtar Command
~ ashram of, VIII:127
~ and building the light quotient, III:28
~ and Wesak, X:153

communication, III:174, VI:50–51, 131, VIII:98, 158, IX:232, X:238–39
~ with the ascended masters, I:213, VI:113–15, 202–3, VII:32, 45, VIII:123–25, IX:177–78, X:7, 76, 238
~ with cetaceans, X:214, 239
~ and channeling, IX:177
~ fifth-dimensional, VI:47
~ fourth-dimensional, III:150
~ glamour of, IX:260–62
~ gossip, V:111, VI:130, VII:102–3, IX:76, 103, 259–60, X:208, XIII:162
~ and the negative ego, IX:201–2, 233, 272–74, XIII:26, 137–38, 148, 161
~ and parenting, XIII:87
~ primary *vs.* secondary, XIII:138
~ public speaking, VIII:158, IX:206–7, X:33
~ in relationships, VII:95, VIII:113, 137, IX:27, XIII:12, 17–18, 23–24, 26–27, 29, 45, 47, 53, 118–21, 126–27, 136, 138–39, 141, 144–45, 159, 161–62, 164, 168–69, 172–73, 176, 178
~ and spiritual leadership, IX:27, 209
~ through energy, VI:113
~ with the unborn child, XIII:79–80

Communism, IV:14, V:107, 180–81, VI:178, IX:7, 243–44. *See also* China; Russia; Soviet Union
~ fall of, I:224, 240, III:141, VI:6, IX:106, 114, 131, 133, XI:116
~ and the third ray, VI:179

community, VIII:105, 156, 160, IX:92–93, 95

compassion, VIII:5, 10, 116

computers, IV:66
~ of the Ataien, IV:102

Confederation of Planets. *See* Galactic Confederation of Planets

Confucianism, I:237, IV:284, V:119–20
    ~ and the five great relationships, V:121
    ~ and Taoism, V:117, 121
Confucius, IV:327, V:119–21
    ~ as an incarnation of Djwhal Khul, I:237, V:119, VI:147
    ~ writings of, V:119, 121
conscious mind, III:104, IV:258, V:169, VI:58, 158, 213, 221, 239,
    VII:39, 42, 74, 155, VIII:11–12, 15, 84, 90, 92, 112, 117, 159,
    X:7, 108, 130–31, 143, 156, XI:35, XII:95, 103, XIII:74, 121, 151,
    155. *See also* middle self
    ~ and the Huna teachings, IV:158–59, 162
    ~ integration of, VI:100, 103, X:4
    ~ mastery of, VI:60
    ~ and the negative ego, X:114
    ~ reprogramming of, VII:30, 41, 45–46, 48, 140, 161
consciousness, I:45, 74, 180, 224, 228, 239, 251, 271–74, 287,
    III:178, IV:139, 158, 235, 266, V:20–22, 61, 129, VI:97, 104, 108,
    158, VII:28, 92, VIII:112, IX:74, 221, X:236. *See also* Buddha con-
    sciousness; Christ consciousness
    ~ abundance, VIII:83–84
    ~ and aging, I:78
    ~ of angels, IV:121
    ~ of animals, IV:147, IX:120–22
    ~ Anointed-Christ-Overself, VI:90
    ~ Aryan, VI:166
    ~ ascended-master, I:219, VIII:12, 24, IX:92, 121, 140, 157,
        179, 213, X:39, XI:160, XIII:180
    ~ and ascension, I:28, 30
    ~ astral, IV:269
    ~ Atlantean, VI:166
    ~ atmic, IV:270
    ~ Brahmic, V:66
    ~ brain, **I:58**
    ~ Buddhic, IV:270
    ~ and the building of the antakarana, I:44, 46
    ~ cosmic, I:178–80, 209, V:42
    ~ cosmic planes of, III:180
    ~ Creator-level, I:17
    ~ and death, I:74
    ~ and devas, IV:129–30
    ~ dimensions of, VI:61–62, **VI:62**, VI:63, **VI:63**
    ~ divine, I:40, V:63, 65
    ~ during dream time, IV:193
    ~ ego, V:31, VIII:79
    ~ eighth-dimensional, VI:62–63
    ~ elohim, VI:90

consciousness, (cont.)
~ energy fields of, VI:56
~ evolution of, IV:281
~ expansion of, IX:94
~ and extraterrestrials, I:242
~ fear, IV:74
~ fifth-dimensional, I:215, VI:48–49, 51, 57, 61, 140, 245,
  VIII:116, IX:71, 75, 92, 121
~ fourth-dimensional, I:146, 215, 240, 243, IV:2, VI:49, 51, 57,
  61, 140, 245, VIII:16, IX:71
~ galactic, III:61, 147, 179, VI:90
~ galactic-monadic, VIII:51
~ global, IX:107, 246
~ God-, I:14, 251, 267, IV:258, V:128, VI:110, 139, 159–61,
  VIII:14, 16, 51, 72, 76, IX:7, 120, 122, 136, X:50, 202, 236,
  XI:36
~ group, **I:67,** I:110, 117, 208, 277, 289, III:59, 111–20, 174,
  178, VI:19, 21, 28, 54, 62, 64–65, 89, 97, 172, 175, 198,
  227, VII:12, VIII:105, 107, vii, IX:12–13, 16, 21, 71, 92–95,
  107, 132, 156–60, 179, 186–88, 206, 213, 217, 221–22, 240,
  249–50, 257–58, X:31, 71–72, 138, 149, 185–86, 201–3,
  207, 226, XI:68, 196–97, 221–22, 234–35, XIII:60, 85
~ of hell, IV:273
~ Hierarchical, I:45
~ I Am, IV:270
~ and initiation, IV:180–82, VI:172
~ and the Kriya technique, I:164
~ Lemurian, VI:166
~ between lives, I:87–103
~ logoic, I:40
~ lower-self, IX:121–22
~ Mahatma, I:214, 216
~ mass, I:206, 239, III:172, VI:48, 102, 137, 139–40, VII:28,
  IX:52, 138, X:51
~ mind map of, VI:56–57, **VI:57,** VI:58
~ monadic, I:27, 118, IV:301, 310, VI:90, VIII:51
~ negative-ego, VI:65, 102, 138, 190, 240, 244, VII:154, 161,
  VIII:21, 79, IX:96, 109–10, 123, X:51, XI:36
~ ninth-dimensional, VI:63
~ and the Order of Melchizedek, I:228
~ Paradise-Sons, VI:90
~ of plants, IV:145
~ poverty, VIII:83–84, IX:50, 92, XI:163
~ prosperity, VI:209, IX:92, XI:163
~ punishment, IX:71, 73, 98
~ race, I:7
~ and the rays, I:133

consciousness, (cont.)
>   ~ saint, IX:225
>   ~ self-, VI:172
>   ~ seventh-dimensional, VI:62, 245
>   ~ Shamballa, I:45
>   ~ Shiva, V:89
>   ~ sixth-dimensional, VI:62, 245
>   ~ solar, VI:90
>   ~ solar-monadic, VIII:51
>   ~ soul, I:93, 118, IV:139, 256, 300–301, 310, V:72, IX:51
>   ~ during soul travel, IV:194, 198, 200
>   ~ spiritual, I:74, IV:256, 310, VII:49, 92–93, 135, X:82
>   ~ splitting of, I:186, 194
>   ~ third-dimensional, I:215, 240, 243, VI:49, 51, 57, 140, 245,
>   VIII:16, IX:96, 120–21, 123
>   ~ third-eye, V:168
>   ~ transcendental, V:21
>   ~ transformation of, I:216, XIII:106–8
>   ~ twelfth-dimensional, VIII:116
>   ~ twelve faces of, III:231
>   ~ of unconditional love, I:18
>   ~ unity, VI:61, 63, VIII:76
>   ~ universal, III:147–48, VI:90
>   ~ universal-monadic, VIII:51
>   ~ unmani, V:169
>   ~ victim, I:59, IV:74, 78, 139, VI:61, 137, XI:38, XIII:146, 156
>   ~ witness, VI:221
>   ~ and the year 2012, I:225

consciousness cord, I:44–47
>   ~ and physical death, I:77, 81

Constantine, V:175

consumerism, IX:135. *See also* materialism

Contragate, IV:3. *See also* secret government

Cooper, Milton William, IV:16, 18

core fear matrix removal, I:281, III:69–73, 201–2, VI:119, 214, 231,
    240, VII:144–45, VIII:32–33, 119, IX:58, 183, X:33, 156,
    XI:52–53, 66, XII:10–11, 64, 93–94, 96. *See also* fear

Corinne, Heline, IV:214

cosmic actualization, IX:121

cosmic body, VI:26, IX:188–89. *See also* group body

Cosmic Book of Knowledge, III:229

cosmic-cellular clearing, VI:239

Cosmic Christ, I:141–42, 146, 157, IV:257, V:8, XI:249. *See also*
    Sathya Sai Baba (Cosmic Christ)
>   ~ coming of, I:243

Cosmic Consultant, III:105

Cosmic Day, I:10–11, 209, 214, 219, 247, III:143–44, 152, 173, 198, 243, **VI:3,** VI:6, 9, 26, 42, 67–71, 73, 76, 79, 116, VIII:21, 65, XI:17, 201, XII:129
~ completion of, I:221
~ premature ending of, III:143–45, 152

cosmic fire, I:31, 35, III:47, VIII:60–61, XI:29, 53

cosmic heart, III:61, 81
~ anchoring of, I:284, III:38, VIII:57, XI:31

Cosmic Hierarchy, I:197, **I:199, III:238, VI:3**

cosmic integration and alignment, III:44, 54–55, IV:45–46

cosmic law. *See* law, spiritual

cosmic logoi, I:183, **I:184, III:238,** III:243, 250, **VI:3**

cosmic masters, I:141, 198, 202, 205, 207–10, VIII:xxiii, XII:84, 115, XIII:99. *See also* ascended masters; galactic masters; universal masters

Cosmic Night, I:214, III:143–44, 152, 243, VI:67–71, 73, XI:17, 201, XII:129

cosmic telephones, I:243

Cotton, Nephi, IV:21–22

Council Chambers of the Sacred Planets, III:181

Council of Elohim, III:199, 220, 223, 227, 229–30, 232, **III:238,** III:243, **VI:3**

Council of Twelve, cocreator, **I:199,** I:202, 215, 217, III:62, X:146, XI:60

Council of Twelve, cosmic, III:222, 231–32, **III:238,** III:242–43, 250, 256, 259, **VI:3,** VI:10, 42, 65, 77–78, 80, 83, 116, 201, IX:10, 220
~ ashram of, VIII:127

Council of Twelve for this Cosmic Day, III:198, **III:238,** III:242, **VI:3**

Council of Twelve, galactic, VI:116

Council of Twelve, multiuniversal, **III:238,** III:242, **VI:3,** VI:116

Council of Twelve, personal, III:106

Council of Twelve, solar, **III:238, VI:3,** VI:116, XI:148

Council of Twelve, universal, III:242, VI:116

Council on Foreign Relations, IV:4–5, 10. *See also* secret government
~ and the television networks, IV:12

A Course in Miracles, I:169, 267, 271, III:8, 23, 69, 73, 89, 205, 265, IV:242, 253, 261, 270, 272, 282, VI:6, 23, 55, 102, 109, 138–39, 202, 227, 244, VII:154, VIII:2–4, 17–19, 62, 75–77, 82–83, 86, 108, 128, 154, 164, xxv, IX:23, 198, 201, 207, 230, X:166, 171, XI:35–37, 44, 91, 144, 162, 216, 260, XII:89, 110–12, XIII:22, 121, 136, 140

Cowan, Walter, I:151

creation, I:1–3, 8, 11, 13, 17, VI:50, 72, 145, IX:136, XII:103
 ~ downward spiral of, I:2
 ~ of Earth, I:10–12
 ~ and free choice, I:1
 ~ goal of, III:145
 ~ and the Kabbalistic tree of life, IV:297–98, 300
 ~ and science, IX:54

creativity, **I:67,** III:145, IV:39, 207, VI:84, 108–9, 187, VIII:98, 123, IX:28, 79, 205, X:37, 73, 75, 93–94, 142

Creator, I:3, 13, 220, 233, IV:300
 ~ and the angels, IV:120
 ~ and the elohim, IV:120
 ~ love/wisdom center of, I:186
 ~ will aspect of, I:111, 117, 186, 189, 191, 222, 277

Creator level, I:17, 215, III:152

cremation. *See* death, physical: cremation

Creme, Benjamin, I:244

crib death, I:91, 106, XIII:78, 83

crime, I:99, IX:98, 150–53. *See also* judicial system (U.S.); prison system (U.S.)

Crombie, R. Ogilvie, III:119, IV:132–35

crossbreeding
 ~ by extraterrestrials with humans, IV:7, 73–75, 79, 97–98

crucifixion, I:79, 138, 170, 278, IV:272
 ~ as initiation, I:25, IV:191

Cruise, Tom, I:18

Crusades, the, IV:274, IX:3. *See also* war

crystals, I:245–46, III:218, VIII:147, X:239
 ~ and the Arcturians, IV:66–67, XIII:174
 ~ in Atlantis, I:8–10, III:149, IV:1, 169, VI:127–28
 ~ and chanting, I:252
 ~ God crystals, VIII:176, 180, XI:257
 ~ and healing, I:246, IV:93, 155
 ~ pseudo-crystals, IV:59–60
 ~ sun crystals, I:9
 ~ technology of, I:8–9, 242, 244, IV:1, 66, VI:231, VIII:29, XIII:174

crystal skull, IV:69

Cuban missile crisis, I:240

cultism, IX:14, 140–43, XII:125

Current Affair, IX:75–76

cyclopes, I:2

D

Dalai Lama, V:105, 107–8, 110–11, 113, VIII:160, 166, IX:53. *See also* Chenrezi; Gyatso, Tenzen; Tibetan Buddhism
    ~ and Agartha, IV:19
    ~ recognition of, V:97–98, 105–6
    ~ reincarnation cycle of, V:100, 105, VII:6, IX:239–40

Dals, IV:37. *See also* extraterrestrials

Dal universe, IV:37–38

dance, IV:39, 323, VII:11, 79, 133, X:37, XIII:177. *See also* arts, the
    ~ and the fourth ray, VII:133, X:56

Daniel, Alma, IV:122

Danielou, Alain, IV:240, 251

Daniel (prophet), IV:122, 288

d'Arc, Jeanne, IV:119

Darjeeling, India, VI:185, **VI:185**

Dark Brotherhood, IV:2–3, 9–10, 23, VI:57, 59, 131, 140, 245, VIII:22, 80, 97, XI:227–28. *See also* Sons of Belial
    ~ and Adolf Hitler, IV:30, VIII:155, IX:3, 99
    ~ and AIDS, IX:117
    ~ and crime, IX:152
    ~ and education, IX:77
    ~ and the Food and Drug Administration (FDA), IX:87
    ~ and fundamentalism, IX:53, 109, 137
    ~ and glamour, I:59
    ~ and the health-care system, IV:12–14
    ~ its capital on Orion, XI:227
    ~ and Lucifer, VI:58
    ~ and the media, IX:148
    ~ and the Moon, XI:227
    ~ and politics, IX:113, 148
    ~ and Saddam Hussein, IX:100
    ~ and the secret government, IV:4
    ~ and twilight masters, VI:130, 143, IX:142

darshan (a visit with a holy man), V:5–6, 44, 82, VII:84, VIII:159–60

Darwin, Charles, V:215

Dass, Ram, VIII:113, XIII:117

Dateline, VIII:157, IX:89

Dattatreya, Lord, I:153, 256, IV:218, V:4, 8, VIII:xx, XII:21
    ~ as an incarnation of Sathya Sai Baba, V:8, VIII:xx

David, King, IV:288
    ~ and the Order of Melchizedek, I:228

David (statue of), VII:97. *See also* Michelangelo

da Vinci, Leonardo, I:121, 125, X:24

Day of Brahma. *See* Cosmic Day

Dead Sea Scrolls, I:171, III:227, IV:288–89, 291–92

death
    ~ of the astral body, I:75, 97, 180, XIII:62
    ~ of the atmic body, I:97, 180
    ~ of the Buddhic body, I:97, 180
    ~ of desire, I:23, 74
    ~ of the etheric body, I:75, 84–85
    ~ of the mental body, I:75, 97, 180
    ~ of the negative ego, I:74
    ~ of the personality, I:74

death hormone, I:82–84, 274, VIII:45

death, physical, I:31, 73–79, 81, 83, 87, 97–98, 180, 267, 271,
    IV:183, 189, 233, V:12, 50, 110, 152, VI:70, 221, VII:2, 12,
    VIII:45, 134, 189, IX:97, 118, 133–34, XI:176, XII:100,
    XIII:61–62, 82, 157. *See also* bardo experience; immortality; rein-
    carnation; suicide
    ~ and the Antares gateway, IV:87
    ~ and the astral plane, I:98, VII:9
    ~ and burial, I:77, IX:118
    ~ of a child, I:91, 106, XIII:78, 83
    ~ compared to birth, I:83
    ~ conscious (mahasamadhi), I:76, IV:198, V:65, 83
    ~ and cremation, I:77, IV:221, IX:118
    ~ and delayed ascension, I:30
    ~ fear of, I:46, XIII:107
    ~ of gardens, IV:145
    ~ and Hinduism, IV:221–22, 227
    ~ and the Huna teachings, IV:165
    ~ illusion of, I:2, 74, 98, 223, IV:273, VII:13, IX:96, 134,
        XIII:157
    ~ and initiation, I:74–75, 84, III:5, IV:180–81, 187
    ~ Moslem traditions for, V:157
    ~ preparation for, I:81–82
    ~ process of, I:84–85
    ~ second, I:74, 97
    ~ for a seventh-degree initiate, III:106

~ and spiritual evolution, XIII:61

~ vs. teleportation, III:106

death threats, IV:91

decadelta light encodements, VIII:63

Declaration of Independence, V:241

deforestation, IV:13

de Gabalis, Comte, V:240

de Gergy, Madame, V:240–41

dematerialization, III:255, IV:165, 168, VI:49, 70, 80, 123, 129, 134, 208, IX:128. *See also* ascended masters: advanced abilities of

democracy, VI:178–79, IX:244. *See also* leadership: democratic; political system (U.S.)

Democrats, IX:44, 47, 49, 81, 95, 128, 148. *See also* political system (U.S.)

Denaerde, Stefan, IV:45–46

denial, I:271, V:15–16, VI:219, VII:29–30, 43, 49, VIII:92–93, XIII:129

de Pompadour, Madame, V:241

depression, IV:138

Deros, IV:58. *See also* extraterrestrials

desire, I:77, 156, 265, III:5, 103, IV:57, 187, 225, 261, 265, V:11–12, 31, 50–51, 75, 82–83, 150, **VI:17,** VI:173, 175, 180, XI:42

~ animal, I:65

~ for ascension, VI:141

~ and building the light quotient, III:24

~ carnal, I:65, 269

~ death of, I:23, 74

~ and the first ray, VI:191

~ for God-realization, I:66, 103, 156, 265, III:1, 103, IV:219, V:23, 77, VI:201, VII:90, VIII:8, IX:139, XI:42, XIII:49

~ higher-self, VI:140, VII:30, VIII:8

~ lower-self, VI:140, VII:30, XII:95

~ mastery of, I:200, III:1, VII:9, 26

~ material, I:60, 65–66, 88–89, 98, 265, III:1, 103–4, IV:57, V:21, 53, 108

~ spiritual, III:103–4

desire body, IV:259, VI:18, 174, IX:127, 129, 135

~ between lives, I:93

~ mastery of, I:265, VI:60, 167, 240, 249, VII:25, IX:4

The Destiny of the Nations, VI:177, 179, 182, 186

detachment, I:108, 117, 268, III:118, IV:232–33, 240, 254–56, 258, 261, 263, 270, 324, 328, V:30, 83, 95, 128, VI:139, 159–60, 172–74, VIII:9, 130, IX:2, 14, 21, 28, 33, 70, 150, 198–99,

211–13, X:19, 114, 119, 198, XI:36, 113, XIII:146, 152, 156, 158.
See also attachment
~ and spiritual leadership, IX:198–99, 212–13
devachan, VII:63–64. *See also* mental plane
~ and physical death, I:75, 84
devas, I:195, IV:129, 131–32, 139–40, 142–45, 151–53, VII:7,
109–10, 113, 119–20, IX:110, X:96–97, 101, 213–15, 226, 239.
See also angelic kingdom; brownies; dryads; dwarves; elementals;
elves; fairy folk; fauns; goblins; hamadryads; nature spirits;
nymphs; Pan (god of the nature spirits); pygmies; satyrs; sylvestres;
trolls
~ astral, IV:139
~ and the elementals, IV:135
~ evolution of, I:191, III:181, IV:122–23, 129–30, VII:19, 109,
119, X:23, 34, 96–97, 213–15, 239
~ green, IV:129
~ hierarchy of, IV:122, 129
~ human oppression of, VII:110
~ lunar pitris, IV:129–30
~ of magnetization, IV:129
~ Overlighting Deva of Healing, I:38, III:38, 80, 97
~ and the Path the Solar Logos Himself Is On, III:181
~ rate of vibrational frequency of, VII:110
~ and the rays, X:24, 35, 44
~ solar pitris, IV:122, 129–30
~ violet, IV:129
~ and Wesak, X:152–53
~ white, IV:129
devil. *See* Satan
devotional songs, V:25, 64, VIII:96, XII:29. *See also* bhajans; music
~ singing of, I:155, 252
~ and yoga, I:163, IV:249
Dhammapada, V:96, VIII:160. *See also* Buddhism
Dharamsala, India, V:105, 107
dharma (life path), I:28, 269, IV:219, 225, 263, V:94, 96, 100, 111,
113, VIII:8, 160, X:2. *See also* spiritual path
Dickens, Charles, X:64
Diegel, Patricia, VIII:xix, xxii, XI:157
Diet for a New America, IV:149–50
dimensions, I:16, 91, 197, III:139–40, 146, 150–51, 192–93, 240–41,
245, IV:260, **IV:267**–68, VI:87, 90, 115, 127, VIII:40, 42, 56,
XI:31, 191, 257, XII:118
~ Agam Lok, **IV:196**
~ Alakh Lok, **IV:196**
~ Alaya Lok, **IV:196**

~ anchoring of, III:37
~ and angels, IV:121
~ Animi Lok, **IV:196**
~ and the arts, III:148
~ and ashrams, **VI:204**
~ Atma Lok, **IV:196**
~ and bodies, VI:204, **VI:204**, VI:205, **VI:205**, VI:206
~ and the chakras, III:193, VI:205–6
~ and color, **IV:195**–96, IV:197
~ eighth, III:16, 142–46, 152, 174, **III:238, VI:3,** VI:10, 19, 49, 54, 62, **VI:62,** VI:63, 66, 86, **VI:204**
~ eleventh, III:147, **III:238,** III:239, **VI:3,** VI:62, **VI:62, 204,** XI:120
~ fifth, I:36–37, 215, 274, 277, III:4, 14, 140, 142–43, 149–51, 196, **III:238,** III:239, 249, IV:64, 206, **VI:3,** VI:6, 10–11, 37, 47–49, 51, 57, 61–62, **VI:63,** VI:140, **VI:205,** VI:223, 245, VII:131, VIII:63, 116, IX:8, 92, 99, 102–3, 110, 115, 122–23, 128, 134, 138, 169–70, 179, X:202, 237--38, 240, XI:98, 143, 160, 187
~ first, III:140, **III:238, VI:3**
~ forty-eighth, **III:238, VI:3,** XI:191, 210
~ forty-ninth, **III:238,** III:241, 245, **VI:3,** XI:31, 191
~ and the four-body system, III:149–50
~ fourth, I:125, 146, 179, 205–6, 212, 214–15, 217, 240, 243, III:14, 105, 141–42, 144, 150, 153, 177, 179, 196, **III:238,** IV:2, 206, 315, **VI:3,** VI:6, 10, 47–49, 51, 57, 59, 61–62, **VI:63,** VI:127–29, 140, **VI:205,** VI:245, VII:131, VIII:16, IX:99–100, 169, X:146, 175, 189, 202, 237, XI:98
~ higher, III:147–48, **VI:204**
~ Hukikat Lok, **IV:196**
~ invocation for, III:48
~ and the Kabbalistic tree of life, III:148, **IV:303**
~ and light quotient, VI:205–6
~ and mantras, IV:249
~ merging with, III:48
~ ninth, III:16, 142–47, 149, 153, 237, **III:238, VI:3,** VI:10–11, 19, 49, 54, 62, **VI:62,** VI:63, 86, **VI:204,** XI:120, 187, 210
~ and the rays, I:131–32
~ second, III:140–41, **III:238, VI:3**
~ and the seven levels of initiation, III:4, **III:4,** III:139–40, VI:205–6
~ seventh, I:36, 222, III:16, 142–43, 146, 153, **III:238, VI:3,** VI:10, 62, **VI:62**–63, **204,** VI:245, IX:179
~ sixth, I:36, 277, III:4, 10, 14, 16, 142–43, 147, 149, 152–53, **III:238,** III:239, **VI:3,** VI:10–11, 62, **VI:63, 204,** VI:245, IX:138, 179, XI:98

~ and sound, **IV:195,** IV:196, **IV:196,** IV:197, 249

~ and sports, III:149

~ Sugmad, **IV:196**

~ Sugmad Lok, **IV:196**

~ tenth, III:146–47, **III:238,** III:239, **VI:3,** VI:62, **VI:62, 204,** XI:120

~ third, I:215, 222, 240, 243, III:14, 141–42, 148, 150, **III:238, VI:3,** VI:10, 37, 47–49, 51, 57, 62, **VI:63,** VI:71, 127–29, 140, **VI:205,** VI:209, 223, 245, VII:131, IX:8, 38–39, 99–100, 102, 110, 114, 122, 139, 169, X:146, 175, 189, 202, 237

~ thirty-sixth, **III:238, VI:3**

~ travel between, III:148, IV:79, 102

~ twelfth, III:147, 193, **III:238,** III:239, **VI:3,** VI:27, 62, **VI:62,** VI:134, **VI:204,** VI:208–9, 221, VIII:51, 107, IX:128, XI:120

~ twenty-fourth, **III:238, VI:3**

~ and vortexes, III:149

dinosaurs, I:7–8

~ in the inner Earth, IV:27

Dionysus, V:136

discernment, I:174, III:56, VII:78, VIII:84, 128–29, 132, IX:17, 33–34, 38, 64, 86–87, 227, 269, 273–74, 276, X:47, 104, 113, 230, XI:6, 268, XIII:44, 50, 123, 129

~ spiritual, **I:71, IV:267**–68, IV:274, 282, VI:49–50, 137–38, 217–18, 228, VII:80, VIII:5, IX:74, 77, 136, 143, XI:198, XIII:138

disciples, I:21–24, 28, 56, 66, 84, 92, 97, 108–13, 116–18, 144–45, **I:199,** I:200, 263–65, III:1–2, 16, 70–71, 176, **IV:130,** IV:257, 268, VI:33, 57, 144, 156, 165, 172–75, VII:36, 75, 89, 154, IX:183, 211–12, X:52, 116, 118, XII:131, XIII:66. *See also* chela

~ the accepted disciple, VI:165, 168–69, VII:23–24

~ and the antakarana, I:43–49

~ of ascended masters, V:2, 15, 25, 29–31, 36–37, 41, 49–50, 85, 113, 141–44, 150, 164, 223–24, VII:72, X:139

~ chela in the light, VI:165–68

~ chela on the thread, VI:165, 169–70

~ chela within his master's heart, VI:165, 172

~ chela within the aura, VI:165, 170–72

~ differences among, VI:187

~ and glamour, I:59–60

~ of Jesus, I:9, 31, 142, 160, 171, 175–76, 217, 237, 241–42, IV:171, 288, V:133–34, 194, VI:148, 171, XI:84

~ little chelaship, VI:165–66

~ and overshadowing, I:142–43

~ and the rays, VI:186–87, 190–91

Discipleship in the New Age, Volumes I and II, VI:165

disease, I:78, III:55–56, 104, IV:8–9, V:67, VI:240, VIII:33, 35, 77, 143, 149, IX:55–56, 59, 61–63, X:243, XII:128, XIII:108. *See also* AIDS; Alzeimer's disease; cancer; healing
> ~ clearing of, VI:126, XII:127–28
> ~ and dairy products, IX:86
> ~ and physical death, I:76–77
> ~ and pollution, IX:86
> ~ sexually transmitted, XIII:129–32
> ~ and sugar, IX:59

Divine Father. *See* Father, the

Divine Life, V:65. *See also* Sivananda, Swami

Divine Life Society, V:63–66

Divine Mother. *See* Mother, the

divine plane, I:16, 132. *See also* logoic plane; logoic plane, cosmic

The Divine Pymander, V:124. *See also* Hermes-Thoth

divorce, IX:46, 148–49, 187, XIII:52, 93–96, 116, 119, 127–28, 139, 152
> ~ causes of, XIII:153–54
> ~ in Islamic teaching, V:159
> ~ and unconditional love, XIII:25, 95

Dix, Betty J., IV:59

Djwhal Khul (ascended master), I:1, 16, 41, 70, 138–39, 177, 186, 189–90, 241, 275, 281, 283, 285, III:4, 15, 17, 34, 56, 62, 64, 67, 69–70, 83, 91, 95, 101, 103, 105, 123, 125, 169, 197, 201, IV:10, 317, V:35, 93–94, 97, 108, 242, VI:49, 94, **VI:112**, VI:126, 171, 193–94, 225, 237, 242–43, VII:16, 18, 79, 148, VIII:34–35, 42–43, 46–49, 58, 64, 68–69, 75, 94, 96, 114, 127, 131, 159–60, 164, 178, IX:2, 9, 29, 176, 200, 205, X:23, 33, 82, 156, 159, XI:19–20, 39, 45, 51–52, 76, 100–101, 108, 111–12, 158, 174, 188, 191, 202, 218, 242, XIII:55, 109
> ~ and the Affirmation of the Disciple, XII:5
> ~ and the ascension ceremony, XI:10
> ~ ascension of, I:187, VI:6
> ~ ashrams of, I:275, 284, III:66–67, 100, 119, **VI:64**, VI:224–25, IX:93, 179–80, XI:30, 53, 107, 110, 113
> ~ and the building of the antakarana, I:47
> ~ as Chohan of the second ray, III:257, VI:241, **VII:19**, X:14, 32–33, 140
> ~ computer of, VIII:61
> ~ golden orb of, III:122
> ~ healing seat of, VI:35–36
> ~ his prayer for the manifestation of money, III:165–66
> ~ his system of pattern removal, III:191
> ~ and initiation, I:21

~ initiations of, VI:22

~ and the levels of delusion, I:57–58, 61, 63–65, 67

~ light-quotient building program of, I:283–84, III:29, 39, VI:115, VIII:38

~ and the Mahatma, X:149–51

~ meditations given by, I:51–56

~ other lives of, I:171, 237, V:119, 141, 203, 226, VI:147

~ and the paths to higher evolution, III:168, 177, XI:98

~ personality of, X:207

~ quotations from, I:13, 21, 57, 105, 144, 197, 205, III:1, 187, IV:29, VI:104, 152–54, VII:32, 34, 107, VIII:126, xxv, IX:139, X:28, 44, 59, XI:36, 65, 175, 268, XII:78–80, XIII:31

~ and the second ray, I:120, X:30, XI:70

~ and the soul or monadic mantra, I:50, 258–59, III:54, VI:199, VIII:95, XII:2–3

~ Synthesis Ashram of, VI:35, 49, 115, 118–20, 144, **VI:204,** VI:231, VII:112, 143–45, VIII:107, 127, 161, 183, IX:177–78, 193, X:32–33, 149–52, 156, XI:218–19, 240, 250, XIII:67

~ and the Theosophical Society, V:201–3, 217–18, 225–26, 228–29, VII:84

~ and the Tibetan Foundation, I:202, 207

~ and Wesak, VIII:138, IX:93, 200, XI:175, 226, XII:83–85

DNA, III:105, 192–93, 206, **III:238, VI:3,** VI:210, IX:136

~ anchoring of, I:38, 272, III:19, 50, 128, 194, 199, 241, 257, 266, IV:35, VI:26–27, **VI:62,** VI:87, 130, VIII:45, X:225, XI:32, 94, 268

~ and the Arcturians, III:83–84

~ as evidence, IX:67–68

~ experiments by Grays, IV:73

~ sacred-letter grid of, VI:130, VIII:56–57

Dogon tribe, IV:69–70. *See also* extraterrestrials

Dog Star. *See* Sirius

Dome of the Rock, V:156

dominions (heavenly governors), **IV:123,** IV:124. *See also* angelic kingdom

Donahue, IX:147

Donaldson, Sam, IX:77

Doors of Mithra. *See* Parsi religion

Doyle, Sir Arthur Conan, IV:140

Draconis, IV:73

dreams, IV:194, VII:74–75, VIII:98, 110, IX:55, 236–37, XII:100–101

~ about Sathya Sai Baba, I:154, VIII:xix, XI:105–6, 157, 169–71
~ and discipleship, VI:168
~ and the higher self, IV:159
~ and initiation, IV:182
~ and intuition, VII:74–75
~ and physical death, I:98
~ and the planet Neptune, I:97

dream state, III:16, IV:193, 259, V:87, 111, VI:69, 71, 74, 203, VII:35–36. *See also* sleep state
~ and the Arcturians, IV:67–68
~ and ascension, XI:157–71
~ and astral travel, IV:165
~ and extraterrestrials, VII:132
~ and the initiation process, IV:180–81
~ lucid dreaming, I:271, IV:180, 194, 203
~ and repetition of the name of God, I:251–52

Dreyfuss, Richard, XI:231

drug addicts, I:98
~ between lives, I:93–94

drug industry. *See* health-care system, drug manufacturers

drugs, I:269, IV:3, 30, 269, V:88, VIII:143, 149, IX:84, 117–18, 166
~ and Baha'i, IV:328
~ and the CIA, IV:9, 17
~ legalization of, IX:145–46
~ for medical purposes, IX:145–46
~ prior to physical death, I:82–83
~ in the prison system, IX:72
~ and the secret government, IV:4, 9, 17

dryads, IV:122, 134, **IV:135**. *See also* devas; elementals: gnomes (nature spirits of earth); nature spirits

duality, IV:237, V:51–52, 123, 126–27, VI:51, 137–40, 190, 223, IX:7, 120, X:234
~ transcendence of, I:156, 267, IV:224, 235, 258, 262, V:15, 86, 128, VIII:16, IX:5, 7, 128, XI:36

Dulce, New Mexico
~ extraterrestrial base at, IV:6–7 (*See also* bases, extraterrestrial)

The Dulce Papers, IV:7

durdalis, **IV:135**. *See also* devas; elementals: gnomes (nature spirits of earth); nature spirits

Durga (Hindu warrior goddess), IV:219

dwarves, IV:131. *See also* devas; nature spirits

dweller on the threshold, I:57–58, 66–67, 118, 264, 271, IV:180, 189
~ dispelling of, I:66–67, VIII:21
~ and its remedy, the angel of the presence, **I:58**

E

Earth, I:2, 11, 32, 77–78, 181–82, 189, 213–17, 281, III:9, 178,
   198–99, **III:238,** IV:51, 124–26, 129, **IV:130,** IV:133, 154,
   VI:3, VI:68, 145, 245, VII:54, 86, 134, 144, VIII:94, 191, IX:97,
   X:85, 213, 236–37, XI:42, 142, 225. *See also* Agartha; environment; hollow Earth; Mother Earth; pollution
   ~ antakarana for, I:45
   ~ ascension of, III:12, 119, 196, 201, VI:77, 223, VII:16,
      IX:8–9, 133, X:221, XI:173
   ~ astral body of, VII:2
   ~ aura of, VI:126, IX:104
   ~ catastrophes of, I:8–9
   ~ chakras of, III:131, 149
   ~ colonization and conquest of, IV:2–3, 36, 73, 75, 77
   ~ and color healing, **IV:212**
   ~ creation of, I:10–12
   ~ and the divine feminine, XIII:16–18, 128
   ~ evolution of, I:25, 143, 186–87, 201, 206, 209–10, 219,
      III:169–70, 196, 200, IV:2, 58, VI:6, 10, VII:16, 20, 32,
      85–86, 130–31, IX:37, 99, 107, 109, 120, 163, 167, X:34,
      52, 55, 93, 108, 146, 179, 238, 244, XI:4–5
   ~ extraterrestrial bases on, IV:6–8, 17, 43, 66, 74–75, VI:127,
      VII:132
   ~ in the fifth dimension, III:196, VI:6, 10, IX:99, 115, 170,
      X:238
   ~ in the fourth dimension, I:205–6, 212, 214–15, 217, 240,
      243, III:105, 141–42, 144, 150, 177, 179, 196, IV:2, VI:6,
      10, X:146
   ~ Golden Age of, I:125, 145–46, 226, 241–42, IV:68, 70, 85,
      VI:222, 224, VII:133, IX:78, 119, 133, X:20, 37, 39, 45, 69,
      122, 148, 153, 168, 176, 178, 214, 217, 221, 225–26, 228,
      231, 236, 243–44, XI:143, XIII:19
   ~ grid points of, I:182, III:56–57, 152, 171, 176, IV:60–61, 66,
      169, 206, VIII:64, 103, X:245
   ~ group body of, X:67
   ~ healing of, VIII:20, X:148, XI:206–7, 226–27
   ~ initiations of, I:277, III:11–12, 187, IX:133, X:221, 244

~ light quotient of, X:232
~ and the Mahatma energy, I:213–17
~ mystery school of, I:11, III:12, 87, 198, IV:109, 262, 269,
    V:176, VI:23–24, 72, VII:130, VIII:12, 20–21, 94, 117–18,
    IX:37, 96, X:52
~ and the Order of Melchizedek, I:281
~ pollution of, IV:8, 11–13, 152
~ and the rays, **I:131, VI:82,** IX:38, X:92, **XI:177**
~ as a sacred planet, **I:131,** I:205–6, III:11, 105, 141, 176,
    182, IV:2, **VI:82,** VIII:xiii, IX:115, X:34
~ in the seventh dimension, I:222
~ shifting axis of, I:224
~ and Taurus, **XI:177**
~ in the third dimension, VI:10, IX:38–39, 99, X:146
~ as "Urantia," VI:73
~ vibrational frequencies of, IX:254–55, XIII:81–82
~ and the violet transmuting flame, X:241
Earth Day, IV:152
Earth, history of, I:4, **I:5,** I:134, 214, 216–17, 225, 228, 240,
    III:169–70, 198, IV:38, 49, VII:110, 130, 151–52, X:93–94, 228,
    XI:25–26, 187, 219
~ Age of Melchizedek, XI:5–6
~ Aryan age, I:44, 66
~ ascension in, I:31, 33
~ Atlantean times, I:3, 7–10, 44, 58, **I:59,** I:63, 142, 214, 231,
    237, 241–42, 244–45, IV:38, 70, 147, X:179, 216, 226 (*See
    also* Atlantis)
~ cycles in, I:145, IV:239, X:41
~ and dinosaurs, I:7–8
~ Egyptian times, I:9–10, X:179, 226 (*See also* Egypt)
~ the Electrical Wars, I:6–7, 182, IV:1
~ extraterrestrial invasions in, IV:17
~ Lemurian times, I:7–8, 44, 58, **I:59,** I:65, 134, 242, IV:38
    (*See also* Lemuria (Mu))
~ mass ascension in, I:6, 29, XI:173
~ pre-Atlantean times, X:216
~ pre-Lemurian times, I:6, 182, III:12, IV:1
~ and the sixth ray, I:124
earth spirits, **IV:135.** *See also* devas; elementals: gnomes (nature spir-
    its of earth); nature spirits
Earth star, **I:52,** I:53, 55–56
Easter, VIII:139, XII:77, 89
Eastwood, Clint, IX:134
Easwaran, Eknath, IV:233, V:72–74, VIII:166
Ebe, IV:5. *See also* extraterrestrials

Eckancar (mystery school), IV:195, 197, 249, V:168, VIII:167, IX:121

Eckankar: The Key to Secret Worlds, IV:200. *See also* Twitchell, Paul

Eckhart, Meister, I:124
    ~ as a walk-in, IV:31

ecology. *See* environment

economics, IX:50–51, 107, 148
    ~ cosmic, IV:46
    ~ homelessness, IX:91
    ~ minimum wage, IX:80, 147
    ~ prophecy for, III:99
    ~ and unemployment, IX:92
    ~ U.S. trade agreement, IX:164–65
    ~ and the welfare system, IX:78, 80–81, 130

ecstasy. *See* drugs

Ecuador
    ~ blocked grid point in, IV:61

Edenic state, I:1

Edgar Cayce foundation, V:246

Edgar Cayce on the Dead Sea Scrolls, IV:296

Edinburgh, Scotland, IV:134

Edison, Thomas, I:120, IV:11, V:211

educational system, VII:47, IX:45–46, 77, 116–17, 137, XIII:73, 153
    ~ and abuse, IX:149–50
    ~ and crime, IX:150–52
    ~ spirituality in, IX:77–78
    ~ and spiritual leadership, IX:77

education, spiritual, IX:49–50

Edwards Air Force Base, IV:5

ego, I:2, 155, 222–23, 225, 263, IV:10, 115, 180, 189, 202, 225–26, 235, 261–62, 281, V:20, 60–61, 75–76, 96, 168, VI:57, 85, 217, 220, 245, VIII:133, IX:75. *See also* negative ego
    ~ advanced, I:134
    ~ and the antakarana, I:46
    ~ Atlantean, I:134
    ~ battle between walk-ins and walk-outs, IV:31–32
    ~ and the group-body consciousness, XI:221–22
    ~ spiritualized, VII:27
    ~ and spiritual leadership, IX:6
    ~ transcendence of, V:30–31, 65

egotism, I:76, V:13, VI:140, 219, 225, VIII:128, IX:108, 162

Egypt, I:9–10, 28, 173, 230, 237, III:56, 131, IV:167, 170, V:123, 133–34, 245, X:226–27, XI:1
    ~ and the Annu, IV:23

~ art of, I:3, X:93
~ and Atlantis, IV:167–68
~ Eighteenth Dynasty, IV:93
~ entrance to the hollow Earth in, IV:25
~ and extraterrestrials, I:10, IV:1, 168–69, 175, VII:133
~ and Hermes-Thoth, IV:168, V:123
~ immigrations to, IV:171
~ initiation in, I:9, 37, 173, 231, 236, IV:93, 170–71, 174–77, 179–92, VI:69, VIII:134, X:226–27, XI:2, XII:107
~ King Zoser, IV:174–75
~ pyramids of, I:9–10, 242, 245, IV:70, 167–70, V:242, VII:133 (*See also* Great Pyramid)
~ and Ra-Ta, IV:171–73, V:245
~ temples of, IV:70, 168
~ Third Dynasty, IV:157, 174
~ the Virgin Mary in, V:187
~ vortexes of, III:149

Egyptian Freemasonry Lodge, V:242

Egyptian government
~ and underground tunnels, IV:24

Egyptian mysteries, I:237, IV:167–73, 175–77, V:135, XII:119

Egyptians, I:231, 242, IV:168, 174, 180, 192, VII:134
~ art of, I:3, X:93
~ and the Huna teachings, I:236, IV:157
~ mantras of, I:257, XII:22
~ prophecies of, IV:174
~ and the Ra, IV:93
~ and third-dimensional Sirians, IV:69–70
~ writings of the hollow Earth, IV:25

eighth ray, I:126–29, **I:135**, III:108, 203, **III:238, VI:3,** VI:39–40, **VI:41,** VIII:49, X:13, **X:13, XI:76.** *See also* rays, twelve
~ and color healing, **IV:210**
~ and the Kabbalistic tree of life, **IV:311**

Einstein, Albert, IV:14, V:211, IX:136

Eisenhower, Dwight D., IV:5–6, 10, 47–48

eka body, III:218–19, 227, VI:25, VIII:59, XI:196

Elam (ruler of the physical plane), **IV:195**

The Elder Brother, V:226, 230. *See also* Tillet, Gregory

Eldridge (battleship), IV:15

Electoral College, IX:48. *See also* political system (U.S.)

Electrical Ones, I:6–7, 182

electricity
~ and Atlantis, I:9

electromagnetic body, III:218–19, 227, VI:25, XI:149–50, 154

~ and the physical body, XI:151

electromagnetism, IV:23

El Elyon, V:133

elementals, IV:122, 129, 131, 134, 139–40, 142, VII:110–11, 113, 119, IX:110, X:25. *See also* devas; nature spirits
 ~ astral, IV:138–39, X:199
 ~ clearing of, VI:241, VIII:29
 ~ and disease, IX:86
 ~ emotional, X:199
 ~ evolution of, VII:111
 ~ gnomes (nature spirits of earth), IV:122, **IV:128, 130,** IV:131, 134–35, **IV:135,** IV:136, 141–42, 153–54, VII:7, 109, 111
  Gob, IV:136
  and the mineral kingdom, IV:136, 153–54
 ~ and love, IV:136
 ~ negative, I:34, 39, 284, III:50, IV:138, VI:33, 87, 101, 119, 228, VII:111–12, VIII:34, 125, IX:55, 86, XII:69–70, 121, XIII:174
 ~ of the plant kingdom, IV:129
 ~ salamanders (nature spirits of fire), IV:122, **IV:128,** IV:131, 135, **IV:135,** IV:137, VII:111
 ~ sylphs (nature spirits of air), IV:122, **IV:128,** IV:129, **IV:130,** IV:131, 135, **IV:135,** IV:137–38, 188, VII:111
 ~ undines (nature spirits of water), IV:122, **IV:128,** IV:129, 131, 135, **IV:135,** IV:136–37, 188
 ~ and violet devas, IV:129
 ~ and Wesak, X:153

elements, Earth, IX:168
 ~ air, **I:184,** IV:131, 135
 ~ earth, **I:184,** IV:131, 135
 ~ fire, **I:184,** IV:131, 135, 137
 ~ and the Kabbalistic tree of life, **IV:304**
 ~ water, I:100, **I:184,** IV:12, 14, **IV:130,** IV:131, 135, 209

The Elephant Man, VII:97

11:11, I:233, 283, III:29, XI:160

eleventh ray, I:127, 129, **I:135,** III:204, **III:238,** IV:309, **VI:3,** VI:39, **VI:41, X:13,** XI:45, **XI:76.** *See also* rays, twelve
 ~ and color healing, **IV:210**
 ~ and the Kabbalistic tree of life, **IV:311**

Elijah (prophet), III:224, 226, IV:285, 288, 290, V:156
 ~ as an incarnation of John the Baptist, I:171, IV:277, 290
 ~ and the Order of Melchizedek, I:228

Elisha (prophet), IV:288, 290

Elizabeth I, V:240

Elkins, Don, IV:93

El Morya (ascended master), I:125, 138, 190, III:48, 95, **III:238,** IV:197, 224, 250, 253, V:242, **VI:3,** VI:108, **VI:112,** VI:248, VIII:160, IX:2, 9, 176, X:28, 71, XI:61, 202–3
 ~ ascension of, VI:6
 ~ ashram of, I:284, VI:107, **VI:204,** VI:225, VIII:126
 ~ as Chohan of the first ray, I:171, 189, **I:199,** I:201, III:257, **IV:121,** VI:144, 163, 214, 241, **VII:19, 117,** IX:1, X:14, 27–29, 73, 141, 152–53, XI:70–71
 ~ other lives of, I:171, 237, IV:277, 287, V:108, 175, VI:148
 ~ sacred glen ascension seat of, III:191
 ~ and the Theosophical Society, V:201–4, 206, 208–9, 215–16, 219–20, 225, 228, 233, VII:84
 ~ and Wesak, X:152

elohim, I:202, III:141, 217, 231–32, IV:119–20, 278, V:154, VI:90, 112, VII:106, 113–14, VIII:62, X:212, XI:53–54, 60, 95, XIII:55, 65. *See also* angelic kingdom
 ~ Apollo and Lumina, **I:199, 203,** III:199, IV:120, VII:113
 ~ Arcturus and Victoria, **I:199, 203,** III:200, IV:120, VII:113
 ~ ashrams of, VIII:127
 ~ Cyclopia and Virginia, **I:199, 203,** III:199–200, IV:120, VII:113
 ~ divine template of, III:220, VIII:62
 ~ Hercules and Amazonia, **I:199, 203,** III:199, IV:120, VII:113
 ~ Heros and Amora, **I:199, 203,** III:199, IV:120, VII:113
 ~ and the Kabbalistic tree of life, **IV:304**
 ~ light packets of information from, VI:115
 ~ Peace and Aloha, **I:199, 203,** III:200, IV:120, VII:113
 ~ Purity and Astrea, **I:199, 203,** III:199, IV:120, VII:113
 ~ and the rays, **I:203,** III:199–200
 ~ seven mighty, **I:199,** I:203, III:54, 199–200, 243, IV:120
 ~ twelve mighty, III:220, 222, 227, **III:238,** III:250, **VI:3**

elohim computers, III:54, 105, 200, VI:37, XI:51
 ~ aligning with, I:285, VIII:62

Elohim Council, **VI:111,** VIII:62

Elohim (God), IV:120, 278

elohim scriptures, III:128, XI:95, 97–98, 114–15

Elohim Vista, III:156

Elohistic Lord's body, **III:238,** III:258, **VI:3,** VI:25, 202–3, VIII:59, XI:195
 ~ and the dimensions, **VI:204**

El Paso, Texas, VIII:103

El Shaddai (God), IV:278
 ~ garment of, III:221, VIII:60, XII:20

elves, IV:122, 129, 131–34, **IV:135,** IV:136, 141, VII:7, 121. *See also* devas; elementals: gnomes (nature spirits of earth); nature spirits
~ in the Findhorn Garden, IV:132–33

The Emerald Forest, IV:152

Emerald Tablets of Thoth, VI:145

Emerson, Willis George, IV:22–23

emotional body, I:18, 63, III:5, IV:105, 193, 241, V:216, VI:18, 61, 72, 100, 102–3, 121, 131, 142, 194, 219, VII:1, 21, 23, 141, VIII:30, 49, IX:79, 129, 135, 140, X:4, 87–88, 108, 110, 113, 120, 199–200, 220, 227, 237, XII:95, XIII:4, 84, 107. *See also* astral body; four-body system
~ and adultery, XIII:117–18
~ appearance of, VIII:4, XIII:7–8
~ and the Atlantean root race, **VI:78**
~ and Bhakti yoga, IV:241
~ clearing of, VI:62, 240, VII:29, VIII:31–32, IX:71, X:56
~ and color, IV:206–7
~ and the fourth dimension, III:142, 150
~ and glamour, I:59–60
~ and integrating soul extensions, VI:93–94
~ integration of, VI:193–94, VII:160–61, XI:17
~ and joy, X:87–88
~ light quotient of, VI:4
~ and the Mahatma energy, I:213
~ mastery of, I:23, 64, 66, 163, 200, 265, III:1, 196, **III:238,** IV:183, 198, 254, 259, 270, **VI:3,** VI:4, 60, 100, 167, 249, VII:9, 25–26, VIII:24, IX:4, XI:267, XIII:139–40, 163
~ and negative extraterrestrials, IV:17
~ and the rays, I:117, 120–22, VI:187, X:19, 39
~ and the repetition of the name of God, I:249, 251–52
~ and the second initiation, I:23, 64, III:1, IV:270, VII:25–26
~ and self-love, X:199–200
~ and sex, XIII:39, 41, 44, 47, 170
~ and the soul, I:106–7, 112
~ during walk-ins, IV:29–30, 32
~ and the yoga sutras of Patanjali, IV:254, 257–58

emotional plane, I:16, 57, VI:59–60, VII:25, 162, X:200, 210, 232, XII:97. *See also* astral plane
~ and the Kabbalistic tree of life, **IV:303**
~ and the sixth ray, VI:180
~ and spiritual etiquette, X:167
~ and the supersenses, **I:71**
~ and synthesis, X:149

emotional ray, I:116, VI:186–87, X:11–13, 128. *See also* rays, seven: configuration of

emotions, I:266, III:69, IV:261, VI:51, 86, VII:26, IX:55, X:18. *See also* love
- ~ the animal kingdom's sensitivity to, IV:148
- ~ of animals, VII:124–25, 127, XIII:69
- ~ and the lower self, IV:158
- ~ mastery of, I:23, III:1, VIII:4, X:200
- ~ negative, I:95, 155, V:70, 86, 108, 112, 250, VI:60, 101, 193, 228, VII:111, 155, VIII:119, IX:121, 230, X:51, 213 (*See also* anger; fear; jealousy)

empowerment, I:99, 118, 265, 269, III:55, 99, 108, 155, 195, IV:3, 9–10, 14, 30, 73, 78, 226, 255–56, V:50, 253, VI:14, 40, 103, 107–8, 174, 197, 221, 245, VII:45–51, 53, 157, VIII:6–7, 9–10, 20, 22, 49, 68, 73, 80, 82–83, 97, 105, 110, 112, 117, IX:1–2, 4, 22, 92, 184, 212–13, 218–19, 223, 228–29, 259, X:11, 16, 25, 41, 44, 71, 94, 137, 140–41, 153, 176, 200, 206, 212, 227–28, XI:29, 40, XII:95, XIII:10–11, 34, 115, 121, 150, 161, 177, 181
- ~ and ascended masters, I:265, VIII:7, 123, 127–29
- ~ and manifestation, VIII:82, 84
- ~ and money, XIII:34–35
- ~ and spiritual leadership, IX:1–2, 19, 50, 116, 173, 198, 223, 234–35
- ~ techniques for, IX:4–5

Encyclopedia Britannica, IX:48

energy, I:34, 163, 247, III:35, 98, 106, 110–11, 114, 148, 157, 226, IV:17, 61, 66, 71, 105, 131, 159–60, 170, 205, 228, 246, V:95, 125, 154, 169, VI:12, 18, 24, 32, 36, 51, 94, 137, 203, 210, 230, 236, VII:2, 107, 110, 125–26, 150, VIII:31, 79, 104, 136, 147, vii, IX:36, 50, 124, 127, 157, 173, 206, 213, 217, 220, 260, 263, 272, X:107, 245, XI:52, 231, XII:1–2, 11, XIII:60, 145, 149, 168, 171, 176
- ~ and the antakarana, I:43–44, 47–48, 51, 54, 56, 77, 113
- ~ ascension energy, III:54, IV:181, VI:193–94
- ~ and color, IV:206–7, **IV:208,** IV:209, 211, VIII:179
- ~ conserving, VIII:142, 148
- ~ of the dimensions, III:140, 142, 150, 152
- ~ divine use of, I:124, 272, III:87, 197–98, IV:258, V:110, VI:14, 37, 141, VII:101–2, VIII:24, 92, 148, 154, 184–85, IX:62, 160, 226, X:21, 172
- ~ fifth-dimensional, VI:47
- ~ fourth-dimensional, I:178
- ~ and healing, III:68, 97–98, 100, 107–8, IV:60, VII:20, 79, VIII:184, X:243
- ~ of holy days, VI:150–53, XII:78–79, 85
- ~ increasing, I:36, 54, III:52, 79, 95, 101, 124, 255, IV:124, 162, 265, 293, VI:17, 26, 33, 52, VIII:102, 147, XI:42
- ~ and light-quotient building, III:23–24, 27, 29

~ negative, I:53, III:58, 202, VII:144, VIII:29, 114, XII:12, XIII:137

~ and physical death, I:84–85

~ of planets, I:94–96

~ of plants, IV:139–40, 142–44, 153, VII:113

~ Purple Positive Energy Plate, III:120–21, VIII:142, 144, 151

~ of the rays, I:118–28, 131, 189–96, 268, III:104, 203, IV:210, VI:39, 42–43, 45, 177–80, 186–91, VII:19, 79, 81, 116, 143, 156, VIII:7, 34, X:15, 17–18, 20, 22–25, 27–29, 33–35, 39, 41, 43, 46, 73, 83, 93, 120, 140–41, 153, 212, 226, 242–43, XI:256

~ and the seven paths to higher evolution, III:170–73, 176–78, 182

~ shifting, VIII:79–80, IX:133, XIII:106

~ spiritual, III:53, 205, 246, V:77, VI:113, VII:63, VIII:40, 97, 103, 139, IX:114, X:34, 54, 112, 215, XI:33

~ tablets of, III:221

~ and technology, I:9, 242, 244, 246, IV:11–13, 59–60, 66, 74, 81, 89, VI:127, VII:143, IX:104, 110–11

~ and thought, I:249, IV:194, 202, 256, V:126, VIII:78

energy body, III:39, VI:92

energy codes, III:230, VIII:58

energy cords. *See* aka cords

energy evaluations, XI:213

energy fields, IV:25, VI:56, 94, VII:93, VIII:33–34, 42, 130, 145, X:55, 193, XI:27, 237, XIII:175

energy, Mahatma. *See* Mahatma energy

energy rushes, III:9, 230, VII:81–83, 85

England. *See* Great Britain

enlightenment, I:226, IV:243, 256, V:22, 24, 29, 35, 94–95, 108–10, 112–14, VI:155, 164, 215–16, IX:117. *See also* nirvana; samadhi (enlightenment); wheel of rebirth: liberation from

Enoch (ascended master), I:39, 208, III:62, 220, IV:197, 291, 293, 314–15. *See also The Book of Knowledge: The Keys of Enoch;* keys of Enoch

~ as an incarnation of Jesus, I:169, 175, 236, IV:288, VI:147

~ covenant of, I:227

~ and Melchizedek (Eternal Lord of Light), I:234

Entertainment Tonight, IX:75

The Enthronings of the Great Mother, V:135. *See also* Orpheus

environment, IV:13, 152, VIII:20, 130, 154, IX:107, 109–12, X:213. *See also* Earth; pollution

~ and Eco yoga, IV:250

~ meditations for, XII:67–69

Environmental Protection Agency, IX:111

E

Enviroprotect, III:34

epikinetic body, III:218–19, 227, VI:25, VIII:59, XI:195–96

Eskimos, VII:134
   ~ writings of the inner Earth, IV:25

Esola, Commander, III:190

Esoteric Astrology, VI:175

Esoteric Buddhism, V:207. *See also* Sinnett, A.P.

Esoteric Healing, VI:170

Esoteric Psychology, I:129, 132, 135, VI:184, X:16. *See also* Bailey, Alice A.

Essassani, IV:103. *See also* extraterrestrials

Essene Brotherhood, I:171–72, 236, IV:277–78, 284, 287–96, V:174–75, VIII:130, XII:120. *See also* Judaism; Kabbalah
   ~ angelology of, IV:293–94
   ~ Great Sabbath, IV:294
   ~ hadoth, IV:290
   ~ history of, IV:287–89
   ~ initiation into, IV:289–90, 294–96
   ~ and Jesus, I:172, 231, 235–36, IV:175, 274, 280, 287–88, 290, IX:123
   ~ Judy, I:172–73, 175, IV:291, IX:123
   ~ and the Order of Melchizedek, I:231, 235–36
   ~ the practici, IV:292
   ~ prayers of, IV:293–95
   ~ Sevenfold Vow, IV:294–96
   ~ the therapeutici, IV:292

The Essene Gospel of Peace, IV:296. *See also* Szekeley, Edmond Bordeaux

Essenian Christosism, V:174

E.T., IV:5, VII:97

Eternal Self, I:155, 264, 267, 269–70, 273, III:116, 205, IV:217, 225, 227–29, 232–36, 261–62, 272, V:1, 8, 11–12, 28, 47–51, 57–60, 66, 82, 88–90, 112, VI:8, 161, 215–16, 221, VIII:5, 75, IX:45, 80, 96, 127, XI:35, 249. *See also* Atman (self)
   ~ merging with, IV:260, 263, 265, V:24–25

etheric body, I:18, 45, 53, 58, 65, 67, 112, 249, III:49, 128, 190, 194, **III:238,** III:239, IV:130, 164, 240, 258, **VI:3,** VI:18, 26, 37, 71, 119, 122, 203, VII:1–3, 7–8, 10, 138, VIII:43, 61, IX:55, 129, X:4, 86, 88–89, 141, 220, 227, XIII:4, 84, 103. *See also* four-body system
   ~ anchoring the twelve strands of DNA in, I:38, III:241, VI:26–27, VIII:45, XI:32
   ~ and the chakras, III:21
   ~ clearing of, III:201, IV:105, VI:45, 126, 240, VIII:31, 33–34
   ~ death of, I:75, 84–85

~ and the fourth dimension, **VI:205**

~ healing of, I:283, III:55–57, 192, VI:120, VII:2, 7–8, VIII:31–32, IX:84

~ and joy, X:88

~ light quotient of, VI:4

~ mastery of, IV:259, VI:4, 60

~ and past lives, VI:126–27

~ and physical death, I:77, 81

~ and plastic surgery, IX:108

~ and sex, XIII:170

~ stabilization of, X:89

~ of the three selves, IV:159

~ and the yoga sutras of Patanjali, IV:258

etheric healing team, I:283, III:57. *See also* Great White Brotherhood Medical Unit; healing; Lorphan (doctor); MAP (Medical Assistance Program)

etheric plane, **IV:195,** IV:197, VI:181, VII:7–8, 12, 110, 131, 162, IX:114, X:210, 232, XII:97

~ incarnation of masters on, VII:16

~ and maya, I:57, **I:58,** I:65

~ and spiritual etiquette, X:167

~ and the supersenses, **I:71**

~ and synthesis, X:149

~ thought and emotional forms in, VII:104, 111

etheric ray, X:12–13, 128. *See also* rays, seven: configuration of

etiquette, spiritual, X:163–83, 235

~ and competition, X:174–77

Europe, **I:5,** V:239, **VI:78.** *See also* individual countries and cities

~ art of, X:93

~ and Saint Germain, V:239–40

~ and the "white root race," I:3

euthanasia, III:125, IX:84, 96–97, 126, XI:176

evolution, I:191, III:12, IV:130, **IV:130,** IV:154, 161, VI:208, 237, IX:136

~ angelic, I:191, 204, III:181, IV:121–23, **IV:130,** IV:133, VII:32, 65, 83, 109, 118, 120–21, X:23, 34, 45, 96–97

~ of animals, I:101, 186, IV:147–48, 150, V:111, VII:111, 124–27, X:213, XIII:69–70

~ and color, IV:206

~ of consciousness, IV:281

~ devic, I:191, III:181, IV:122–23, 129–30, 133, VII:19, 109, 111, 119, X:23, 34, 96–97, 213–15, 239

~ of Earth, I:25, 143, 186–87, 201, 206, 209–10, 219, III:169–70, 196, 200, IV:2, 58, VI:6, 10, VII:16, 20, 32, 85–86, 130–31, IX:37, 99, 107, 109, 120, 163, 167, X:34, 52, 55, 93, 108, 146, 179, 238, 244, XI:4–5

~ of the mineral kingdom, I:186, IV:153

~ of the monad, I:15, 107, 109, VI:89

~ of nations, VI:177–91

~ of the oversoul, VI:89

~ of plants, I:186

~ of religion, IV:280–82, 284

~ and the seventh ray, VI:187

~ of the solar system, I:202, X:91–92

~ of the soul, I:92, 107, 109, 112, 115, VII:12, 14

~ of a universe, VI:75

~ war-like stage of, IV:38

~ of Zeta Reticulum, IV:97–98

evolution, cosmic, I:6, 17, 19, 40–41, 51, 179–80, 187, 198, 200, III:146, 183, 242, VI:44, 47, 88, 143–44, 207, X:236, XII:129

~ council levels of, V:95

~ and mantras, I:250

~ seven paths to higher evolution, I:30, 40, **I:40,** I:41, 177, 200, III:7–8, 167–70, 172–83, **III:184**–85, VIII:132, XII:106

Path of Absolute Sonship, **I:40,** I:41, 177, III:8, 168, 182, **III:185, VI:8**

Path of Earth Service, **I:40,** I:41, 177, III:7, 167–70, **III:184, VI:8**

Path of Magnetic Work, **I:40,** I:177, III:7, 167, 170–72, **III:184, VI:8**

Path of Sirius, **I:40,** I:41, 177, 187, III:7, 167–69, 176–79, 183, **III:184**–85, IV:69, **VI:8**

Path of Training for Planetary Logos, **I:40,** I:177–78, III:7, 167, 172–76, **III:184, VI:8,** XI:98

Path the Solar Logos Himself Is On, **I:40,** I:177, III:8, 168, 180–82, **III:185, VI:8**

Ray Path, **I:40,** I:177, III:8, 168, 179–81, **III:185, VI:8**

~ of a Solar Logos, I:183, **I:184**

evolution, human, I:15–17, 21, 23, 31, 51, 116, 124, 143, 162, 181, 186, 188, 200, IV:126, **IV:130,** IV:149, 161, V:16, VII:1–2, 4–5, 11, 20, 22, 150, IX:136, 267, X:52, 186, 190, XIII:56

~ acceleration of, I:240, III:12, 15, 125, VI:118

~ cosmology of, I:198, **I:199,** I:200–202, 204

~ and the evolution of angels, I:204, III:181, IV:121, 123, VII:109, 118, 120–21, X:45, 97

~ and the evolution of devas, IV:129–30, VII:109, X:96–97, 213–14, 239

~ and extraterrestrials, VII:130, 132

~ of incarnated personalities, I:63, 109, 112

~ and Kriya yoga, I:163–64

~ and Sanat Kumara, I:178

~ spiritual, I:75, 90, 94, 99, 198, 280, III:7, 12, 19, 25, 43,

85–89, 109, 146, 193, 195, IV:211, 262, V:50, VI:7, 11, 18,
61, 92, 96, VII:8, 13–14, VIII:47–51, 56, IX:12, 97, 257,
X:2, 52–54, 75–76, 103–4, 112, 133, 185–86, 205–6, 229,
235, 238, XI:47, 149, 266, XII:118, XIII:4, 49–51, 53,
57–58, 104, 113–15, 143, 146–47, 150, 154–55, 162, 166

evolution, universal, VI:74

existentialism, V:16

exousiai, IV:120. *See also* elohim

The Externalization of the Hierarchy, I:142, VI:152, XII:3–4. *See also*
Bailey, Alice A.

extraterrestrials, I:8, 231, 242, 245, 271, 279, III:9, 149, IV:1–103,
109, 115–16, 169, VII:129–36, VIII:167, IX:32, 105, 115, 130,
161–63, 165, X:55, 235, XI:205, XII:65–66, 106. *See also*
Arcturians; Ashtar Command; Grays; Pleiadians; secret government;
UFOs; Zeta Reticulum
    ~ Alabram, IV:95
    ~ Alpha Centaurians, IV:83
    ~ Andromedans, IV:89–90
    ~ appearance of, III:78, IV:2, 4–5, 38, 46, 64
    ~ Ataien, IV:101–2
    ~ and Atlantis, I:8–9, 231, IV:1–2, 168
    ~ bases of, IV:6–8, 17, 43, 53, 66, 74–75, VI:127, VII:132,
        IX:105, 162, XI:227
    ~ Cessna, IV:81–82
    ~ Dals, IV:37
    ~ Deros, IV:58
    ~ and disease, IX:86
    ~ Dogon tribe, IV:69–70
    ~ Ebe, IV:5
    ~ and Egypt, I:10, IV:1, 168–69, 175, VII:133
    ~ and the emotional body, IV:17
    ~ and the environment, IX:111
    ~ Essassani, IV:103
    ~ and genetics, IX:136, 165–66
    ~ with group consciousness, III:178, IV:65, 69, 73, 97, 102
    ~ humanoid, IV:5, 79
    ~ Hydra, IV:71
    ~ Iargans, IV:45–46
    ~ and implants, IV:74, 77–78, 105–6
    ~ Kantarians, IV:70
    ~ Lyrans, IV:38, 85, 99
    ~ Martians, IV:47–49
    ~ and the media, IX:74
    ~ modern history of, IV:4–18
    ~ negative extraterrestrials, I:9, 247, III:99, IV:2–3, 5–7,
        16–17, 30, 36, 56, 58–59, 64, 73, 77–79, 93–94, 97, 101,

E

VI:71, 126, VII:130, 132–35, VIII:97, IX:86, 105, 165, XI:227
~ and the New Age, IV:2, 71, 112
~ and Nikola Tesla, IV:10–11
~ Nors, IV:52–53
~ Omnipotent Highness Krill, IV:6
~ Orions, IV:41–42
~ positive extraterrestrials, I:215, 226, III:25, 84, IV:5, 16, 59, 79, 168, VI:224, VII:130–33, 135, VIII:124, IX:32, 105, 133, 162, X:6, 42, 117, XIII:102
~ and possession, IV:30
~ Procyonians ("the Swedes"), IV:79
~ protection against negative beings, IV:77–78
~ Proxima Centauri, IV:91
~ Ra, IV:93–94
~ Reptilians, IV:5, 7, 9, 42, 77–79, VII:134
~ Rigelians, IV:74
~ Sirians, IV:69–70, 83, VII:133, XI:205
~ technology of, I:246, IV:10, 15, VI:119, 129, XI:29
~ telepathic rapport with, XIII:102
~ Ummites, IV:43–44
~ Valiant Thor (Martian visitor), IV:47–48
~ Vegans, IV:38, 99
~ Venusians, IV:51–54, VII:131
~ and Wesak, X:152
Eye of Horus, III:63–64, VIII:57, XI:95
Eysmnje. See Venus
Ezekiel (prophet), IV:285, 288
Ezra (prophet), I:170, IV:288

F

Fairies, IV:140. *See also* Gardener, Edward

fairy folk, IV:122, 129, **IV:130,** IV:131, 133–34, 137–38, 140–42, 154, VII:109, 111, 113, 131, X:226. *See also* devas; nature spirits

Faith (archangel), **I:199,** III:199
    ~ and the first ray, **I:204, IV:123, VII:115,** X:94

fakir (Moslem holy man), V:1–2, 5

"fall of man," I:2–3

family. *See* relationships: familial

fasting, III:203, IV:201, 323–24, V:185, VIII:142–43

Father, the, I:14, 17, 40, 106, 170, 200, 254, III:247–49, IV:120, 301, VI:2, VII:106, 148, VIII:63, X:53, 76, 159, 183, 197, 244, XII:19, XIII:2, 57, 65, 89, 101, 120
    ~ ascension seat of, VI:31, 35, XI:262
    ~ Eye of Divine Creation, III:220
    ~ and the Kabbalistic tree of life, **IV:307**
    ~ merging with, X:116

Fatima, Portugal, V:179–83

fauns, IV:122, 131, 134. *See also* devas; nature spirits

FBI, IV:15, V:252, IX:45, 71, 100–101, 130

fear, I:225, 269, 273, III:25, IV:74, 138, V:25, 66, VI:101, 218–19, 240, VIII:4, 79, IX:50, 117, 161, X:17, XI:41, XIII:23. *See also* core fear matrix removal; emotions: negative
    ~ and cults, IX:142
    ~ and economics, IX:92
    ~ and healing, IX:88
    ~ illusion of, I:2, 120, 122–23, 155
    ~ and initiation, IV:180, 182, 187
    ~ and manifestation, VIII:71, 84
    ~ of physical death, I:46, XIII:107
    ~ and the secret government, IV:15
    ~ and soul travel, IV:195

Federal Reserve System, IX:168–69

Federation of Free Worlds, IV:94

Federation of Planets, VII:135, IX:107

Federation of United Worlds, IV:58

feminine principle, III:199, 255, VI:56, 184, 197, VIII:15, 99, 112, 178, X:215, XI:40, XIII:2, 16–18, 55, 57, 100, 128–29, 177–78

feminism, IX:120

Fenner, Herr Horst, IV:91

Ferguson, Marilyn, IX:131

Festival of Humanity, III:29, VI:149, 155, VIII:139, XI:174, XII:14, 77, 87–89

Festival of the Buddha. *See* Wesak Festival

Festival of the Christ, I:139–40, III:29, VI:149–50, 153, VIII:139, XI:174–75, XII:14, 77, 79, 85
   ~ meditation for, XII:86–87

Feuerstein, George, IV:247, 251

fifth kingdom, I:24, VII:17, 130, 132, IX:121, 163, X:206, 234, 236, XI:44
   ~ and channeling, III:127

fifth ray (of Concrete Science or Knowledge), I:116, 122–23, 126–27, 132, **I:134**, I:192–94, **I:199,** I:201, III:108, 203, **III:238, IV:121,** V:239, **VI:3,** VI:39–40, **VI:41,** VI:182, **VI:184,** VI:185–86, 188–89, **VII:19, 117,** VIII:49, IX:185, **X:12,** X:13–14, 19–20, 24, 37–39, XI:70, **XI:75,** XI:111. *See also* rays, seven; rays, twelve
   ~ and the Ajna chakra, **I:130**
   ~ and Archangel Raphael, **I:204, IV:121, 124, VII:115,** X:95, 153
   ~ and Austria, **VI:183**
   ~ and color healing, **IV:210**
   ~ corresponding professions, **I:130**
   ~ and Cyclopia and Virginia, **I:203,** III:199–200
   ~ and Darjeeling, India, **VI:185**
   ~ and Elohim Vista, III:156
   ~ and the fourth ray, X:39
   ~ and France, **VI:182**
   ~ and Gemini, **XI:177**
   ~ glamour of, I:62, X:19–20
   ~ Hilarion as Chohan, I:192–94, **I:199,** I:201, III:257, **IV:121,** VI:144, 163, 214, 241, **VII:19, 117,** X:14, 38–39, 152–53, XI:70–71
   ~ and the Kabbalistic tree of life, **IV:311**
   ~ and London, England, **VI:185**
   ~ and the mental body, I:122–23
   ~ and the mental plane, **I:132**
   ~ and the Moon, **I:132**
   ~ and the New Age, I:123, 194, X:39
   ~ and the Olympics, IX:249

~ and the Path of Magnetic Work, III:171
~ and the planet Mercury, **XI:177**
~ and the planet Venus, **I:131, VI:82**
~ qualities of, I:123, **I:129, 132,** I:194, IX:62, X:24
~ as a ray of attribute, I:116, X:28
~ and the second ray, VI:189
~ and spiritual leadership, I:192–94, IX:43, 185
~ and the Synthesis Ashram, VII:145
~ and the third initiation, VI:188–89
~ and the Virgin Mary, **I:204, IV:124, VII:115,** X:95, 153
~ and Wesak, X:153

film industry, VII:130, IX:74, 134–35, X:37. *See also* arts, the; media
~ effects of, VII:97–98
~ and the negative ego, X:37
~ and sex, IX:138–39

Findhorn garden, III:119, IV:132–33, 139, 142, 144, 147–48, 151, VII:119

The Findhorn Garden, IV:142, VII:119

fire letters, I:280, 284, III:19, 45, 205, 219, VI:213, VIII:55–56
~ anchoring of, VI:115, XI:54, 94

fire spirits, **IV:135.** *See also* devas; elementals: salamanders (nature spirits of fire); nature spirits

first ray (of Power, Will or Purpose), I:11, 81, 116, 118–19, 126–28, 130, 132, **I:134,** I:171, 189, 192, **I:199,** I:201, III:108, 203, **III:238, IV:121,** V:72, 95, **VI:3,** VI:39–40, **VI:41,** VI:107, 177, 185–86, **VII:19, 117,** VII:156, VIII:7, 49, IX:1, 19, 46, 113, 185, **X:12,** X:13, 16, 19–20, 22, 27–29, 73–74, 141, XI:45, 70, 73, **XI:75,** XI:111, 175, XII:3. *See also* rays, seven; rays, twelve
~ and the Ancient of Days, **VI:179**
~ and Archangel Faith, **I:204, IV:123, VII:115,** X:94
~ and Archangel Michael, **I:204, IV:121, 123, VII:115,** X:19, 94
~ and Aries, **XI:176**
~ in Atlantis, VI:178
~ and China, **VI:182**
~ and color healing, **IV:210**
~ corresponding professions, **I:130**
~ and the crown chakra, **I:130**
~ El Morya as Chohan, I:171, 189, **I:199,** I:201, III:257, **IV:121,** VI:144, 163, 214, 241, **VII:19, 117,** IX:1, X:14, 27–29, 73, 141, 152–53, XI:70–71
~ and the Festival of Humanity, VI:155, XII:87
~ and the fifth initiation, VI:191, **XI:127**
~ and Geneva, Switzerland, **VI:185**
~ and Germany, **VI:182,** VI:183
~ glamour of, I:61, X:16

~ and Great Britain, **VI:182,** VI:183
~ and the Great Divine Director, III:156
~ and Hercules and Amazonia, **I:203,** III:199
~ and India, **VI:182**
~ and the Kabbalistic tree of life, **IV:311**
~ in Lemuria, VI:178
~ and the Manu, I:189, 200–201
~ and Mars, **XI:176**
~ and Master Jupiter, I:189
~ and Melchizedek (Universal Logos), **VI:179**
~ and the Olympics, IX:249
~ and the plane of divinity, **I:132**
~ and the planet Pluto, **I:131, VI:83**
~ and the planet Uranus, **I:132**
~ and the planet Vulcan, **I:131, VI:82**
~ qualities of, I:119, **I:129,** I:190, VI:178, IX:22, X:22
~ and Raja Yoga, **I:132**
~ as a ray of aspect, I:116, X:28
~ and the Ray Path, III:179–80
~ and Sanat Kumara, **VI:179**
~ and Shamballa, VI:178, **VI:179**
~ and spiritual leadership, I:189, IX:1–2, 43, 185
~ and the Synthesis Ashram, VII:145
~ and vows, VI:223
~ and Wesak, VI:151–52, X:153, XII:78

fission, I:4

five-body system, VI:4, 203. *See also* four-body system; nine-body system; seven-body system; twelve-body system

Florence, Italy, VII:79

flugelrads, IV:19, 27. *See also* Agartha

The Flying Saucer, IV:21
~ and Admiral Byrd, IV:20

fohat energy, III:170–71

Food and Drug Administration (FDA), IV:12–14, IX:59, 87, 111

Food Is Your Best Medicine, VIII:142

Forbes, Steve, IX:143

Ford, Arthur, I:95

forgiveness, I:93, 103, 267, III:24, 71, 100, 155, 190, IV:41, 160, 261, 272, V:30, 154, 166, 170, 189, VI:130–31, 137–38, 173, 223, VII:59, 153–55, 161, VIII:3, 83, 117, 130, IX:41, 69, 73, 98, 134, 144, 194, 231, X:157–58, XI:37, 228, XII:15, XIII:27–30, 52, 95, 133–34, 136, 156, 159
~ self-, VIII:9, 83, 113, IX:37, X:111, 158, 210, XIII:30, 136

Fortune, Dion, IV:311

Fossa, Zandria, IX:11

four-body system, I:84, 126, 284, III:10, **III:238,** III:239, VI:1,
  VI:3, VI:52, 61, 86, 121, 135, 203, 216, 219, VII:1, 3, 23, 32, 39,
  54–56, 62, 77, 81–82, 138, 158, VIII:58, 116, IX:94, 122, X:4,
  72–73, 109, 128, 220–21, 227, 237, 244, XIII:25, 99–100, 111.
  See also emotional body; etheric body; five-body system; mental
  body; nine-body system; physical body; seven-body system;
  twelve-body system
      ~ and the antakarana, I:44–45, 49
      ~ and the ascension meditation treatment, I:287
      ~ balancing of, I:266, III:199, VI:100, VIII:15, 44
      ~ clearing of, I:281, 285, III:69–70, VII:107, VIII:29, 31–32,
        X:174
      ~ and death, I:84–85
      ~ development of in utero, XIII:76–77, 79–80, 84
      ~ and immortality, I:78
      ~ and integrating soul extensions, VI:93–94
      ~ integration of, III:30–31, VI:103, 210, VII:91, VIII:14–15,
        30, 44, 99, 110, X:4, 89, 108–10, 113, 120, 155–56, 198–99,
        229, XI:17, 21, 37, XII:95–96, XIII:5, 14, 108
      ~ and joy, X:86, 90
      ~ and levels of light quotient, I:33, III:29–31
      ~ and the Mahatma energy, I:216, X:147
      ~ mastery of, VI:60, 249, VII:3, 96
      ~ and rising vibrational frequencies, XIII:106
      ~ and romantic relationships, XIII:4–5, 8–9, 15, 144
      ~ and sex, XIII:39, 44, 46–47
      ~ and the solar system, XI:42
      ~ stabilization of, VI:193–94, 209
      ~ and the ten dimensions of reality, III:149–50
      ~ during walk-ins, IV:32
      ~ and yoga, I:164, IV:241
Four Corners, the, IV:6. *See also* Dulce, New Mexico: extraterrestrial
  base at
fourth kingdom, III:127, VI:189, 223, VII:17, IX:121, X:234, XI:44
fourth ray (of Harmony through Conflict), I:116, 121–22, 126, 128,
  132, **I:132, 134,** I:192–93, **I:199,** I:201, III:104, 203, **III:238,**
  IV:121, V:239, **VI:3,** VI:39, **VI:41,** VI:185–86, 189–90, **VII:19,**
  VII:79, 116, **VII:117,** VII:133, VIII:101, IX:185, **X:12,** X:13–14,
  18–19, 23, 36–37, 39, 56, 92–93, 98, XI:70, **XI:75,** XI:111. *See
  also* rays, seven; rays, twelve
      ~ and Archangel Gabriel, I:193, **I:204, IV:121, 124,**
        VII:115, X:24, 95
      ~ and Archangel Hope, **I:204, IV:124, VII:115,** X:95
      ~ and Atlantis, VI:189
      ~ and Austria, **VI:183**
      ~ and Brazil, **VI:183**

~ and the chakras, I:121, **I:130**
~ and color healing, **IV:210**
~ corresponding professions, **I:130**
~ and Earth, **I:131, VI:82**
~ and the emotional body, I:121–22
~ and the fifth ray, X:39
~ and the fourth initiation, VI:189–91, **XI:127**
~ and Germany, **VI:182**
~ glamour of, I:62, X:18
~ and India, **VI:182**
~ and Italy, **VI:182,** VI:183
~ and the Kabbalistic tree of life, **IV:311**
~ and Libra, **XI:177**
~ and the Moon, **I:131, VI:83**
~ and the Olympics, IX:249
~ and Pallas Athena, III:156
~ Paul the Venetian as Chohan, I:192–93, **I:199,** I:201, III:257, **IV:121,** VI:144, 163, 214, 241, **VII:19,** VII:116, **VII:117,** X:14, 35–37, 152, XI:70–71
~ and the plane of the intuition, **I:132**
~ and the planet Mercury, **I:131, VI:82**
~ and the planet Saturn, **I:132**
~ and Purity and Astrea, **I:203,** III:199
~ qualities of, I:122, **I:129,** I:193, X:23–24
~ as a ray of attribute, I:116, X:28
~ and the second ray, VI:190
~ and spiritual leadership, I:192–93, IX:43
~ and the Synthesis Ashram, VII:145
~ and Tokyo, Japan, **VI:185**
~ and Venus, **XI:177**
~ and Wesak, X:153

France, IV:43, V:179
~ and the feminine principle, VI:184
~ and nuclear weapon testing, VI:126
~ and the rays, **VI:182,** VI:183

Francis of Assisi, Saint, I:124, V:71, VII:106, IX:170
~ as an incarnation of Kuthumi, I:237, V:71, VI:148, VII:106, X:42

Franklin, Benjamin, V:242
~ as a walk-in, IV:31

Frederick the Great, V:239–40, 243

free choice, I:13, 101, 251, 264, 276, III:88, 99, 197, 255, IV:1, 3, 9, 58, 67, 79, 275, 319, V:151, 160, VI:36, 74–75, 86, 138, 173, 242, VII:20, 47, 57, 59, 84, 115, 157, IX:55, 112, 142, 182, X:23, 72–73, 113, 134, 140, 142, 173, XI:28, 75, XIII:17, 176
~ and abortion, IX:96

~ and angels, I:204, IV:120–21, 123
~ and creation, I:1
~ and the Essene Brotherhood, IV:290
~ and the fourth ray, VI:190
~ of the middle and lower selves, IV:158
~ misuse of, VII:86
~ and prophecy, I:239–40
~ and reincarnation, X:128
Freemasonry, V:230, 241–43
free speech, IX:103, 271–74
free will. *See* free choice
French Revolution, V:241, 243
From Enoch to the Dead Sea Scrolls, IV:294–96. *See also* Szekeley, Edmond Bordeaux
Froude, J.A., V:175
Fry, Daniel, IV:51
Fuhrman, Mark, IX:64–65, 70, 158
Futureplex homeopathics, III:34, 111, VIII:149–51

G

Gabriel (archangel), I:172, **I:199,** III:199, IV:122, V:155–57, 159, 161, X:35, 37
  ~ and Christianity, I:237
  ~ and the fourth ray, I:193, **I:204, IV:121, 124, VII:115,** X:24, 95
  ~ and the Kabbalistic tree of life, **IV:304**
  ~ and Mohammed, I:175, 236–37

Gaia. *See* Mother Earth

galactic activation, VI:53

galactic actualization, IX:121

galactic body (11th), **III:238,** III:240, **VI:3,** VI:12, 53, 87, 194, 203, 206, XI:136, 150. *See also* twelve-body system
  ~ anchoring of, VI:13–14, 19, 23, 44, 53, **VI:62,** VIII:59, XI:120, 148, 154, 187, 192, 210, 252
  ~ and the eleventh dimension, **VI:204**

Galactic Center. *See* Galactic Core

Galactic Command, IV:64

Galactic Confederation of Planets, IV:38, 57–58, 94, 107

Galactic Core, I:205, 210, 212, 234, 274, III:128, 142, 150, 171, 174, 176–77, VI:6, 34, **VI:41, 116,** XII:115
  ~ accessibility of, I:206
  ~ ascension seat in, III:44, 147, 187, 258, VI:32, 43, 115, XI:100
  ~ attunement to, I:207
  ~ merger with, III:61
  ~ and Sirius, III:179

Galactic Council, IV:53

Galactic Hierarchy, I:187, 189

Galactic Logos, I:117, 181, 187, **I:199,** I:202, 234, X:145–46, 236. *See also* Melchior (Galactic Logos)

galactic masters, I:206, 274, III:176, VI:72. *See also* ascended masters; cosmic masters; universal masters

galactic monadic group, **III:238,** III:243, 256, **VI:3**

galactic plane, VI:206

Gallup Poll, IV:112

Gandhi, IX:74, 134

Gandhi, Indira, I:118

Gandhi, Mahatma, IV:221, V:17, 46, 69–70, 76, 211, VI:133, VII:16, VIII:165, IX:99, 113–14, 126, 231, X:71, 130, XI:228, XII:109–10. *See also* ahimsa (nonviolence)
  ~ ashram of, V:46, 74
  ~ and the *Bhagavad-Gita*, V:69, 71, 74–75
  ~ quotations from, I:155
  ~ and repetition of the name of God, I:249, IV:218, V:9, 74, VIII:96
  ~ and Satyagraha, V:70–76
  ~ as a walk-in, IV:31
  ~ and yoga, I:160, IV:243

Gandhi, the Man, V:72–73. *See also* Easwaran, Eknath

Ganesha (Hindu elephant-headed god), IV:219, VIII:69, IX:240, XI:224
  ~ ceremony of, VI:124

Ganges River, IV:221, V:56, 80, XI:161. *See also* Hinduism; India

Garabandal, Spain, V:188–89

Gardener, Edward, IV:140

Garden of Eden, V:160. *See also* Adam and Eve

Garment of Light, III:226

Garment of Shaddai. *See* El Shaddai (God): garment of

Gateway Ministries, VIII:159

Gathas, V:66

Gaver, Jessyca R., IV:329

Gaya (city), V:93

Gelugpa, V:98

Gematrian body, III:218–19, VI:25–26, VIII:59, XI:195

Gemini. *See also* astrology
  ~ and color healing, **IV:212**
  ~ and the fifth ray, **XI:177**
  ~ full moon in, VI:149, VIII:139
  ~ and London, England, **VI:185**
  ~ and Mercury, **XI:177**

Gemstone Guardians, IV:155–56

gemstones, III:218, IV:136, 153, VIII:147. *See also* mineral kingdom
  ~ and healing, IV:155–56
  ~ hierarchy of, **IV:154**

genetic engineering, IX:165–66
  ~ cloning, IV:73–74, 97, IX:165–66 (*See also* extraterrestrials)
  ~ and the negative ego, IX:165

genetic line clearing, III:57, VI:126, 237–38, VIII:35

Geneva, Switzerland, VI:185
> ~ and the first ray, **VI:185**
> ~ as Leo, **VI:185**
> ~ and the second ray, **VI:185**

Genghis Khan, IX:2

genies, IV:176. *See also* angelic kingdom

Germany, III:141, IV:4, 14, IX:131, 133
> ~ East, I:224, VI:6, IX:106–7
> ~ and the hollow Earth, IV:23
> ~ and the masculine principle, VI:184
> ~ Nazi, I:250, IV:23, IX:3, 99–100, 245, 271, 276 (*See also* Hitler, Adolf; World War II)
> ~ and the rays, **VI:182,** VI:183
> ~ reunification of, I:240
> ~ rods of power in, I:206

ghrina (dislike), V:67

Gibran, Khalil, VII:97

Gibson, Mel, IX:93

Gifts of the Gemstone Guardians, IV:155–56

Giri Bala, V:55–56

glamour, I:57, 60, 65–66, 70, 271–72, III:71, 89, 170, 230, IV:180, 189, 193, 261–62, 273, VI:58–59, 85, 136, 138, 167, 216, 245, VIII:6, 22, 84, 92, IX:99, 122, 132, 138, 157, X:71, XI:34, 269, XII:96–97. *See also* illusion; maya
> ~ of the ascended master, IX:262–64
> ~ of ascension, VI:134, VIII:18, X:107–24, XII:129
> ~ of the astral body, IX:75
> ~ and the Atlantean root race, I:58, **I:59**
> ~ of channeling, X:121–23
> ~ of control, X:112–13
> ~ of devotion, I:61
> ~ dissipation of, I:60, 66–67
> ~ and the emotional body, I:59–60
> ~ of the family, I:60
> ~ and the fourth ray, VI:190
> ~ of initiation, VI:104, 134, VIII:133, IX:264–67, X:107, XI:21–22
> ~ and its remedy, illumination, I:57, **I:58**–59, I:61
> ~ of materialism, I:60
> ~ in the media, IX:75
> ~ national, I:60
> ~ of the pairs of opposites, I:60, 68
> ~ of psychic abilities, III:97
> ~ of the rays, I:61–63, X:15–21

~ and the second initiation, I:23
~ of sentiment, I:60
~ of the spiritual path, I:61
~ of words, IX:260–62

Glamour, A World Problem, I:57, 61, 64–65, 67. See also Bailey, Alice A.

gnomes. See elementals: gnomes (nature spirits of earth)

Gobi Desert
~ and Shamballa, I:186, III:125
~ and the "yellow root race," I:3

goblins, IV:131, 136. See also devas; nature spirits

God, I:3, 9, 14, 38, 40, 45, 88, 101, 155, 163, 183, 187, 197–98, 204, 213, 220, 225–26, 263, 266–70, 273–74, III:102–3, 107, 116–17, 141, 144–45, 167, 195, 222, 250, 256, IV:38, 64, 102, 119–21, 125, 139, 161, 180, 197, 225, 259, 270, 274, 283, 292, 315, V:8, 11, 20, 25, 31–32, 36, 40, 45, 50, 60–61, 66, 87–88, 90, 112, 149, 155, 166, 171, 177, 236, 250, VI:13, 65–66, 72, 75, 79, 83, 95, 108–9, 116, 142, 202, 215, 217, 219, 221, 223, 229, 245, VII:1, 3–4, 6, 33, 35–36, 53, 56, 63, 68–69, 77, 88, 92, 101, 137, 148, 157, VIII:12, 49, 75, 108, 111, 113, 119, 134, ix, xv, IX:61, 91, 93, 98, 103, 107, 127, 136, 143, 220, 241, 264, X:2, 17, 22, 30, 42, 44, 50, 57, 70–71, 77, 79–80, 82, 85, 99, 116, 119, 136, 138, 140, 142, 157, 188, 193, 196, 199–200, 203, 206, 211, 219, 245, XI:35, 216, 249, XII:87, XIII:10, 57, 59–60, 82, 85, 100, 119, 125, 137, 154. See also Ancient of Days; Brahma (God); Brahman (God); Creator; El Shaddai (God); Father, the; Jehovah (Yod Hay Way Hay); Mother, the; Yahweh; YHWH (God)
~ anchoring God crystals, VIII:176, 180, XI:257
~ anchoring God's heart, XI:257–58
~ anchoring God's lightbody, VIII:177
~ anchoring the God seed packets, XI:257
~ and the angelic kingdom, IV:120–21, 125
~ ashram of, VI:42, **VI:204,** VI:225, VIII:127, X:201
~ attunement to, IV:143, VII:132, 136, X:20, 47–48, 80, 90, 105, 154, 179, 226, XIII:160
~ and the bardo experience, I:79
~ chakras of, XI:203
~ city of, VIII:103
~ and the coming of the Mahatma energy, I:216
~ covenant with the Jewish people, IV:278–80, 286
~ and creation, I:1–2, 8, 11, 13, 17
~ and the divine plan, I:4, 108–9, 143, 146, 204, 213, 222, 233, 278, III:145, 151, 171, 227, 253, IV:3, 7, 10, 115, 123–24, 128, 149, V:72, VI:23, 50, 74, 76–77, 79, 88, 131, 163, 168, 233, 245, VII:17, 32, 80–81, 87, 98, 100, 151, 164, VIII:18, 82, 84, 135, 181, 187, IX:9, 28, 39, 99–100, 113–14, 116, 131, 171, 175, 188, 202, 243, X:2, 8, 18, 25,

29, 43, 45, 49–50, 58, 72–73, 81, 98, 179–80, 182, 188, 196, 201, 205–6, 228, 232, 239, XI:21, 70, 242, XIII:19, 33, 48, 60, 87, 132, 154
~ the I Am, I:200, 257, IV:278–79, 297, 300, 317–21, VIII:75
~ inbreath and outbreath of, I:219–21, 225, IV:259, V:127
~ joy of, X:81–82, 86, 89
~ and karma, VII:60, 67
~ love/wisdom aspect of, I:190, VI:151, VII:53, X:108, XII:78
~ merging with, IV:269, VI:69, VIII:62–64, X:140, 236
~ and Metatron, I:255, XII:20
~ names of, I:49, 249–54, III:200, 224, 231, IV:120, 173, 249, 278, 300, **IV:302,** V:52, 159, 161, 167, VII:113, VIII:75, 96, XII:19–23, 99
~ practicing the presence of, III:24, VI:134, VIII:3, 110, 184
~ and the rays, I:115, 124, VI:191
~ relationship with, VIII:10, X:76–77, XI:267, XIII:2, 20, 99–110, 135–36, 181
~ as the ultimate parent, XIII:88–89
~ union with, I:124, 163, 204, IV:180, 187, 217, 242, 244, 247, 249, 270, 324, V:137, 160, 170, VIII:75–78, 82, IX:122, X:79, 81, 86–87, XII:133, XIII:31, 65, 99–110
~ will aspect of, III:176–77, 179–80, 203, 230, VI:155, VIII:126, XI:73
~ and yoga, I:163, IV:240, 242–44
God-actualization. See God-realization
Godek, Gregory, XIII:181
God-flame, I:30
God-force, I:2, III:107, VIII:17, IX:136, X:7
~ activation of, XII:5
Godhead, I:14, 17, 51, 117, 180, 198, **I:199,** I:202–3, 212, 217, III:54, 62, 146, 152, **III:238,** III:241–42, 245, 256, 258, IV:288, VI:2, **VI:3,** VI:9, 25, 41, 243, IX:261, X:92, 143, 149, 161, 198, 246, XI:17
~ ascension seat of, VI:31, 34–35, VIII:65–66, XI:199, 203, 231–34, 246, 253–55
~ merging with, III:241
God-realization, I:83–84, 92, 95, 160, 222, 267–68, 273, III:15, 51, 196, IV:63, 105, 183, 224, 325, V:25–26, 32, 50, 52–53, 65, 88, 165, VI:66, 104, 141, 158, 161, 207, 217, 219–20, 244, 248–49, VIII:11, 13, 21, 76, 84, 134, IX:117, 121, X:49, 110, 114–16, 118, 132, 134, 179, XI:83, 266–67, XIII:113–15, 117
~ and the chakra chambers, III:17–18
~ desire for, I:66, 103, 156, 265, III:1, 103, IV:219, V:23, 77, VI:201, VII:90, VIII:8, IX:139, XI:42, XIII:49
~ and love, IV:232, VIII:2
~ and the Mahatma energy, I:216

~ and mantras, I:49, 251, 253, IX:121
~ and sexuality, IV:247, VIII:12
God's body, **VI:205**
God-self, I:267, III:146, IV:68, VII:4–5, 18, VIII:189, xiii, X:48, 87, 122–23, XI:36
Goelitz, Jeffrey, IV:153
Golden Rule, IV:285, VI:142, VIII:5, IX:80
Golden Tablets of Orpheus, V:135–36. *See also* Orpheus
Goldman, Ron, IX:156
Goldsmith, Joel, VIII:3
Gonzalez-Balado, Jose Luis, V:192
Good Friend (a spirit), IV:153
Gopal, Ram, I:161–62, V:41–42
Gorakhpur, India, V:39
Gore, Al, IV:16, IX:97, 110
~ and the environment, IV:152
~ initiations of, IX:113
Göring, Hermann Wilhelm, IV:23
Gospel of Peace, IV:292–93. *See also* Essene Brotherhood, the
Govinda galaxy, III:60, VI:74, VIII:65
Govindan, Marshall, I:165, VI:162
Graffner, Franz, V:242
Graf, Steffi, IX:63
grand universe, IV:113–14, VI:73
Granth Scripture, V:161. *See also* Sikhism
Grant, Joan, IV:167, 177
gratitude, IV:207, V:192, VIII:85–86, 119, IX:202, 263, XIII:52, 163
Grattan, Brian, I:175, 211, 213–14, 216, 218, 241, 243, 247, VIII:166, XI:31, 33, 98, 188
~ as an incarnation of Zoroaster, I:217, V:133–34
~ ascension of, V:133
~ other lives of, I:176
~ twelve-initiation system of, I:276–77, III:7, 266, VI:1–2, XI:24
Grays, IV:5, 7, 9, 17, 73–75, 79, VI:71, 127, VII:134–35, IX:61, 162. *See also* extraterrestrials; Zeta Reticulum
~ Beeletrax, IV:75
~ from Draconis, IV:73
~ drawing of, **IV:74**
~ health of, I:247
~ Omnipotent Highness Krill, IV:6
~ and the Reptilians, IV:77
~ from Rigel, IV:73–74

~ species of, IV:2, 73
~ technology of, IV:6–7, VI:71
~ and treaty with United States, IV:6, 67, 73–74
~ from Ursa Major, IV:73
~ from Zeta Reticulum, IV:5–6, 17, 73–75, VI:71

Great Bear constellation, I:131, **I:199**, I:202, 205, III:182, **III:238,** III:255, **VI:3**. *See also* Logos of the Great Bear; Lord of the Great Bear Star System

Great Britain, VII:109. *See also* London, England
~ and the masculine principle, VI:184
~ and the rays, **VI:182,** VI:183–84

Great Central Sun, III:46, 63, 127, 201, 245, 255, IV:66, 170, VI:191, X:145, XI:131, 202
~ ascension seat in, VI:31, VIII:65
~ cosmology of, VI:116
~ and the healing modules, III:124
~ lightbeings from, III:38, 52
~ and the seven paths to higher evolution, III:170
~ at the Source level, VI:116, **VI:116**

Great Central Sun, galactic, VI:116, **VI:116,** XI:202

Great Central Sun, multiuniversal, VI:116, **VI:116,** XI:202

Great Central Sun, universal, VI:116, **VI:116,** XI:202

The Great Divine Director, **I:199,** III:156

Great Flood, the, I:9, IV:23, 25, 168–69, 283. *See also* Atlantis

The Great Invocation, I:55–56, 140, 250, 259–60, VI:190, VII:107, XII:3–5, 12, 85, 87, 89, 91. *See also* prayers

Great Ocean: The Dalai Lama, V:106–7

Great Pyramid, I:36, 241, III:131, IV:169–71, VIII:102, IX:52, 115, X:93, 226–27. *See also* Egypt; Hall of Records; pyramids; Sphinx
~ and Agartha, IV:20, 23
~ ascension seat in, I:279, VI:32, VIII:41
~ building of, I:173, 203, 242, 245, IV:93, 169–71, 174
~ capstone of, IV:170–71
~ Chamber of Rebirth, IV:171
~ extraterrestrial spacecraft under, I:246
~ Hall of Judgment, IV:190
~ and the initiation of Jesus, IV:274
~ King's Chamber, I:36, III:32, 56, IV:171, VI:32, 69, 145, XI:28
~ meditation at, III:250–53
~ and the Order of Melchizedek, IV:174–75
~ Pit of the Fiery Ordeal, IV:189
~ Queen's Chamber, IV:190
~ and the Ra, IV:93
~ sarcophagus of, IV:179–81, 186, 189–90, VI:69

~ as a temple for initiation, I:9, 173, 231, 236, IV:93, 170–71, 174–77, 179–92, VI:69, VIII:134, X:226–27, XI:2, XII:107

~ Well of Life, IV:171, 190

Great Spirit, IV:151

Great Transition. *See* initiation: eighth

Great White Brotherhood Medical Unit, I:38, III:38, 80, 97. *See also* healing; Lorphan (doctor); MAP (Medical Assistance Program)

Great White Brotherhood of the Spiritual Hierarchy, I:16, 30–31, 139, 237, IV:26, 55, 58, 60–61, 168, 283, V:204, 226, 239–41, VI:171, VII:32, XI:71, 206, 227. *See also* Great White Lodge; Spiritual Hierarchy

~ and the Alice Bailey books, I:139, 144

~ and the Great Pyramid, I:173, IV:168–69

~ and the Order of Melchizedek, I:235, IV:26, 170

~ and the soul mantra, I:258–59

~ and the Theosophical movement, I:139, 142, 144, V:201, 204, 207, 211, 213–14, 219, 223, 229, 233

~ *vs. the Dark Brotherhood,* IV:3, VI:140

Great White Lodge, III:101, 177, **III:238,** III:243, 255, **VI:3, 41,** VI:43, 53, 115, 125, 189, 195, **VI:204,** VII:32, 34, 133, VIII:64, 127, IX:220, XI:152–53, 174, 227. *See also* Great White Brotherhood of the Spiritual Hierarchy; Sirius

~ ascension seat of, VI:32–33, 115

~ light packets of information from, VIII:54

~ and Shamballa, III:178–79

Greece, I:173, V:123

Greek Mystery School, I:237, V:135, 147

Greeley, Father Andrew, IV:112

greenhouse effect, III:150, IV:13, 152, IX:109. *See also* pollution

Greenland

~ rods of power in, I:206

Green Party, IX:46, 111. *See also* political system (U.S.)

grief, XIII:157

griffin, IV:186

Gross, Darwin, IV:195, VIII:167

Gross, John-Roger, VIII:167

grounding, I:56, III:53, 203, 257, VIII:40, IX:115, X:34, 153, XI:26, XIII:4, 57

~ and the seventh ray, VI:180, 210, IX:114, X:228

grounding cord, I:50, III:200, VIII:101, XI:33, XII:11

group body, III:116–18, VI:34, 94, VIII:60, 105, 136, IX:188–89, 217, 221–22, X:65–69, 185–96, 244, 247, XI:221–22. *See also* cosmic body

group-module monadic family, VI:64–66

group-monadic actualization, IX:121

group-monadic body (9th), III:239, VI:96, 203, XI:150. *See also* twelve-body system
    ~ anchoring of, VI:19, 86, 97, VIII:59, XI:136, 154
    ~ and the eighth dimension, **VI:204**
    ~ and the ninth dimension, **VI:204**

group-monadic family, VI:63–64

group soul, VI:238

group-soul actualization, IX:121

group-soul body (8th), III:239, VI:203, XI:136, 150, 195. *See also* twelve-body system
    ~ anchoring of, VI:19, **VI:62,** VI:86, VIII:59, XI:136, 154
    ~ and the seventh dimension, **VI:204**

group-soul extension, VI:87

Gualdi, Signor, V:243

guardian angels, I:89, IV:123, **IV:128,** VII:83, 117–18, 120. *See also* angelic kingdom
    ~ between lives, I:91–92

Guillain-Barré Syndrome, IX:60

Gulf of Thailand, IV:61

Gulf War, IX:100, 153–54. *See also* war

gunas (the rajasic, the sattvic and the tamasic), IV:228–29, VI:160

gun control, IX:101–4

Guthrie, Kenneth Sylvan, V:143

Gyatso, Tenzen, V:105. *See also* Dalai Lama

H

Habakkuk (prophet), IV:288

Haeri, Shaykh F., IV:324

Haggai (prophet), IV:288

Haich, Elizabeth, IV:167, 177, 181, 183, VIII:134, XI:6
~ and initiation in the Great Pyramid, IV:176–77, 181–83
~ and Ptahhotep, IV:181–82

Hail Mary, V:184, VII:107. *See also* prayers
~ as a mantra, I:258, XII:23

Hall, Manly P., IV:167

The Hall of Ignorance, I:18, 22

The Hall of Learning, I:19
~ and the path of probation, I:21–22

Hall of Records, I:9, 142, 241–42, IV:170. *See also* Great Pyramid; Sphinx

The Hall of Wisdom, I:19, 22, 25

Halloween, IX:119

hamadryads, **IV:135**. *See also* devas; elementals: gnomes (nature spirits of earth); nature spirits

Hamlet, IX:28

Handel, George Frederick, VII:97, X:36

Hands across America, IV:153

Hanna Kroeger specialists, IX:58

Hanuman (Hindu monkey god), IV:219, V:10, 23

Harary, Keith, IV:203

Hard Copy, IX:75–76, 138

Harivamsa, V:9

harmlessness, IV:264–65, V:16, 111, 176, VI:173–74, VII:5, IX:29, X:242, XIII:43, 46, 147. *See also* ahimsa (nonviolence); nonviolence

Harmonic Convergence, I:178, 212, 214, 216–17, 233, 242, III:29, 93, 141, 144, 177, 179, 196, IV:152–53, VI:6, 34, 236, X:146, 161, XI:33, 39, 214

harmonics. *See* music

Harrison, Benjamin, IX:48

Harris, Robert, IV:14

Hatengdi, M.U., V:77, 79, 83–84

Have an Out-of-Body Experience in 30 Days, IV:203

Havona (the central universe), IV:113, VI:73

Hawaii, VIII:68. *See also* Huna teachings
> ~ blocked grid point in, IV:61
> ~ language of, IV:158
> ~ war in, IV:165

Hayes, Rutherford B., IX:48

healing, I:38, **I:71,** I:283, III:49, 57, 97–98, 104, 107–8, IV:169, 202, **IV:267,** V:2, 176, 213, 217, VI:45, 118–22, 125–26, 231, 236, VII:17, 20, 73, 79, 105–6, 108, 114–15, 117–18, 120, 155, VIII:4, 28–29, 32, 34–35, 39, 46, 78, 80–82, 88–89, 103, 110, 143, 168, 171, 176, 184, xxi, xxii, IX:35, 58, 61, 82–84, 88, 170–71, X:55–57, 95, 141, 156, 159, 174, 242–43, XI:99, XII:12, 60, 124, XIII:108, 110, 173. *See also* Great White Brotherhood Medical Unit; Lorphan (doctor); MAP (Medical Assistance Program); individual methods of
> ~ activations for, XI:255–56
> ~ affirmations for, VI:117, IX:83
> ~ and AIDS, I:243, IV:9
> ~ and the Arcturians, III:38, 79, 98
> ~ and the ascended masters, III:39, VI:118–20, VII:20, 82, VIII:31, IX:61
> ~ attitudinal, I:95, 224, 266, III:73, IV:261, V:127, VII:26, 85, 106, 140, 159, 161, VIII:4, 15, 21, 80, 110, X:17, 141, XI:35, XIII:137, 150, 158
> ~ the aura, I:53–54, III:34, VI:120, VII:112, VIII:34
> ~ and building the light quotient, III:124–25
> ~ and the chakras, **IV:208**
> ~ with chanting, I:251, 253, IV:172, VII:105–6, 108
> ~ and cloning, IX:165
> ~ with color, I:246, III:107, IV:172, 205–7, **IV:208,** IV:209–12, **IV:212,** IV:213–15, VIII:32–34, IX:83, X:36–37, 39, XII:107
> ~ with crystals, I:246, IV:93, 155
> ~ of the Earth, I:126, 128, VIII:20, X:148, XI:206–7, 226–27
> ~ energy evaluations, XI:213
> ~ by the Essene Brotherhood, IV:292
> ~ of the etheric body, I:283, III:55–57, 192, VI:120, VII:2, 7–8, VIII:31–32, IX:84
> ~ and gemstones, IV:155–56
> ~ and the Huna prayer method, IV:162–64

~ on the inner plane, VIII:31–32, 182, IX:35, 58, 83
~ and Kriya yoga, I:163
~ and Mahatma energy, I:215
~ with meditation, IV:172
~ with minerals, IV:155
~ with music, IV:172, **IV:208,** IV:213–15, V:142, IX:83, X:36–37, 39
~ and the Pleiadians, III:99–100
~ and Pythagoras, V:140
~ and the rays, I:126, 128, III:107–8
~ with sound, I:246, 250, IV:205, **IV:208,** VII:105, 107–8, X:36–37, 39, XII:107
~ in the Temple of Sacrifice and the Temple Beautiful, IV:172
~ and virbhuti ash, I:153–54
~ by the Virgin Mary, V:179, 186
~ visualization for, VI:117
~ with water, I:99–100, IV:209

Healing with Music and Color, IV:214

health-care system, IV:12–14, IX:81–90. *See also* medicine, Western
~ drug manufacturers, IX:84
~ and the elderly, IX:79–80, 84, 89
~ health insurance, IX:82, 90
~ HMOs, IX:87–89
~ Medicare, IX:89–90
~ pharmacies, IX:85
~ reform of, IX:79–80, 82–83
~ and veterans, IX:90

heaven, IV:273, VIII:94

Heaven on Earth seal of protection, III:122–24

hedonism, IV:3

Helena, Lady, XI:62

Heliopolis, Egypt, I:173, 231

Heliopolis school, IV:175

Helios (Solar Logos), I:39–40, 131, 187, **I:199,** I:202, 206, 284, III:32, 49, 62, 124, 132, 170, 174–76, 182, **III:238,** III:246, 255–56, 258, IV:2, 206–7, **VI:3,** VI:43, 51–52, 77, 115, 117, 230, VII:19, IX:9, 179, XI:28, 59, 116, 148. *See also* Solar Logos; Vesta
~ ashram of, VI:225, VIII:127, IX:200
~ and building the light quotient, III:38
~ chakras of, VI:77, XI:42
~ copper-gold ray of, **VI:41,** VIII:50
~ crystals of, XI:257
~ Golden Chamber of, I:279, III:44–45, 187, VI:32, 230, 234
~ and the keys of Enoch, IV:315
~ light rods of, XI:259

~ and the Path of Magnetic Work, III:171
~ and the Path the Solar Logos Himself Is On, III:180–81
~ and the Ray Path, III:179
~ and the rays, I:116–17, 120, 126
~ and Sanat Kumara, I:186
~ seed packets of, VIII:179, XI:257
~ and the solar body, III:254, XI:28

hell, I:73, 87–89, IV:272–74, V:153, 181, VI:138

Hellraiser, VII:97

Henry, Patrick
~ as an incarnation of Mohammed, I:175, VI:148

Hept-Supht, IV:173

herbalism, V:240, VIII:143, IX:56, 85, 87, X:89. *See also* healing
~ and AIDS, IX:117
~ and the Essene Brotherhood, IV:292

Hercules, I:119, VI:181

Hermes-Thoth, I:9, 28, 37, 78, III:56, 101, 121–23, 200, 253, IV:167, 170, 175, 190–91, V:123, 125, 128, VI:242–43, VIII:57, 102, XI:28, XII:105. *See also* Hermetic Principles; Mercury (Roman messenger god)
~ as an incarnation of Gautama Buddha, I:237, IV:168, 198, V:123, 128, VI:145, 148, 243
~ and building the Great Pyramid, IV:174
~ Emerald Tablets of, VI:145
~ and the Hermetic rites, V:147
~ and soul travel, IV:198
~ writings and teachings of, I:231, IV:179, V:124, 130–32, VI:1, 68–69, VII:104, X:2, 35, 66, 151

Hermetic Principles, VIII:15. *See also* Hermes-Thoth
~ the principle of cause and effect, V:124, 128–29
~ the principle of correspondence, V:124–25
~ the principle of gender, V:124, 129–32
~ the principle of mentalism, V:124–25, VIII:78, 80
~ the principle of polarity, V:124, 126–27, VIII:79–80
~ the principle of rhythm, V:124, 127–28
~ the principle of vibration, V:124–26

heroin. *See* drugs

Hersheiser, Orel, VIII:165

Hicks, Roger, V:107

hieroglyphics, V:136

High Council of Mars, IV:48

higher mind, I:13, 18, 46, 96, 223, VI:50–51, 175, VIII:79, IX:55, X:7. *See also* higher self; soul; superconscious mind
~ organization of, VI:47, 56–58
~ and the spiritual triad, I:43, 109–10, IV:300

higher self, I:13, 17–18, 111, 116, 211, 264, 272, III:1–2, 23, 53, 69,
80, 153, 246, V:126, 177, VI:25, 91, 124, 136, 139, 166, 172,
174–75, 199, 221–22, VII:5, 9, 21–24, 27, 30–31, 41–42, 50,
63–64, 67, 77, 154–55, 157, 161, VIII:11, 14, 21, 43, 99–100,
190, IX:5, 61, 89, 121, 143, X:2, 9, 48–49, 71, 73, 108, 129,
133–35, 138, 156–57, 188, 199, XI:28, 36, XII:3, 97, 103, XIII:80,
84, 151, 165. *See also* higher mind; soul; superconscious mind
    ~ attunement to, X:49, 72
    ~ on the Buddhic plane, VII:11–12, 21
    ~ and channeling, VII:79–80
    ~ and dreams, intuition and premonition, IV:159, VII:73
    ~ evolution of, I:107
    ~ and the Huna teachings, IV:158–65
    ~ and the Kabbalistic tree of life, IV:300–301
    ~ and the Mahatma, I:214
    ~ merging with, I:23, 25, VI:19
    ~ merging with the lower self, X:86–87
    ~ and the prebirth bardo experience, I:91
    ~ and the rays, VI:180, 188
    ~ and reincarnation, X:129
    ~ shadow body of, IV:159–60

Hilarion (ascended master), I:142, III:48, **III:238**, IV:224, **VI:3,
112,** IX:9, 62, X:18
    ~ ashram of, I:284, **VI:204,** VI:225, VIII:127
    ~ as Chohan of the fifth ray, I:192–94, **I:199,** I:201, III:257,
        IV:121, VI:144, 163, 214, 241, **VII:19, 117,** X:14, 38–39,
        152–53, XI:70–71
    ~ divine mission of, X:38–39
    ~ and the Theosophical Society, V:203
    ~ and Wesak, X:152–53

Hill, Napoleon, IX:51

Himalayan Mountains, I:159–61, 174, III:95, IV:197, 221, V:39–42
    ~ Wesak Valley in, V:95, VI:150–51, 154, VIII:138, X:152,
        XI:174–75, 262, XII:77, 81 (*See also* Wesak)

Himalayan school (for ascended masters), IV:253

Himis, Tibet, I:173–74

Himmler, Heinrich, IV:23

Hinduism, I:236–37, 255, III:103, IV:217, 219, 221–22, 231, 250,
254, 256, 259–60, 263, V:9, 11, 17, 29, 36, 88, 112, 161, 169,
VI:124, VII:63, VIII:160, X:76, XI:2, 161. *See also* caste system; India; *Itihasa;* maya; Patanjali; Sikhism; yoga
    ~ and Agartha, IV:20
    ~ avatars of, IV:218
    ~ and the coming of the Kalki Avatar, I:137, IV:220
    ~ cosmology of, IV:221–22
    ~ and death and cremation, IV:221–22, 227

~ and dharma (life path), IV:219, 225, 263
~ and the Divine Mother, IV:218–19
~ and the ego, IV:282
~ and Jainism, V:16
~ and karma, IV:119, 220, 229
~ mantras of, I:255–57, XII:20–22
~ and marriage, IV:221
~ and reincarnation, VII:6
~ trinity of (Brahma, Vishnu and Shiva), I:147, 153, 255,
    IV:161, 218, 250, VIII:xx, XII:20–21, 119
~ and yoga, IV:220

Hira, Mount, V:159

Hiroshima, Japan, I:9, IV:19–20, 27, 54, 56, VI:126, IX:245–46

Hislop, Jack, I:150–51

Hispanics
    ~ and AIDS, IV:8

History of European Morals, V:175

Hitler, Adolf, I:250, VIII:155, IX:2–3, 7, 99–100, X:42. *See also* Germany, Nazi; World War II
    ~ and the hollow Earth, IV:23
    ~ and music, X:37
    ~ Nazi law of, IX:271
    ~ negative karma of, I:89
    ~ and the regions of hell, I:88–89
    ~ as a walk-in, IV:30

HIV. *See* AIDS

Hodson, Geoffrey, IV:128, 141

Hogan, Hulk, IX:123

hollow Earth, I:237, IV:19–28, 70, 168–69, VII:133–34, IX:168,
    XII:106–7. *See also* Agartha; Annu; Anunnaki
    ~ and Arcturians, IV:68
    ~ ascended masters in, I:275, XI:16, 72, 77
    ~ ascension seat in, VI:32
    ~ entrances to, III:149, IV:20–23, 25
    ~ inhabitants as descendants of the Atlanteans and Egyptians,
        IV:168

The Hollow Earth, IV:21–23, 28. *See also* Bernard, Raymond

Holmes, Ernest, I:121, VIII:78

holograms, IV:39, VII:133

holographic communicator, IV:48

Holy Grail, X:226

Holy Land, IV:93. *See also* Israel; Jerusalem; Middle East

Holy Mother, V:28. *See also* Nikhilananda, Swami

Holy Spirit, I:17, 45, III:220, 223–24, 226, VIII:61–62, 99, 158,

IX:81, 92, 143, 176, 236, XI:168, XIII:144, 155, 173. *See also*
Shekinah (Holy Spirit)
    ~ baptism by, III:55
    ~ gifts of, III:222, VIII:61
Homecoming: Reclaiming and Championing Your Inner Child, IX:230
Home of Compassion (in Melbourne), V:193
homeopathy, VIII:143, 149–50, IX:56, 58, 85–87, X:89. *See also* heal-
ing
    ~ and AIDS, IX:117
Homestead Air Force Base, Florida, IV:5
homosexuality, IX:45, 137, XIII:1–2, 18, 92, 147. *See also* relation-
ships, romantic
    ~ and AIDS, IV:8, XIII:131
    ~ and Christianity, IV:274
    ~ and marriage, XIII:91–92
    ~ and the military, IX:147
Hope (archangel), **I:199,** III:199, X:37
    ~ and the fourth ray, **I:204, IV:124, VII:115,** X:95
Hopi Indians, I:153, V:107, VII:85. *See also* Native Americans
Horus, III:56, 101, 121, IV:188, VIII:41, XI:28. *See also* Egypt
Hosea (prophet), IV:285, 288
How to Build High Self-Esteem, XIII:22
Hsakamim, III:221
Hukikat Purusha (ruler of the Hukikat Lok dimension), **IV:196**
human sacrifice, I:9
Huna Research Associates, IV:158
Huna teachings, I:231, IV:157–58, 162–65, VI:170, VIII:108,
    XII:118, XIII:89, 151. *See also* Hawaii
    ~ affirmations of, IV:162
    ~ the "Clearing of the Path," IV:162–64
    ~ and the conscious mind/middle self (the "uhane"), IV:158–65
    ~ and the Egyptian teachings, I:236, IV:157
    ~ and healing, IV:162–64
    ~ and the Huna prayer method, III:21–22, 27, 82, 155–66,
        232–36, IV:161–64, VI:23, VIII:68–69, IX:214–16, XI:10,
        66, 68–69, 83, 93–96, 102–3, 105, 109–10, 121–26, 128,
        141, 182–83, 193–94, 203–4, 259–60, XII:108–9, XIII:2
    ~ and mana, IV:160–64
    ~ and the subconscious mind/low self (the "unihipili"),
        IV:158–65
    ~ and the superconscious mind/high self ("the aumakua"),
        IV:158–65
    ~ ten basic elements of people, IV:159–60
    ~ trinity of God (Ku, Kane and Kanaloa), IV:161

H

The Hunchback of Notre Dame, VII:97

hundredth-monkey effect, I:221, IV:78

Hurlburt, Robert, IV:81–82

Hurtak, J.J., III:217, 232, IV:197, 311, 313–15, VI:25, VII:113

Hussein, Saddam, IX:3, 100

Hyades, IV:38

Hydra, IV:71. *See also* extraterrestrials

hydrogen bombs. *See* nuclear weapons

Hymns of Orpheus, V:136. *See also* Orpheus

A Hymn to Memory, V:176. *See also* Apollonius of Tyana

Hyos Ha Koidesh, **I:199,** I:203, III:221–22, 231–32, **III:238, VI:3, 111,** VI:112, 115

Hyperborea, **I:5,** IV:38, **VI:78**

hyperspace, IV:36

hypnotism, IV:77–78, V:213, 243, 246, VIII:110–11, IX:55, 83, XII:103. *See also* self-hypnosis

    ~ and *dehypnosis,* VIII:93

    ~

I

I Am America Map, VI:227–28

The "I Am" Discourses, I:237, 244–45, 280, III:46–47, 94,
    IV:317–21, V:239–40, 243–44, VI:6–7, 228, VII:148, VIII:163,
    X:240, XII:117, XIII:67. *See also* King, Godfré Ray

I Am Foundation, IX:53

I Am (God). *See* God: the I Am

I Am Presence, I:13, 17, 24, 53, 214, 268, 271, 274, 280–81, 283–85,
    III:2–3, 15, 23, 28, 49, 60, 62–64, 70, 87, 99, 127, 190, 198, 202,
    243, 246, 259, IV:211, 317–21, VI:4, 8–9, 11, 18, 25, 77, 85–86,
    92, 94–95, 103, 117, 126, 163, 198–99, 218, 220, 222, 235, 243,
    VII:5, 12–13, 16, 22, 27, 31–33, 43, VIII:14, 43, 45, 47, 49, 60,
    77, 86, 93, 100, 111, 190, IX:5, 21, 55, 91–92, 94, 136, 143, 146,
    178, 221, 235, X:4, 17, 48, 51, 56, 127, XI:17, 32, XII:3, XIII:59,
    65, 85, 89, 165. *See also* monad; spirit
        ~ and ascension, I:30, VI:216
        ~ attunement to, X:16, 18, 49
        ~ and self-actualization, I:18

I Am Presence, cosmic, VI:8, 200–201. *See also* monad, cosmic

I Am Presence realization, VI:99

Iarchus, V:174, 176

Iarga, IV:45–46

Iargans, IV:45–46. *See also* extraterrestrials

Illuminati, IV:3–4, 14, 78. *See also* secret government
        ~ and the environment, IV:13
        ~ and human health, IV:12–13
        ~ and Nikola Tesla, IV:11

illumination, V:94
        ~ as the remedy for glamour, I:57, **I:58**–59, I:61

illusion, I:57, 59–60, 63–66, 97, 270–72, III:71, 89, 230, IV:132,
    180, 189, 193, 220, 261–62, V:11, 21–22, VI:59, 85, 138, 167,
    172, 190, 193, 202, 207, 212, 215–17, 219, 221, 245, VIII:6, 19,
    21–22, 84, 92, IX:45, 92, 99, 106, 120–21, 132, 135, 170, X:8, 17,
    110, 117, 149, 200, XII:96–97. *See also* glamour; maya
        ~ and the Aryan root race, I:58, **I:59**

~ clearing of, I:66–67, XII:72–73
~ of death, I:2, 74, 98, 223, IV:273, VII:13, IX:96, 134, XIII:157
~ of fear, I:2, 120, 122–23, 155
~ and its remedy, intuition, I:57, **I:58**–59, I:63–64
~ seven ways of, I:64

imagination, IX:55, 252, X:18

Imam Mahdi, I:137, IV:281. *See also* Islam

Imhotep, IV:175. *See also* Egypt

immaculate conception, I:171–72, 174

Immaculate Heart, V:180

immigration, IX:107

immortality, I:4, 28, 45, **I:67,** I:78, 156–57, 160, 270, III:95, 197, IV:232, 235, V:16, 52, 75, 93, 137, 175, VI:12, 26, 61, 221, VIII:2, 45, IX:96, XI:12, 188, XII:88. *See also* death, physical
~ and Christianity, IV:273
~ conditional, I:73
~ of elementals, IV:135
~ of Saint Germain, V:239–40

The Immortal Sage, V:144. *See also* Bernard, Raymond

Imperishable Sacred Land, **I:5, VI:78**

implants, I:34, 39, 246, 271, 284, III:98, 258, IV:74, 77–78, 105–6, VI:87, 101, 219, VII:134–35, IX:55. *See also* extraterrestrials: negative
~ and channeling, VI:228
~ and disease, IX:86
~ function of, IV:105
~ on pets, VIII:34
~ in the prison system, IX:72
~ removal of, III:50, IV:105, VI:17, 33, 119, 241, VII:134, VIII:29, 125, X:46, XII:69–70, 121, XIII:174

Incas, IV:169

Independent party, IX:128, 160. *See also* political system (U.S.)

India, I:75–76, 149, 160, 173, 250, III:130, IV:169, 171, 173, 217, 221–22, V:1–2, 8, 15, 20, 28, 36–37, 39–40, 45, 57, 66, 72–73, 76, 82–83, 85, 105, 107, VI:183, 185, **VI:185,** VII:54, 150, VIII:190. *See also* Calcutta, India; Ganges River; Hinduism
~ art of, X:93
~ and the feminine principle, VI:184
~ and the Hindu caste system, IV:220, V:15, 72
~ poverty of, V:193–94
~ and the rays, **VI:182**
~ rods of power in, I:206
~ saints of, V:63
~ vortexes of, III:149

India Mirror, V:208

individualism, I:96, 134, IV:102, VIII:107–8, XIII:55
    ~ in romantic relationships, XIII:27–29, 51, 53, 142, 146, 169

individualization, VII:72, 153
    ~ of angels, IV:122–23
    ~ of animals, IV:147–48, VII:111, 125–27, X:213, XIII:69–70
    ~ of devas, IV:122

Indra (Hindu war and water god), IV:219

initiation, I:9, 14, 16, 18–22, 25, 31, 33–35, 37, 57, 66, 78, 84, 97, 144, 197, 212, 235, 241, 271, III:1–2, 6, 24, 81, 116, 139–40, 146, 175, 192–93, 237, 240, 245, IV:179–83, 187, 191–92, 240, 259, 269–70, V:135–36, 232, VI:1–2, 5, 7, **VI:17,** VI:23–24, 49, 51, **VI:62,** VI:63, 81, 86, 95, 100, 104, 113, 122–23, 137, 139, 141, 144, 173, 177, 187, 193, 200, 208, 214–16, 218, 222, 230, 232–33, 246, VII:4–6, 9, 21–22, 34–36, 55, 64, 71, 89, VIII:44, 132–34, IX:22, 97, 264, 266, X:1–2, 4, 34–35, 109–13, 115, 133, 178, 220, 225, 232, XI:3, 26, 33–34, 61, 64, 68, 72, 87, 134, 173, 186–87, 209, 266, XII:94, XIII:65, 114
    ~ and the accepted disciple, VII:23–24
    ~ of Al Gore, IX:113
    ~ Amrita, IV:189
    ~ of angels, VII:109
    ~ and ankhs, IV:185–90
    ~ of Apollonius of Tyana, V:173, 175
    ~ ascension activation, declaration and integration, I:32–33
    ~ and the aura, XI:132
    ~ and the bardo experience, I:83
    ~ of Bill Clinton, IX:81, 113
    ~ and the bodies, VI:205–6
    ~ and the chakras, III:13–14, 17, VI:205–6, XI:23–24, **XI:127**
    ~ and channeling, VI:228
    ~ and competition, X:110–11
    ~ correlation with the cosmic initiations, III:4
    ~ as death and rebirth, I:74–75, 84
    ~ and the dimensions, III:4, 139–40, VI:205–6
    ~ of Djwhal Khul, VI:22
    ~ of the Dogon tribe, IV:70
    ~ of Earth, I:277, III:11–12, 187, IX:133, X:221, 244
    ~ eighth, I:276, III:4, 10–11, 169, 240, 266, VI:62, 86, 247, **XI:127,** XI:176
    ~ eleventh, I:276, III:169, VI:247, XI:252, 265
    ~ of the Essene Brotherhood, IV:289–90, 294–96
    ~ fifth, I:18, 25–26, 32, 34, 44–45, 48, **I:59,** I:64, 97, 186, 197, **I:199,** I:200, 211–12, 277, III:3–4, **III:4, 11,** III:24, **III:139,** III:177, 219, **III:238,** III:240, IV:253, 263, 269–70, 300, 310, V:173, 175, 230, **VI:3,** VI:8, **VI:17,**

I

VI:32–34, 43, 53, 59–60, 62, 103–4, 107, 163, 191,
VII:31–32, **XI:127,** XI:194 (*See also* adepts)

~ first, I:19, 21–22, 58, **I:59,** I:64, 67, 97, 144, 197, **I:199,**
I:200, 265, III:1, **III:4, 139, 238,** IV:240, 270, V:223,
VI:3, 17, VI:166, 187–88, VII:24–25, X:107, **XI:127**

~ fourth (crucifixion), I:18, 24–25, 32, 44, 48, 50, **I:59,** I:66,
74, 77, 97, 105, 108, 110, 170, 197–98, **I:199,** I:200, 268,
277, III:2–3, **III:4, 11,** III:24, **III:139,** III:176, **III:238,**
IV:261, 270, V:108, 175, 209, 227, 230, **VI:3, 17,** VI:18,
33, 43, 59, 160, 163, 168, 189–91, 222, VII:30–31, VIII:10,
133, xxi, XI:11, **XI:127** (*See also* arhat; renunciation)

~ for fundamentalist Christians, VI:129–30

~ glamour of, VI:104, 134, VIII:133, IX:264–67, X:107,
XI:21–22

~ in the Great Pyramid, I:9, 173, 231, 236, IV:93, 170–71,
174–77, 179–92, VI:69, VIII:134, X:226–27, XI:2, XII:107

~ and group monadic mates, XIII:60

~ of Jesus, I:138, 170–71, 173, III:10, IV:184, 274, V:173,
175, VI:22, VIII:134, IX:184, XI:64

~ of John the Baptist, IV:184

~ and the Kabbalistic tree of life, IV:300, 310

~ Kalachakra, V:107

~ of Krishna, I:176, IV:224

~ light quotient level for, I:32–33, 36, 277–78, 283, III:3, 6,
8–10, 24, 76, **III:238,** VI:3, **VI:3,** VI:205–6, 216, XI:16,
43, 163, 265

~ of Lord Maitreya, I:138, 176, 278, III:10, IV:224

~ misconceptions about, VI:132–34

~ of Mohammed, I:175

~ and the negative ego, IX:266, X:110–12, XI:21–22

~ and the nine-body system, **VI:17**

~ ninth (the refusal), I:74, 198, 276, III:4, 7, 11, 147, 169, 240,
VI:62, 247, **XI:127**

~ into the Order of Melchizedek, I:207, 230–32, 236, 281,
III:10, IV:157, 174–75, 181, 191, VI:215, VIII:64, XI:1–3,
5–6

~ and the path of probation, I:19, 21–22, 44, 65, **I:199,** I:200,
III:1, V:228, 232, VII:22–23, 33

~ a personal experience of, XI:19–24, 63–91, 93–155, 188–93,
196–234, 236–40, 242–43, 265

~ and the planes, III:4, **III:4**

~ of planets, VI:77

~ of Plato, IV:184

~ at the Pythagorean mystery school, V:144

~ and the rays, VI:187–91, XI:73, **XI:127**

~ of Sanat Kumara (Planetary Logos), I:178, 186, 205,
III:11–12

initiation, (cont.)

  ~ second, I:23, 58, **I:59,** I:64, 67, 74, 97, 176, 197, **I:199,**
    I:200, 265, III:1–2, **III:4, 139,** III:176, **III:238,** IV:270,
    V:223, 233, **VI:3, 17,** VI:59, 187–88, VII:25–27, X:107,
    XI:127

  ~ the seven gradations of evolvement, XI:22, 24

  ~ seventh (resurrection), I:32, 35, 40, 97, 197–98, 200,
    276–79, 283, III:4, **III:4,** III:5, 7–11, **III:11,** III:13–14, 16,
    19, 24, 50, 76, 106, 116, 118, **III:139,** III:142, 147, 169,
    177, 193–94, 205, 219, **III:238,** III:239–40, IV:181,
    VI:1–2, **VI:3,** VI:8, 11, **VI:17,** VI:18–19, 23, 35, 37, 59–62,
    VI:63, VI:67, 92, 99, 101, 103–4, 107, 162–63, 201, 203,
    208–9, 220, 222, 233–34, VII:18, 33–36, 90, VIII:47, 122,
    IX:199, X:13, XI:3, 31, 40, 72–74, 82, 91, 98, **XI:127,**
    XI:130, 163, 168, 176, 186–87, 196, 199, 267 (*See also* res-
    urrection)

  ~ shaktipat, V:86–87

  ~ in Sikhism, V:161

  ~ sixth (ascension), I:18, 26–40, 45, 48–49, 64, 78–79, 97,
    197–98, **I:199,** I:200, 212, 264, 276–77, III:3–4, **III:4,**
    III:5–8, **III:11,** III:14–15, 24, 76, **III:139,** III:140, 142,
    167, 176–77, 219, **III:238,** III:239–40, IV:69, 268–70, 300,
    310, V:108, 129, 240, VI:1, **VI:3,** VI:6, 8, 10–11, **VI:17,**
    VI:35, 43, 59–62, **VI:63,** VI:87, 92–93, 99, 107, 163, 167,
    208–9, 215, 233–34, VII:18, 32–34, VIII:42, IX:199, X:13,
    XI:3, 13, 16, 40, 43, 72–74, 84, 98–99, **XI:127,** XI:130,
    132, 173, 176, 186, 199, 248, 266 (*See also* ascension)

  ~ sublevels between, I:276–77

  ~ tenth, I:276, III:169, VI:247, XI:252, 265

  ~ third, I:18, 23–25, 32, 46–47, 58, **I:59,** I:64, 66–67, 74, 97,
    106, 108, 110, 117–18, 197, **I:199,** I:200, 211, 264–65,
    271, 277, III:2–3, **III:4, 11,** III:24, **III:139, 238,** III:240,
    IV:269–70, 310, V:233, **VI:3,** VI:8, **VI:17,** VI:56, 59, 82,
    130, 163, 167, 170, 172, 188–89, 222, VII:25–31,
    IX:183–84, X:107, 127, 186, 229, XI:98, **XI:127,** XI:227
    (*See also* soul merge; transfiguration)

  ~ thirtieth, VI:23

  ~ twelfth, I:276–77, III:7, 169, 194, VI:248, XI:252, 265–66

  ~ twentieth, VI:23

  ~ of the United States, IX:158

  ~ of Vywamus, III:191, XI:116

Initiation, IV:167, 176–77, 181, 183, VIII:134, XI:6. *See also* Haich,
  Elizabeth

initiation, cosmic, I:212, III:12, 63, VI:2

  ~ first, III:4, 177

  ~ second, III:4, 177

  ~ third, I:205, III:4, 177, XI:91

initiation, galactic, III:193

Initiation, Human and Solar, I:21, 41, 67, III:168, 185, IX:264. *See also* Bailey, Alice A.

Initiation in the Great Pyramid, I:230, IV:171, 184, 191, VIII:134, XI:6. *See also* Chaney, Earlyne

initiation, universal, III:193

inner child, I:266, VI:60, 100, 103, 108, 249, VII:40, 42, 45, 50, 154, VIII:111, 116, IX:4, 129, 224, X:199–200, XI:267, XII:95, 103, XIII:73–74, 76, 79, 104, 114, 138–39, 151, 153. *See also* self-parenting

inner Earth. *See* hollow Earth

inner occult vision, VII:7

inner plane, I:3, 15, 36, 77, 94, 112–13, III:43, 59–60, 197, V:88, VI:22, 67, 92, 103, 207, 244, VII:17, 65, IX:13, 51, 157, X:129, 140, 149, 189. *See also* spiritual world
  ~ ashrams on, VI:135, VII:143, VIII:127, IX:9–10, 115, 219–20, X:71, 202
  ~ classes on, I:33, 269, 283, III:61, 170, 173–74
  ~ healing on, VIII:31–32, 182, IX:35, 58, 83
  ~ and initiation, III:3–4, VII:30, 36, XI:5
  ~ between lives, I:90, 93, VII:62, XIII:83
  ~ science on, I:194, IX:102, X:38
  ~ service work on, VI:202, VII:16, VIII:183
  ~ sex on, XIII:60–61

inner self, VI:197, VIII:110–12

inspiration, I:57, **I:58**–59, I:66

instinct, **I:67, VI:17,** VI:18, 86, 175, VII:73
  ~ of animals, **I:67,** IV:147
  ~ and the Moon, I:96

integrity, VIII:11–12

intent, III:1, 24, 41, 62, 68, 112–13, 115, 170, IV:203, 244, V:109–10, VI:108–9, 168, VII:10, 23, 28, 57–58, 63, 65, 73–74, 116, 139, 158, IX:273, X:7, 36, 57, 102, 123, 139, 152–53, 185, 188, 219, XI:34, 187, XIII:1, 3, 68, 104, 175
  ~ in the building of the antakarana, I:47–48, 280
  ~ divine, VII:13, 23, 80, 87, 132, 148, IX:253, 271, X:56, 72, 102, 148, 154, 176, 181–82, 209–10, 212, 215, 218, 229, 238, XIII:66, 91–92, 121

interdependence. *See* consciousness: group

Interdimensional Federation of Free Worlds, IV:57–58, 115

International Order of the Star, V:233, 235

Internet, IX:73, 75. *See also* media

interplanetary communication, IV:11

Interplanetary Confederation of Planets, IV:57–58, 94

interplanetary travel, I:94–97, IV:11

intragalactic patrol, IV:37

intuition, I:44, **I:71,** I:120, 223, III:107, IV:159, 225, **IV:268,**
    VI:17, VI:18, 23, 47, 50–51, **VI:57,** VI:77, 86, 113, 174–75, 181,
    184, 203, 218, VII:73, 78, VIII:7, 98, 133, 170, IX:23, 55, X:24,
    121–22. *See also* Buddhi (intuition)
        ~ development of, VII:73–74, 77
        ~ higher, VII:73–76, 79
        ~ as the remedy for illusion, I:57, **I:58**–59, I:63–64
        ~ and the spiritual triad, I:43, 109–10, IV:300

intuitional plane. *See* Buddhic plane

Inxtria, IV:89. *See also* Andromeda

Iran
        ~ and Baha'i, IV:327
        ~ and the "white root race," I:3

Iraq, IX:100, 107. *See also* Hussein, Saddam; war

Iraqgate, IV:3. *See also* secret government

Iroquois, I:9. *See also* Native Americans

Irwin, Lord, V:73

Isaac (son of Abraham), IV:279, V:156

Isaiah (prophet), IV:285, 288

Ishmael (son of Abraham), IV:279. *See also* Islam

Ishta (beloved Deity), V:52

Ishvara, IV:257, 260, 264–65

Isis, I:37, III:56, 101, 121, IV:170, 173, V:99, **VI:112,** VII:16,
    VIII:41, 178, XI:2, 28. *See also* Egypt
        ~ and initiation, IV:191–92
        ~ and Iso, IV:173

Isis Unveiled, V:201, 205, 211, 213, 215. *See also* Blavatsky, Madam

Islam, IV:278–79, V:25, 155–58, 160–61. *See also* Koran; Moslems;
    Ramadan; Sikhism; Sufism
        ~ and Archangel Gabriel, I:175, 236–37
        ~ coming of the Imam Mahdi, I:137, IV:281
        ~ and the ego, IV:281–82
        ~ fundamentalist, V:4
        ~ mantras of, I:257, XII:22
        ~ pillars of faith, V:156–60
        ~ and Sufism, IV:323–24

Isle of Paradise, VI:73–74

Iso. *See* Isis; Ra-Ta (prophet)

Israel, I:241–42, IV:285–86. *See also* Holy Land; Jerusalem; Middle
    East

Israfil (angel), V:156, 160

I

Issa, I:173–74. *See also* Jesus

Italy, VII:79. *See also* San Damiano, Italy
    ~ art of, X:93
    ~ and the fourth ray, **VI:182,** VI:183
    ~ and the masculine principle, VI:184
    ~ and the sixth ray, **VI:182**

Itihasa, V:9. *See also* Hinduism; Mahabharata; Ramayana

It Takes a Village, XIII:85. *See also* Clinton, Hillary

J

Jackson, Jesse, IX:231

Jackson, Michael, IX:65–66, 148

Jacob (grandson of Abraham), IV:122, 279, 287

Jagannatha Temple, IV:221. *See also* Hinduism

Jainism, V:15–17. *See also* Mahavira

Jaipur, India, IV:26

James (disciple of Jesus), IV:288

Jampolsky, Jerry, III:73, IX:230

Jansen, Olaf, IV:22–23

Japan, V:100, VI:126, 129, IX:79, 99. *See also* Hiroshima, Japan; Nagasaki, Japan; Tokyo, Japan
~ art of, X:93
~ and medicine, VIII:89
~ and Shintoism, IV:325

japa (repetition of the name of God), IV:244–45, V:30–32. *See also* chanting: repetition of the name of God; mantras

Jaques, Annie, V:210

Jaredites, V:197

Jason and the Argonauts, V:136

jatharigni (digestive fire), V:67

Javits, Jacob, V:107

Jayrambati, India, V:28

jealousy, XIII:128, 149–50. *See also* emotions: negative

Jefferson, Thomas, V:242

Jehoshua
~ as an incarnation of Jesus, I:170

Jehovah (Yod Hay Way Hay), I:227, IV:120, 278, V:153

Jeremiah (prophet), IV:285, 288

Jerome, Saint, IV:292

Jerusalem, I:229, III:227, V:156. *See also* Israel
~ and the Order of Melchizedek, I:228

Jeshua
~ as an incarnation of Jesus, I:169, 236, VI:147

Jesus, I:160, 172, 176, 228, 250–51, III:131, 194, 224, 226, IV:51,
57, 153, 174, 253, 280, 314, 327, V:25, 182, 186, 191–93, 199,
209, VI:59, 108, 207, 229, 248, VII:16, 111, 147, VIII:xvii, IX:54,
176, 194, 239–40, 262, 270, X:71, 120, XI:20. *See also* Sananda
   ~ affirmations of, IV:317–18
   ~ ascension of, I:25, III:10, VI:6
   ~ ashram of, I:284, VIII:127
   ~ baptism of and the second initiation, I:23, VI:188, **XI:127**
   ~ birth of, I:172, 175, 222, 229
   ~ birth of and the first initiation, I:22, VI:187, **XI:127**
   ~ as Chohan of the sixth ray, I:192, 194–95, **I:199,** I:201,
      III:48, 257, **IV:121,** VI:163, 214, **VII:19,** VII:79, **VII:117,**
      XI:70–71
   ~ and Christianity, I:73, 144, 241, IV:271–75, 281, 283, 287,
      VI:180, IX:137–38
   ~ crucifixion of, I:79, 138, 170, 278, III:10, IV:272, V:174–75,
      IX:239–40
   ~ crucifixion of and the fourth initiation, I:25
   ~ disciples of, I:9, 31, 142, 160, 171, 175–76, 217, 237,
      241–42, IV:171, 288, V:133–34, 194, VI:148, 171, XI:84
   ~ and the Essene Brotherhood, I:172, 231, 235–36, IV:175,
      274, 280, 287–88, 290, IX:123
   ~ and the Festival of Humanity, VI:155, XII:87
   ~ and the Festival of the Christ, VI:150, XII:85
   ~ and healing, VII:82, X:141
   ~ initiations of, I:138, 170–71, 173, III:10, IV:184, 274, V:173,
      175, VI:22, VIII:134, IX:184, XI:64
   ~ and Judaism, I:141, 172, IV:277, 287
   ~ and Lord Maitreya, I:25, 138–43, 170, 175, 195, 236, 278,
      III:10, 177, IV:31, 223–24, 272, 274, 287–88, V:99, 174–75,
      227, **VII:19,** X:30, 41, 120
   ~ and love, I:143, IV:288, V:95, IX:194
   ~ miracles of, I:147, 152, 250, V:78, VII:54
   ~ and Mohammed, I:175, 236, IV:278
   ~ necklace of rejuvenation of, III:122, XI:90
   ~ other lives of, I:2–3, 169–71, 175, 207, 227, 234–36, IV:198,
      277, 284–85, 287–88, V:141–42, 151, 153, 173–75, VI:147,
      XI:1, 5
   ~ and the rays, I:124, X:20, 24, 40–41
   ~ resurrection of and the fifth initiation, I:25
   ~ resurrection of and the seventh initiation, **XI:127**
   ~ sayings of, I:27, 84, 185, 204, 270, III:72, 139, 205, IV:193,
      260, 287, V:191–92, VI:102, 109, 138, 142, VII:4, 18, 57,
      141, 147, 162, VIII:9, 17, 19, 22–23, 92, 105, 154, IX:7, 34,
      78, 128, 140, 144, 166, 221, 240, 270, 276, X:21, 42, 83,
      104, 161, 166–67, 205, 208, 215, XI:37, 108, XIII:1, 128,
      136, 159

~ transfiguration of and the third initiation, I:24, VI:188
~ travels of, I:173–74
~ unknown years of, I:173–75, 195
Jethro (prophet), I:228
Jewish mysticism. *See* Essene Brotherhood; Judaism; Kabbalah
Jews, VI:72, 81, IX:99–100. *See also* Judaism
~ art of, X:93
~ persecution of, IV:282
jinah (saint), V:17
jiva (soul), V:22
Jivatman (Eternal Self), V:11–12
Jnani (a knowledge yogi), V:24
Joel (prophet), IV:288
John of Penial, I:142
~ as an incarnation of Kuthumi, IV:171, VI:148, IX:115
~ and the Hall of Records, I:9, 242, IV:170–71
John Paul II, Pope, V:107. *See also* Pope, the
John, Saint. *See* John the Beloved
Johnson, Magic, VIII:165, XI:68
John the Baptist, I:173, 231, IV:175, 285, 288, IX:240
~ initiation of, IV:184
~ other lives of, I:171, IV:277, 290
John the Beloved, IV:288, XI:84
~ as an incarnation of Kuthumi, I:237, IV:171, VI:148
~ ascension of, I:31, 142, 171
~ and the Hall of Records, I:9, 241–42
~ and Kriya yoga, I:160
Johrei, III:107, V:99–100, VIII:168
Jonah (prophet), IV:288
Jones, Jim, IX:141
Jones, Stanley, V:73
Jophiel (archangel), **I:199,** III:199, 253
~ and the second ray, **I:204, IV:121, 123, VII:115,** X:94
Jordan, Michael, IX:123, XI:68
Joseph (husband of the Virgin Mary), I:172–73, IV:277, 288
~ as an incarnation of Saint Germain, I:171, 237, V:239, VI:148
~ and Archangel Gabriel, I:237
~ other children of, I:174–75
Josephus (philosopher), IV:289–92
Joseph (with the coat of many colors)
~ as an incarnation of Jesus, I:169–71, 236, IV:277, 287, VI:147

Joshua (prophet), IV:285, 288
    ~ as an incarnation of Jesus, I:169–71, 236, IV:277, VI:147
Jot Niranjan (ruler of the astral plane), **IV:195**
journaling, I:252, 269–70, III:19, 24, 57, 72, 86, 127, IV:202–3,
    VII:26, 29, 145, 154–55, 158, 162, VIII:4, 69, 73, 111–13,
    117–20, 170, XIII:26, 104, 132, 137, 139, 159, 162, 172
Journey to the Center of the Earth, IV:20
Judaism, I:171, 236–37, III:217, IV:52, 277–81, 284–88, 290,
    VII:146–47, VIII:165, XI:2. *See also* Essene Brotherhood; Jews;
    Kabbalah
        ~ covenant with God, IV:278–80, 286
        ~ and the ego, IV:274, 281–82
        ~ holy places of, V:156
        ~ and Jesus, I:141, 172, IV:277, 287
        ~ mantras of, I:254–55, XII:19–20, 22
        ~ and the Messiah, I:137, 141, 144, 243, IV:283
        ~ and the name of God, I:251, IV:278, 300, **IV:302**
        ~ and the Order of Melchizedek, I:230, 235
        ~ and reincarnation, VII:6
        ~ teachings of, IV:284–86
judgment, VI:48–49, 101, 138, VIII:113, X:53, 71, 104, 157–59, 183,
    196, 208, 216, 220
        ~ in romantic relationships, XIII:19, 28–30, 37, 50–51,
            133–34, 138, 147, 165, 168
        ~ self-, X:53, 104, 111, 197, 201, 211, 246, XIII:30
Judgment Day, I:243, V:156, 160
judicial system (U.S.), IX:63–70, 130, 144, 156, 158–60. *See also*
    crime; prison system (U.S.)
        ~ and African Americans, IX:156, 158–59, 161
        ~ attorneys, IX:64, 66–67
        ~ and the death penalty, IX:98
        ~ and expert testimony, IX:68
        ~ juries, IX:64–66
        ~ and the media, IX:65–66, 148
        ~ and the negative ego, IX:64, 66–67, 69–71, 101
        ~ and the police, IX:66–67, 69–71, 100–101, 130
        ~ racism in, IX:63–66, 70, 156, 158–61
        ~ tools for handling for the lightworker, IX:36–37
Jung, Carl, I:67, 106, VII:153, VIII:79, 114, 159, IX:14, XIII:164
    ~ and the vertical/horizontal aspects of life, III:108–9
Junner (teacher of Jesus), I:173
Jupiter, VI:83, XI:41–42
        ~ ascension seat of, VI:36
        ~ and color healing, **IV:212**
        ~ cometary collisions of, XI:41–42

~ energy qualities of, I:95–96
~ and the Kabbalistic tree of life, **IV:302**
~ and the rays, **I:131, 133, VI:82, XI:177**
~ and Sagittarius, **XI:177**
Jupiter, Master (of the first ray), I:189, V:230
Jurassic Park, IX:122

K

Kabbalah, I:254, III:217, 224, IV:120, 278, 284, 286–87, 297–313, V:153, VII:106, 146, VIII:165, X:159. *See also* Essene Brotherhood, the; Judaism

Kabbalah: Your Path to Inner Freedom, IV:302, 311

Kabbalistic tree of life, I:68, III:217, 257, IV:247, 286–87, 297–98, **IV:298,** IV:299, **IV:299,** IV:300–302, **IV:302,** IV:303–5, **IV:306**–7, IV:308–10, **IV:310,** IV:311–12, VIII:55, 61, 165, XII:108, 128
~ and the angels, IV:124, **IV:303**–4, IV:305
~ "climbing Jacob's ladder," IV:309, **IV:311**
~ and color, **IV:304, 308**–9
~ and the dimensions, III:148
~ and the Earth elements, **IV:304**
~ and the Lord's Prayer, **IV:305**
~ meditation of, III:187–89
~ and Metatron, I:203, **IV:303,** X:159, 161, 232, XI:241–43
~ personality-level triad, IV:301, **IV:307**
~ and the planes, **IV:303**
~ sephiroths of, I:68, III:148, 227, IV:300–302, **IV:302, 304,** IV:305, **IV:305, 308**–9, VIII:55, 161–62, IX:5
    Binah (Understanding), **IV:298**–99, IV:300, **IV:302**–8, **310**–11, VI:42
    Chesed or Gedulah (Mercy), **IV:298**–99, IV:300–301, **IV:302**–8, **310**–11
    Chokmah (Wisdom), **IV:298**–99, IV:300, **IV:302**–8, **310**–11, VI:42
    Daath, IV:305, **IV:307,** IV:310, **IV:311**
    Geburah (Severity), **IV:298**–99, IV:300–301, **IV:302**–8, **310**–11
    Hod (Splendor), **IV:298**–99, IV:301, **IV:302**–7, **309**–11
    Kether (Crown), **IV:298**–99, IV:300, **IV:302**–4, IV:305, **IV:305**–8, **310**–11, VI:42
    Malkuth (Kingdom), **IV:298**–99, IV:301, **IV:302**–4, IV:305, **IV:305**–7, **309**–11
    Netzach (Victory), **IV:298**–99, IV:301, **IV:302**–8, **310**–11

Tiphareth (Beauty), **IV:298**–99, IV:300–301, **IV:302**–4, IV:305, **IV:305**–8, **310**–11

Yesod (Foundation), **IV:298**–99, IV:301, **IV:302**–4, IV:305, **IV:305**–7, **309**–11

~ soul-level triad, IV:300–301, **IV:307**

~ supernal or spiritual-level triad, IV:300, **IV:307**

~ and the tarot, IV:305, **IV:306, 308**–9

~ ten branches of, **IV:302**

~ three-dimensional, IV:309, **IV:310**

~ three pillars of, **IV:299**, IV:302–3, **IV:307**

Kabir (the poet-saint), I:160, IV:194, 197–98, V:2, 160–61, 163–65, VII:97, VIII:165–66

~ as an incarnation of Sathya Sai Baba, IV:194, V:160, 163, VI:147, VIII:165

~ and the Middle Way, V:164, 170

~ poetry of, V:167–72

~ quotations from, V:165–68, 172

~ and Sabda yoga, IV:249

~ teachings of, V:165–72

Kabir, the Weaver of God's Name, V:168. *See also* Sethi, V.F.

Kahjian (teacher of Jesus), I:173

kahunas, III:155, IV:158, 161, 163–65, VIII:68

Kailas, Mount, IV:221. *See also* Hinduism

kaivalya (emancipation), IV:254, VI:160–61

kaizen, VIII:108, IX:223

Kali (Hindu goddess of war and destruction), IV:219, V:23, 29, X:71

Kali Yuga, I:147, V:20

Kalki Avatar, I:137, IV:220

Kalmelchizedek (Source), I:234, III:144

Kal (the devil), V:167

kama (lust), V:8, 12

Kantarian Confederation, IV:70

Kantarians, IV:70. *See also* extraterrestrials

karma, I:27, 91, 111, III:59, IV:31, 272, V:3, 17, 50, 61, VI:70, 86, 118, 139, VII:31, 57–69, 86, 124–25, IX:50, X:113, 131–37, XI:145, XII:102. *See also* Karmic Board; Lords of Karma

~ and abortion, IX:96, XIII:78

~ and adultery, IX:127

~ of the animal kingdom, VII:124–25

~ and ascension, III:5, VI:92, 216, VII:11, XI:21, 44, 129, 248–49, 266

~ astral, VI:162

~ and blood transfusions, IX:85

~ causal, VI:162

~ clearing of, I:82, 269, III:100, 219, IV:262, V:170, VI:92–93, 239, VII:64, VIII:62, 86–87, X:131, 173, 240
~ collective, VI:139, 166, VII:31, 65, 68–69, 86, IX:95, 160
~ and credit cards, IX:135
~ and crime, IX:68–69, 98, 152–53
~ and discipleship, VI:166–67, 173
~ and divorce, IX:149
~ emotional, I:92, XI:249
~ and euthanasia, IX:96
~ and the family unit, V:81, VII:95, X:133–35, XIII:72, 83, 94
~ and grace, I:245, III:99, 190, V:116, 128, VI:217, VII:59–60, 67–68, 85–86, VIII:25, 87, 134, IX:69, X:110, XIII:115
~ and Hinduism, IV:219–20, 229
~ and initiation, IV:180, 185, 190, VI:93, XI:266
~ and Jainism, V:15
~ and the Lords of Karma, I:188, VII:65
~ mental, I:92, VI:160, XI:249
~ and murder, I:93, V:142, VII:68–69
~ negative, I:89, V:216, VII:58, 61, 86, X:240
~ and occupations, X:135–37
~ and organ transplants, IX:85
~ past-life, IV:262, V:50, VI:18, 55, X:128, 131–39, XI:29
~ and the permanent atoms, IV:190, VII:62–63, 66, XIII:84
~ physical, I:92, XI:249
~ planetary, I:239, IV:167, VII:86
~ positive, VII:58–61, 65, XI:249
~ and the rays, X:127–28
~ and reincarnation, III:2, VII:66–68
~ of romantic relationships, X:61–62, 64, 138–39, XIII:72, 83, 94, 156
~ and service work, VIII:18
~ and siddhis, IV:269
~ and walk-ins, IV:30–31
~ and war, VII:68–69, VIII:21, IX:99–101
Karmic Board, III:156, VI:94, VIII:75, 97, XI:80. *See also* karma; Lords of Karma
~ ashram of, VIII:127
Katz, Ginny, IV:155–56
Keaton, Michael, IX:166
Keeper of the Scrolls, III:157
Kennedy, John F., I:97, IV:9, IX:231
~ assassination of, IV:3, 9, 16, IX:129–30, 162
~ other lives of, VI:147
~ and the Warren Commission, IX:162
Kennedy, Robert F., IV:3, 9, 16
Kenya, III:149

key codes, I:280, 284, III:19, 45, 205, VI:213, VIII:55–56
  ~ anchoring of, VI:115, X:212, 225, XI:94

keys of Enoch, III:218, IV:197, 297, 313–15, XII:114. *See also The Book of Knowledge: The Keys of Enoch;* Enoch (ascended master)

The Keys to Theosophy, V:210–11. *See also* Blavatsky, Madam

KGB, IX:244

Khalil, Mr. and Mrs., V:187

Khamael (archangel), I:285, III:53
  ~ and the Kabbalistic tree of life, **IV:303**

Khomeini, Ayatollah, IX:3

Khrushchev, Nikita Sergeyevich, I:240

King, Godfré Ray, I:237, III:46–47, IV:317–21, V:240, 243, VI:226, 229, VII:84, 148, VIII:163, IX:53, X:240, XII:111, 117, XIII:67. *See also The "I Am" Discourses*
  ~ as an incarnation of George Washington, I:244–45, V:242, VI:147, VIII:163

King, Martin Luther Jr., VII:16, IX:114, 231, X:71, 130

King of Kings, VII:97

King, Rodney, IX:63, 71, 130, 159–60

Kittler, Glenn D., IV:296

Kleineas. *See also* Pythagoras
  ~ as an incarnation of Djwhal Khul, V:141, 203, VI:147

Knowers of the Purpose, Custodians of the Will, III:10

Koran, V:66, 155–58, 160. *See also* Islam

Koresh, David, IX:141

Korton (ascended master), III:190

Kosei, V:102

Kowalska, Sister Faustina, I:261–62

Kripalani, J.B., V:71

Krishna (avatar), I:147, 153, 159, 236, IV:200, 219, 224–30, 241–43, 327, V:9–10, 15, 23–24, 36, 69, 71, 74, 231, VI:207, 229, VIII:21, xviii, IX:182, X:51, XI:36, XII:21. *See also* Arjuna; *Bhagavad-Gita;* Hinduism
  ~ as an incarnation of Lord Maitreya, I:138, 176, III:130, IV:218, 223, VI:148, 154, VII:19, XI:225, XII:80, XIII:101
  ~ as an incarnation of Sathya Sai Baba, IV:251
  ~ initiations of, I:176, IV:224
  ~ and Kriya yoga, I:160
  ~ quotations from, I:73, 75–76, 79, 137, VII:154, IX:99, 116
  ~ and the three gunas, IV:228–30

Krishna consciousness, IX:53

Krishna mind, III:23

Krishnamurti, I:139, V:224, 227–28, 230–36. *See also* Theosophical Society; Theosophy
  ~ first initiation of, V:228
  ~ later philosophy of, V:235–37
  ~ and Nitya (his brother), V:227–28, 231–32, 234
  ~ rejection of Theosophy, V:229–31, 235–36
  ~ as a vehicle for Lord Maitreya, I:139–40, V:227, 229–37, IX:6, X:31

Krishnamurti, His Life and Death, V:233–34, 236. *See also* Lutyen, Mary

Kriyananda, Swami, V:44, VI:162, 164, VIII:166

kriyas, V:87

krodha (anger), V:8, 12

Kroeger, Hanna, III:34, VIII:144

Kuever, Julie Ray, VI:164, IX:11

kundalini, I:285, III:15, 54, IV:188, V:226
  ~ and Kriya yoga, I:163, 166
  ~ during physical death, I:81, 83
  ~ planetary, I:285, III:54
  ~ rising of, III:19, 64, IV:189, 246, 303, V:80, 86, 136, VIII:43, IX:122, XI:48, 232, XIII:99–100, 106–7

Kundalini: the Secret of Life, V:91. *See also* Muktananda, Baba

Kung Fu, IX:134

K'ung Fu-Tse. *See* Confucius

Kuthumi (ascended master), I:25, 33, 124, 138, 142, 166, 190, 272, III:48, 67, 95, 193–94, **III:238,** IV:197, 224, 253, V:242, **VI:3, 112,** VI:144, 171, 241, 248, VII:18, 23, VIII:160, IX:2, 9, 176, 200, 205, X:23, XI:202–3, 218–19, XIII:109
  ~ ascension of, VI:6
  ~ ashram of, I:190, 284, VI:35, **VI:204,** VI:225, VII:145, VIII:127, X:32, XI:111–12, 218
  ~ as Chohan of the second ray, I:166, 190, **I:199,** I:201, III:67, 257, **IV:121,** VI:144, 163, 214, **VII:19, 117,** X:14, 30, 140, 149, 152, XI:45, 70–71, 111, 218
  ~ as the future head of the Spiritual Hierarchy, I:146, 243, III:197
  ~ other lives of, I:171, 237, IV:171, V:71, 108, 139, 147, VI:148, VII:106, VIII:98, IX:115, X:42
  ~ as the Planetary Christ, I:243, III:169, VI:35, XI:102, 111, 210, 218
  ~ quotations from, I:43
  ~ and the second ray, I:120, X:32–33
  ~ and the Synthesis Ashram, VII:144–45, VIII:161
  ~ and the Theosophical Society, V:201–3, 206–7, 209, 217–18, 220, 224–28, 232–33, VII:84

L

Laberge, Stephen, IV:203
Ladakh, Tibet, I:173
Lady Fatima. *See* Virgin Mary
Lady Leda, XI:239
Lady Nada, **I:199**, III:156, **VI:112**
Lady of the Light, VIII:178
Lady of the Sun, VIII:178
Lake Shrine Temple, V:46
Lakshmi (Vishnu's wife), IV:219, V:99
Lamont, Lena, IV:132
Lananites, V:197
"land of Shalmali." *See* Lemuria (Mu)
Lanto (ascended master)
    ~ as Chohan of the second ray, XI:111
Laochi, III:107
Lao-tzu, I:237, IV:327, V:115–17. *See also* Taoism
laser technology, IV:39, VII:133
Laughton, Charles, VII:97
law, civil. *See* law, earthly
law, earthly, IX:126, 269–75, 278, X:20
    ~ and the negative ego, IX:270–71
    ~ vs. spiritual law, IX:270–71
law of attraction, I:98, VII:104, XIII:3, 5, 7
law of love and forgiveness, IV:41
Law of One, I:8–9, IV:2, 41, 167, 172, 283, VI:178, X:116
    ~ and the Procyonians, IV:79
    ~ and the Ra, IV:93
law of the mind, I:138, 249
law of vibration, III:179
law, spiritual, I:3, IV:46, V:2, VI:70, VIII:72, 86, IX:126, 269–75, X:67, 85, 108, 130
    ~ and free choice, IV:58

~ shifting of, IX:275–77

Laxmidevi Temple, V:5

Layne, Al, V:246

Lay-oo-esh (Pillar of Light), III:221

Lazarus, I:250

Leadbeater, C.W., I:139, IV:197, V:211, 219–20, 223–34, 242–43, VII:16, VIII:164, IX:6, XI:19. *See also* Theosophical Society; Theosophy

    ~ and the externalization of the Spiritual Hierarchy, I:142

    ~ other lives of, V:141, 226

leadership, IX:184

    ~ democratic, VI:179, IX:7, 13

    ~ dictatorial, VI:179, IX:7, 13

    ~ egotistical, VIII:155, IX:3–4, 44

    ~ laissez faire, IX:7

leadership, cosmic, IX:221

leadership, spiritual, VI:56, 107–10, 141, 210, VII:99, VIII:46, 78, 80–82, 126, 128–29, 136, IX:10, 12, 16–17, 19, 23, 44, 79, 86, 114, 116, 143, 157, 182, 221, 236, X:69, XI:198, XII:123

    ~ archetypes of, IX:185–86

    ~ and the business world, IX:50–51

    ~ and communication, IX:27, 209

    ~ and detachment, IX:198–99, 212–13

    ~ and dreams, IX:236–37

    ~ and the fifth ray, IX:43, 185

    ~ and the first ray, IX:184–85

    ~ and the fourth ray, IX:1–2, 43, 185

    ~ and group consciousness, IX:206

    ~ key qualities of, VIII:102, 115, 155–58, IX:1–6, 13–15, 18, 21–29, 146, 173–74, 178, 181–87, 189–99, 201–14, 217–19, 222–36, 255–57

    ~ and motivational skills, IX:26–27, 192, 209, 231, 233

    ~ and the negative ego, IX:3–4, 20, 29, 44, 177, 187–88, 193, 202, 206–7, 209, 223, 228, 256

    ~ in the New Age, IX:1–29, 256–58

    ~ prayer for, IX:237

    ~ pressures of, IX:174–75

    ~ and prosperity, IX:51, 204–5

    ~ and the rays, IX:182, 186

    ~ and the second ray, IX:2–3, 43, 51, 185

    ~ and the seventh ray, IX:43, 185

    ~ and the sixth ray, IX:43, 185

    ~ spiritual tests of, VIII:131, IX:213

    ~ stages of, IX:183–84

    ~ styles of, IX:195–96

    ~ and the third ray, IX:43, 185

Leaving the Body, IV:201

Lecky, William, V:175

Lemuria (Mu), I:4, **I:5**, I:7, 134, IV:26, 38, **VI:78**. *See also* Earth, history of: Lemurian times; root races: Lemurian; souls: Lemurian
    ~ and the Anunnaki and the Annu, IV:23
    ~ and the "brown root race," I:3
    ~ and the first ray, VI:178
    ~ and glamour, I:65
    ~ healing temples of, I:242
    ~ and maya, I:58, **I:59**
    ~ and the Order of Melchizedek, XI:1
    ~ sinking of, I:8, IV:23
    ~ and the sutratma, I:44
    ~ underground cities of, IV:26
    ~ and the Venusians, IV:52

Lenduce (ascended master), I:282, III:38, 48–49, 62, 100, 172, 202, **III:238**, VI:53, **VI:112**, VI:207, XI:18, 148, 192
    ~ ascension seat of, VI:32
    ~ ashram of, I:279, III:32, 44–46, 61, 85, 135, 147, VIII:127, XI:54–55
    ~ and Vywamus, I:207, III:243, XI:208

Leo. *See also* astrology
    ~ and color healing, **IV:212**
    ~ and Geneva, Switzerland, **VI:185**
    ~ and the Sun, **XI:177**
    ~ and the third ray, **XI:177**

leprechauns, IV:136

Letters on Occult Meditation, IX:264

Letters on Yoga, IV:251. *See also* Aurobindo, Sri

Levi, I:173, IV:177, 184. *See also The Aquarian Gospel of Jesus the Christ*

levitation, VII:17, XI:48. *See also* ascended masters: advanced abilities of

ley lines, IV:169. *See also* Earth: grid points of
    ~ cleansing of, IV:60–61

Lhamo, Lake, V:105–6

Lhasa, Tibet, I:173, V:106
    ~ and Shamballa, IV:19–20

liberation, I:78, 80, 84, 265, 269–70, 272, III:1, 5, 24, IV:224, 227, 255–56, 262, 269, V:12, 15–17, 21–22, 31, 46, 50, 67, 69, 77, 81, 90, 108, 110–12, 137, 168, 209, VI:36, 158, 174, 190, 244, VII:11, 18, 34, VIII:20, 94, 99, X:108, 118, XI:35, XIII:84
    ~ and Jnana yoga, IV:243–44
    ~ from the wheel of rebirth, I:24, 64, 80, 138, 198, 200, 268, III:2–3, 5, IV:188, 219, 222, 232, 269, V:12, 94, 109, 136,

209, VI:1, 59, 61, 67, 123, 160, 163, 208, 222, 244, VII:12, 140–41, VIII:xxi, IX:265, XI:11, 74, 173, 186, 267 (*See also* enlightenment; nirvana; samadhi (enlightenment))

Liberty, Goddess of, **I:199,** III:156, VIII:178
~ and George Washington, I:244

Libra. *See also* astrology
~ and color healing, **IV:212**
~ and the fourth ray, **XI:177**
~ and Venus, **XI:177**

Life and Teaching of Sri Anandamayi Ma, V:49

The Life and Teachings of the Masters of the Far East, VIII:163

life hormone, I:274, VIII:45

The Life of Apollonius of Tyana, V:173. *See also* Philostratus, Flavius

The Life of Pythagoras, V:176. *See also* Apollonius of Tyana

life thread, I:43, 46–47, 51. *See also* silver cord; sutratma
~ and physical death, I:77, 81
~ and the soul, I:113

light, I:1, 22, 38, 40, 126, 280, III:10, 20, 170–71, 205, 222, 226, 229, 232, IV:64, 105, 142, 153, 247, V:66, 128, VI:117, 173, VII:3–4, 33, 53–54, 72, VIII:20, 57–58, 65, 80, 96, 101, 184, X:49–51, 55, 82–83, 108, 179, 211–12, 214, 239, XI:33
~ anchoring of, III:226, 231, VII:99, 137–38, IX:170, X:108
~ and ascension, I:30–31, 35, 213, III:8, 194–95, VII:137
~ and the bardo experience, I:79–83
~ and the cherubim, IV:124–25
~ clear light of God, III:8, IV:189, 191, V:108, 111, 169
~ and extraterrestrials, VI:85, VII:133
~ information packets of, I:36, 39, 282, III:37, 45, 61–62, 83, 100–101, 128, 176, 221, 223–24, 227, 229–31, VI:115, VIII:54–55, IX:236, XI:27
~ keeping the mind steady in, I:46, 48, 60, 64, 66, 81–82, 265, III:23, VI:4, 170, 223, VIII:81, 96, IX:139, X:16, 44, 49, 85–87, 89, 119, 244, XI:36
~ language of, I:207, 221, 274, III:222, VIII:55–56, X:238–39
~ and meditation, IV:259, V:87, 114
~ merging with, I:31, 79–83, 267, III:8, 228, IV:180, 191, 259–60, V:87, 108, 114
~ physicalization of, XI:130–31, 133
~ as a replacement for physical food, VI:12, VIII:46–47, XI:127–33, 258–59
~ and the sixth initiation, I:27
~ of the soul, I:108
~ technology of, I:8, VI:58

lightbody, I:26–27, 40, 216, 251, III:28, 201, 245, 254, IV:193, 270, V:127, VI:40

~ anchoring of, I:126–27, 274, III:239
~ building of, I:212–13, 216
~ of God, VIII:177
~ monadic, IV:270
~ of Mother Earth, I:126
~ and physical death, I:75, 84
~ and the tenth ray, I:126, 128
~ and the zeal-point chakra, III:191

lightbody, galactic, III:245–47, 254

lightbody, monadic, III:245

lightbody, solar, III:219, 245–47, 254

lightbody, soul, III:245

lightbody, universal, III:245–47, 254

Light of a Thousand Suns, III:54

Light of the Soul: The Yoga Sutras of Patanjali, IV:253, 270. *See also*
Bailey, Alice A.
~ excerpt from, IV:254–67, **IV:267,** IV:268, **IV:268,**
IV:269–70

Light on the Path, I:194

light quotient, I:277, III:53, 195–96, 237, 241, 260, 266, VI:1–2, 44,
103, 132, 206, VII:24, 54–55, 78, 132, 137, VIII:44, X:107–8,
113, 222, 232, XI:56, 186, 209, 266
~ and ascension seats, I:280
~ and bilocation, III:42
~ and bodies, VI:205–6
~ building of, I:33, 36–40, 277, 280–81, 283–84, III:7, 23–35,
37–39, 43–44, 46, 52, 54, 61, 63, 76–77, 82–83, 85–86, 108,
124–25, 128, 132, 196, 199, 202, 205, 257, VI:4, 33, 45–46,
87, 92, 95, 100, 115–16, 120, 122, 212, 231, VIII:28, 38, 40,
176, X:227, XI:17, 26, 77, 98, 154–55, 191, 209, 241, 259,
XII:97
~ and chakras, VI:18, 205–6
~ and dimensions, VI:205–6
~ of Earth, X:232
~ for the fifth initiation, I:32, 277, III:3, 24, **III:238, VI:3**
~ for the first initiation, **III:238, VI:3**
~ fluctuation of, VIII:38
~ for the fourth initiation, I:32, 277, III:3, 24, **III:238, VI:3**
~ and immortality, III:197
~ and initiation, VI:60–61, 205–6
~ for the second initiation, **III:238, VI:3**
~ for the seventh initiation, I:32, 277–78, 283, III:9–10, 24, 76,
III:238, VI:3, **VI:3,** XI:163
~ for the sixth initiation (ascension), I:32–33, 36, 277, III:6, 8,
24, 76, **III:238,** VI:3, **VI:3,** VI:216, XI:16, 43

L

~ stabilization of, VI:3–5, VIII:38–39
~ for the third initiation, I:32, 277, III:24, **III:238, VI:3**
light quotient, cosmic, VI:5, 53, 205–7, VIII:39, XI:248, 266, 268
~ anchoring of, III:259–60, VI:63
~ building of, VI:27–28, 87, 115–16
~ for the eleventh initiation, XI:265
~ for galactic completion, VI:27, 53
~ for multiuniversal completion, VI:16, 27
~ for planetary completion, VI:16
~ for solar completion, VI:16, 27, 53
~ for Source activation, VI:27
~ for the tenth initiation, XI:265
~ for the twelfth initiation, XI:265
~ for universal completion, VI:16, 27, 56, **VI:62**
Light Synthesis Chamber. *See* Arcturians: and the Light Synthesis Chamber
lightworkers, III:104, VIII:93, IX:49
~ and the arts, IX:52
~ and the business world, VIII:171–73, IX:33–34, 50–51, 195, 208–9, 213–16, 224–25
~ cosmic, I:215
~ and glamour, X:123–24
~ and physical health lessons, VI:118–22
~ and self-forgiveness, IX:37
~ and sexuality, XIII:46–47
~ and social issues, VIII:154–55, IX:31–41, 112–15, 141, 170–71, 247–48
Lilith (the first female human), I:2
Limitless Love and Light, IV:132
limoniades, **IV:135**. *See also* devas; elementals: undines (nature spirits of water); nature spirits
Lincoln, Abraham, I:119, VII:16
~ as an incarnation of John F. Kennedy, VI:147
~ quotations from, X:201
~ as a walk-in, IV:31
lingam (sacred Hindu icon), XI:161
Lipski, Alexander, V:49
Little Buddha, IX:134
The Lives of Alcyone, V:227, 233. *See also* Leadbeater, C.W.
lobha (greed), V:8, 12
Lo Chi (avatar), I:6
Lodz, Poland, I:261
logoic body, III:239, VI:18, 203, **VI:205**, XI:150, 187
~ anchoring of, **VI:63**, VIII:59, XI:154

~ and the seventh initiation, **VI:17**, VI:18

~ and the sixth dimension, **VI:204**

~ and the sleep state, VI:71

logoic body, cosmic, **III:238**, III:259, **VI:3, 24, 205**, VI:206, XI:155

logoic plane, I:16, 40, **I:184, 197**, I:277, III:4, 8, 139, VI:8, **VI:8**, VI:206, VII:13, 34–35, XIII:64–65. *See also* divine plane

~ anchoring of, **III:139**

~ and the Kabbalistic tree of life, **IV:303, 307**

~ between lives, I:87–89, 92, 97

~ and the seventh initiation, I:200, **III:4, 139, VI:17**, VI:18, **XI:127**

~ sexual expression on, XIII:65

logoic plane, cosmic, I:17, 198, **I:199**, I:202, III:167, 181, **III:238**, III:240, **VI:3**, VI:8, **VI:8, 24**, VI:206. *See also* divine plane

Logos of the Great Bear, **I:199**, I:202, **III:238**, III:255, **VI:3**. *See also* Great Bear constellation; Lord of the Great Bear Star System

Logos of Sirius, **I:199**, I:202

Loltun, cave of, IV:24

London, England, I:140, V:36, VI:185. *See also* Great Britain

~ as Gemini, **VI:185**

~ and the rays, **VI:185**

Long Island, New York, IV:15

Long, Max Freedom, IV:157–58

Lopez, Marcia Dale, I:67–68, 275

Lord Ashtar. *See* Commander Ashtar

Lord of the Great Bear Star System, **VI:111**. *See also* Great Bear constellation; Logos of the Great Bear

Lord of Arcturus, III:80–83, **III:238, VI:3**, VI:32, 52, **VI:112**, VI:115, 121, 193, 195, 212–13, 240–41, VII:112, 132, VIII:28–29, 34–35, 56, 135, XI:93, 130–31, 148, 239, 255. *See also* Arcturians; Arcturus

~ ashram of, VIII:127

~ and cancer, VI:125–26

~ and healing, VI:45, 119

~ and Wesak, X:153, XI:174

Lord of Pleiades, III:190, VI:32, **VI:112**. *See also* Pleiades, the (seven sisters); Pleiadians

Lord of Sirius, III:83, 100–101, 176, **III:238**, III:255, **VI:3**, VI:32, 43, 53, **VI:112**, VI:115, 195, VIII:54, 57–58, 64, IX:179, XI:148. *See also* Great White Lodge; Sirius

~ ashram of, **VI:204**, VI:225, VIII:127, IX:220

~ and the galactic body, III:254

~ scroll of, XI:228, 230

L

~ and Shamballa, VII:133

~ and Wesak, XI:174

Lord of the World, III:179

Lord's Mystical Body, **III:238,** III:258, **VI:3,** VI:25, 202–3, VIII:49, 59, XI:143, 154, 195

~ and the dimensions, **VI:204**

Lords of Civilization. *See* Mahachohan

Lords of Karma, I:188, **I:199,** I:201, III:62, 156–57, 197, **III:238,** V:99, **VI:3,** VI:131, VII:63–65, 68, X:128. *See also* karma; Karmic Board

~ and physical birth, XIII:71–72

Lords of Light, XI:195

Lord's Prayer, I:140, 250, 255, V:184, VII:107, XII:5, 20, 85, 89. *See also* prayers

~ and the Kabbalistic tree of life, **IV:305**

~ as a mantra, I:258, XII:23

Lorphan (doctor), VII:82, VIII:29, 32–33, IX:61, XI:255, XII:124, XIII:110. *See also* Great White Brotherhood Medical Unit; healing; MAP (Medical Assistance Program)

~ and Western medicine, IX:35

Los Angeles, California, VI:185–86, VIII:103, IX:63, 68–70, 156, X:152

~ police department of, IX:158

Lotus Sutra, V:102

Lourdes, France, V:179

love, I:156, 179, 264–65, 268–69, 273, III:55, 59, 69, 71–73, 108, 170–71, 199, IV:64, 136, 273, V:30, 32, 90, 147, 150, 192, VI:59–60, 74, 130–31, 137–38, 168, 197, 223, 232, 240, VII:3–4, 53–54, 71, 112, VIII:2–4, 7, 9, 22, 94, 117, 130, 160, 177–78, 184, 189, viii, IX:83, 124, X:30, 46, 49–51, 55, 82–83, 86, 89, 91–94, 114–16, 166, 177, 181, 196–97, 211–15, 219, 228, 231, 234, 240, XI:38, 40–41, 228, 269, XIII:25, 60–61, 76, 81, 150, 157. *See also* emotions; self-love

~ anchoring of, I:143, VIII:65, IX:170, X:119

~ and the animal kingdom, VII:126, X:213–14

~ and ascension, VI:12–13, 28, 193, 207, VII:33, 35, 39–41, 83, 138–39, VIII:30

~ and Bhakti yoga, IV:240–41

~ and the Christ, IV:288, V:95, VIII:4

~ and devas, VII:7, X:44, 213–15, 239

~ and divorce, XIII:25, 95

~ and the Festival of the Christ, VI:150, XII:85

~ and initiation, IV:183, VII:25–26, VIII:134

~ and marriage, IX:127, XIII:91, 116

~ and the New Age, I:225, III:183, X:40, 161

~ and the planet Venus, I:94, 96

~ and the rays, I:119, 123, 127, VI:191, X:16, 18, 20–21, 23–24, 33, 140–41

~ and romantic relationships, X:138, 220, XIII:21–28, 52–53, 116, 125–26, 135, 150, 152, 156, 166–67, 170–71, 176

~ and Satyagraha, V:71–72

~ and service work, I:18, VII:139, X:118–19

~ and spiritual leadership, IX:2–3

~ and the spiritual path, III:85, VI:173, 175, VIII:110, IX:129

~ transcending, VIII:79, X:118, 134

Love is Letting Go of Fear, III:73. *See also* Jampolsky, Jerry

love principle, I:143, 191, IV:288, V:95, 144

love quotient, X:222, XI:259, 268

~ building of, VIII:177, XI:17, 191, XII:97–98

lower mind, I:46, VI:58, 175

lower self, I:64, 116, 264, 269, 272, III:23–24, 69, 71, 88, IV:138, 158, 174, 268, 271, V:67, 70, 110, VI:4, 57, 122, 172–73, 175, VIII:8, 21, 143, IX:46, 119, 121–22, X:49, 156, 187, 210–11, XI:29, 36. *See also* subconscious mind

~ and adultery, XIII:122–23

~ and the Huna teachings, IV:158–65

~ and initiation, I:23, IV:187

~ and the Kabbalistic tree of life, IV:301

~ merging with the higher self, X:86–87

~ and the *Ramayana*, V:11

~ and the rays, VI:180, 188

~ shadow body of, IV:159–61, 163–65

lower spiritual triad. *See* threefold personality

Lucid Dreaming, IV:203

Lucifer. *See* Satan

Lucis Trust, IX:53

Luther, Martin, I:118

Lutyen, Mary, V:233–34, 236

Luxor, VIII:126. *See also* Serapis Bey (ascended master)

~ ascension seat at, I:30, 279, III:25, 30, 32, 43, VI:32–33, X:34, XI:27, 29, 31

Lyra, I:242, **IV:33,** IV:38, 69, 85, 97, 99

Lyrans, IV:38, 85, 99. *See also* extraterrestrials

L

M

MacArthur, Douglas, I:118

Machu Picchu, III:149

Maclean, Dorothy, III:119, IV:132, 139, 142, 147–48, 151

mada (passion), V:8

Madrid, Spain, IV:43–44

Magdalene, Mary. *See* Mary Magdalene

The Magic Presence, III:47. *See also* King, Godfré Ray

magnetism, III:171–72

Mahaavatar Babaji. *See* Babaji, the Yogi Christ

Mahabharata, I:147–48, 236, IV:218–19, 224, V:9. *See also*
  Bhagavad-Gita; Hinduism

Mahachohan, I:190, 192, **I:199, III:238,** V:218, 228–29, 239,
  VI:3, VII:19, IX:9, X:21, 23, 25, 34, 43–44, 71, 236, XI:210
    ~ ashram of, VIII:127
    ~ and the rays, I:191–95, 201, X:14, 33
    ~ and Saint Germain, I:192, XII:78
    ~ and Sanat Kumara, X:34
    ~ and Wesak, V:95, VI:151, XII:78

mahakalpa, VI:73, 77

Mahamuni Babaji. *See* Babaji, the Yogi Christ

Maharshi, Ramana, I:150, V:57, 59–61, VIII:166
    ~ ashram of, V:64
    ~ and the Eternal "I," V:58–61
    ~ teachings of, V:58–59, 61, VIII:76

Maharshi's Gospel, V:57–59

mahasamadhi (conscious death), I:34, III:106, IV:198, V:65, 83. *See
  also* bardo experience; death, physical

Mahasaya, Lahiri, I:159–62, V:40–45, XIII:132

Mahatma (Avatar of Synthesis), I:36, 38–39, 127, 141–42, 206,
  211–13, 215–17, 274, 280, 282, 284, III:48, 62–63, 91, 139, 146,
  170, 232, **III:238,** III:240, 250, 256, 260, V:133, **VI:3,** VI:6, 115,
  207, VII:82, 144, VIII:49, 62, 127, 176, 178, IX:9, 133, 200, 220,
  235, 237, 279–81, X:92, 145–49, 151, 159–61, 179, 214, 217,

238, XI:27, 32–33, 195, 241–42, 249–50, 255, XII:104, 134, XIII:66, 68, 102. *See also* Mahatma energy
  ~ ascension seat of, XI:199
  ~ ashram of, IX:200
  ~ and building the light quotient, III:27–28, 34, VIII:176
  ~ and building the love quotient, VIII:177
  ~ crystals of, XI:257
  ~ divine mission of, X:145
  ~ first contact with the Earth, I:214
  ~ and the four-body system, X:155–56
  ~ and the group body, IX:221
  ~ and healing, VIII:182
  ~ light information packets from, III:61, XI:27
  ~ message from, VI:250–53
  ~ and the Order of Melchizedek, XI:3
  ~ and the rays, X:92
  ~ seed packets of, VIII:180, XI:257
  ~ and Wesak, IX:200, X:152

The Mahatma Book, VIII:166. *See also* Grattan, Brian

Mahatma consciousness, VII:140–41

Mahatma energy, I:212–17, 247, 274, 287–89, III:194, VIII:62–63, 176, X:145–49, 151–52, 154–59, 161, 211, 230, 236, XI:3–4. *See also* Mahatma (Avatar of Synthesis)
  ~ anchoring of, I:213–17, 247, IX:133, X:147, XI:32, XIII:102
  ~ as an intermediary between the personality and the Godhead, VI:9, X:146
  ~ and cosmic ascension, X:148
  ~ and the evolution of Earth, X:146
  ~ and healing, III:107

Mahatma I & II, I:176, 211, 213, 276, III:7, V:133. *See also* Grattan, Brian

The Mahatma Letters, V:207, 214

Mahavira, V:15–17, VIII:166

Maimonides, Moses, IV:285

Maitreya (Planetary Christ), I:33, 140, 143, 145, 159, 190, **I:199,** I:208, 226, III:2, 63, 77, 101–2, 193, **III:238,** III:242, 257, IV:224, 275, 283, **VI:3,** VI:35, 69, 94, **VI:112,** VI:114, 125, 131, 149, 161, 172, 194–95, 207, 218–19, 225, 230, 237, 243, VII:15, 19, 111, 147, VIII:35, 38, 46, 64, 68–69, 75, 107, 122–23, 126, 131, 178, xvii, xxiii, IX:2, 8–9, 84, 103, 112, 133, 194, 200, 205, 210, 235–37, 262, X:116–17, XI:10, 17, 30, 53, 71, 111, 210. *See also* Buddha Maitreya; Christ, the; Planetary Christ
  ~ ascension of, I:134
  ~ ashrams of, I:144, VI:27, 35, 171, **VI:204,** VI:224–25, VII:145, VIII:126–27, IX:17, 93, 200, 220, XI:71, 218
  ~ and the Avatar of Synthesis, I:141–42, 211, 216

~ coming of, I:137–39, 141–46, 190, 214, 226, 243–44, IV:10, 174, 223, 274, 281, V:95, 224, XIII:67
~ as the Cosmic Christ, I:146, III:169, 253
~ cosmic evolution of, III:169, 197, IV:223, V:176, X:32, XI:98, 101–2
~ current life of, I:140–44, 240, III:51, 194, 243, IV:223, V:100, VI:150, 208, 216, VIII:xviii, IX:114–16, X:30–32, XI:169, 225
~ divine mission of, X:31–32
~ and the Festival of Humanity, VI:155
~ and the Festival of the Christ, VI:150, XII:85, 87
~ and the Great Invocation, I:140, 260, XII:3
~ as head of the Spiritual Hierarchy, I:137, 139, 146–47, 170, 186, 236, III:2, 132, 176, IV:223, VI:9, 114, 150, VIII:xvii
~ and healing, III:49, VII:82, X:141
~ and initiation, I:22–23, VI:144, 163, 214
~ initiations of, I:138, 176, 278, III:10, IV:224
~ and Jesus, I:25, 138–43, 170, 175, 195, 236, 278, III:10, 177, IV:31, 223–24, 272, 274, 287–88, V:99, 174–75, 227, **VII:19,** X:30, 41, 120
~ and Krishnamurti, I:139–40, V:227, 229–37, IX:6, X:31
~ light quotient of, III:31, 241, VI:5, 27, XI:187
~ and love, I:143, XI:242, XIII:109
~ other lives of, I:138, 176, III:130, IV:218, 223, VI:148, 154, VII:19, XI:225, XII:80, XIII:101
~ quotations from, X:32, XIII:89
~ and the rays, I:120, 124, 190, 193, 201, VI:180–81, 184, 190, X:23, 30, 33, 40, 140, XI:218
~ and the Spirit of Peace and Equilibrium, I:141–42
~ and the Synthesis Ashram, VII:144–45
~ and the Theosophical movement, IV:197
~ and Wesak, III:29, VI:125, 151–54, VIII:138, IX:200, X:152–53, XI:174–75, 226, XII:78–81, 84
~ as the World Teacher, I:140–41, X:41
Majestic Twelve (MJ12), IV:5–6, 10. *See also* secret government
mala beads, I:252
Malachi (prophet), IV:288
malathion, IV:12
Malaya, V:64
Maldek, IV:57
manas (mind), IV:300, XIII:69
mana (vital force), IV:160–64, VIII:68
mandalas, IV:247, V:98, 109
Mangalore, India, V:85
manifestation, I:274, III:61, IV:145, V:125, VI:180, VII:3, 10, 57, 59,

104, VIII:7, 68–90, 175, IX:22, X:23, 34, 73, 185, 231–32, XI:98, 163, XII:102

~ and Atlantis, X:216
~ attitudes for, VIII:82–85
~ and devas, IV:143–44
~ five levels of, VIII:81
~ and gratitude, VIII:85–86
~ group, IX:217
~ and the Kabbalistic tree of life, IV:299–300
~ and mantras, I:253
~ placing limitations on, VIII:71
~ prayer to manifest money, III:165–66
~ principles and laws of, VIII:78–82
~ of romantic relationships, III:151, VIII:138, XIII:1–4, 141–42, 177
~ and self-love and forgiveness, VIII:83
~ and service work, VIII:16, 18
~ and spiritual leadership, IX:16
~ stories of, VIII:87–89
~ tools for, VIII:73–75

manifestation and transmutation grid, VIII:74

Manjushri (deity of wisdom), V:113

Man's Eternal Quest, I:162, V:39, XII:110. *See also* Yogananda, Paramahansa

mantras, I:49, 53, 99, 249–58, IV:244–45, 249, 262, V:29–32, 48, 56, 85, 89–90, 98, 168–71, VI:216, VII:105, 107–8, VIII:96, XII:19–23, 99. *See also* chanting; sound; words of power; yoga: Mantra yoga

~ Adonai, I:49, 254, XII:19
~ Adonai H'artez, I:255, XII:20
~ Aham Brahmasmi, I:257, XII:22
~ Ain Sof Ur, I:255, XII:20
~ Alayi (senses), **IV:195**
~ Allahu Akbar, I:257, XII:22
~ Aluk, **IV:196**
~ Amen, IV:196
~ and angels, IX:260
~ Areeeooommm, I:257, XII:22
~ Aum (mind), I:49, 163, 250, 255, 257, **IV:195,** IV:196–97, 234, 244, 254, 257, V:97, VII:105, VIII:95, XII:20–21
~ Au-U Ur-Se-Ur Au-U, I:257, XII:22
~ Ave Maria, I:258, XII:23
~ Baju (intuition), **IV:195**
~ Baruch Ha Shem, I:254, XII:19
~ Barukh Ata Adonai, I:254, XII:19
~ Be Still and Know I Am God, I:257, XII:22

mantras, (cont.)
~ Bismillah Al-Rahman, Al-Rahim, I:257, XII:22
~ Brahma, I:255
~ Brahma, Vishnu, Shiva, XII:20
~ and breath, V:87
~ Buddha, I:258, XII:23
~ Buddhist, I:258, XII:23
~ of the chakras, I:256–58, XII:21, 23
~ Christian, I:258, XII:22–23
~ and death, I:82
~ and dimensions, IV:249
~ Eck Ong Kar Sat Nam Siri Wha Guru, I:257, XII:22
~ Egyptian, I:257, XII:22
~ Eh Hay Eh, I:254, XII:19
~ Ehyeh Asher Ehyeh, I:254, XII:19
~ Ehyeh Metatron, I:255, XII:20
~ El Eliyon, I:254, XII:19
~ Eli Eli, I:254, XII:19
~ elohim, I:49, 251, 254, III:200, IV:120, VI:112, VII:106–7, XI:54, XII:19
~ El Shaddai, I:49, 254, XII:19
~ Erta-Na-Hekau-Apen-Ast, I:257, XII:22
~ galactic-monad, VI:201
~ the Gayatri Mantra, I:255–56, IV:244, XII:20–21
~ God, Christ, Holy Spirit, I:258, XII:22
~ Hail Mary, I:258, XII:23
~ Ham, I:256, XII:21
~ Ham Sa, I:256
~ Hare Krishna, I:256, XII:21
~ Hari Om, I:256, XII:21
~ Hari Om Tat Sat, I:256, XII:21
~ Ha Shem, I:254, XII:19
~ He, XII:23
~ and healing, VII:105
~ Heaven on Earth, III:105–6
~ Heru-Udjat, I:257, XII:22
~ Hindu, I:255–57, XII:20–22
~ Hong Sau, I:163, 220, 256, IV:197, XII:21
~ Hram Hrim, IV:244
~ Hu, **IV:196,** IX:121, XII:23
~ Huk, **IV:196**
~ Hum, **IV:196**
~ Hyos Ha Koidesh, I:255, XII:20
~ I, XII:23
~ I Am, I:257, XII:22
~ I Am God, I:49, 257, XII:22
~ I Am that I Am, I:49, 257, VII:107, XII:22

M

mantras, (cont.)
  ~ I Love, I:49, 257, XII:22
  ~ Isis, I:257, XII:22
  ~ Islamic, I:257, XII:22
  ~ I Will, I:257, XII:22
  ~ Jehovah, I:254, XII:19
  ~ Jesus Christ, I:258, XII:22
  ~ Jewish, I:254–55, XII:19–20, 22
  ~ Kadoish, Kadoish, Kadoish, Adonai 'Tzebayoth, XII:19
  ~ Kala (emotion), **IV:195**
  ~ Krishna, I:256, XII:21
  ~ Lam, I:256, XII:21
  ~ Layoo-esh Shekinah, I:255, XII:20
  ~ the Lord's Prayer, I:258, XII:23
  ~ Mana (memory), **IV:195**
  ~ and Mantra yoga, IV:244–45
  ~ monadic, I:49–52, 54–55, 258–59, III:54–55, VI:199–201,
     XII:2–3, 11
  ~ Moshe, Yeshua, Eliahu, I:255, XII:20
  ~ multiuniversal-monad, VI:201
  ~ Nefer-Neter-Wed-Neh, I:257, XII:22
  ~ Nuk-Pu-Nuk, I:257, XII:22
  ~ O, XII:23
  ~ Om, I:156, 255, 257, 270–71, III:68, IV:196, 227, 237, 254,
     257, VII:105, XII:5, 12, 20–21
  ~ Om Ah Hum, I:258, XII:23
  ~ Om Mani Padme Hum, I:49, 258, V:97, 100, 109, XII:23
  ~ Om Namah Shivaya, I:256, IV:244, V:86, XII:21
  ~ Om Ram Ramaya Namaha, I:257, XII:22
  ~ Om Shanti, I:256, XII:21
  ~ Om Sri Dattatreya Namaha, I:256, XII:21
  ~ Om Sri Rama Jaya Rama Jaya Jaya Rama, I:256, XII:21
  ~ Om Sri Sai Ram, I:256, XII:21
  ~ Om Tat Sat, I:256, XII:21
  ~ Ong, IV:196
  ~ Osiris, I:257, XII:22
  ~ Padme Siddhi Hum, I:258, XII:23
  ~ power of, I:250
  ~ Qadosh, Qadosh, Qadosh, Adonai Tzeba'oth, I:254
  ~ Quan Yin, Avalokitesvara, Chenrazee, I:258, XII:23
  ~ Ra, I:257, XII:22
  ~ Ram, I:49, 256, XII:21
  ~ Rama, I:256, XII:21
  ~ Ra-Neter-Atef-Nefer, I:257, XII:22
  ~ Ribono Shel Olam, I:254, XII:19
  ~ Ruach Elohim, I:254, XII:19
  ~ and Sabda yoga, IV:249

mantras, (cont.)
   ~ Sai Baba, I:256, VII:107, XII:21
   ~ Sai Ram, I:156, 256, VII:107, XII:21
   ~ Sat Nam, I:257, IV:197, XII:21
   ~ Shaddai El Chai, I:255, XII:20
   ~ Shalom, I:255, XII:20
   ~ Shanti, **IV:196**
   ~ Shekinah, I:254, XII:19
   ~ Shekinah Ruach Ha Quodesh, I:255, XII:19
   ~ Shiva, I:255
   ~ Sh'Mah Yisrael Adonai Elohainu Adonai Chad, I:254, XII:19
   ~ Shu, XII:23
   ~ Sikh, XII:21
   ~ Sivo Ham, I:257, XII:22
   ~ six-monad, VI:200
   ~ So Ham, I:49, 156, 163, 220, 255–56, 271, IV:197, 244,
     V:86–87, VIII:101, XII:20
   ~ So Hum, I:220
   ~ solar-monad, VI:200–201
   ~ soul, I:49–52, 54–55, 258–59, VI:199–201, VIII:95, X:72,
     XII:2–3, 11
   ~ and soul travel, IV:199–200
   ~ Sugmad, **IV:196**
   ~ for summoning the devas, X:44
   ~ Tat Twam Asi, I:256, XII:21
   ~ Tibetan Buddhist, V:97
   ~ from the Tibetan Foundation, I:258
   ~ ultimate cosmic monad, VI:201
   ~ of unification, I:55
   ~ universal-monad, VI:201
   ~ Vam, I:256, XII:21
   ~ Vishnu, I:255
   ~ Wa, XII:23
   ~ Western, I:257, XII:22
   ~ word mantras, I:258, XII:23
   ~ Ya, XII:23
   ~ Ya-Fattah, I:257, XII:22
   ~ Ya-Ghaffar, I:257, XII:22
   ~ Ya-Hafiz, I:257, XII:22
   ~ Yahweh Elohim, I:255, XII:20
   ~ Yam, I:256, XII:21
   ~ Ya-Mutakabir, I:257, XII:22
   ~ Ya-Rahman, I:257, XII:22
   ~ Ya-Sabur, I:257, XII:22
   ~ Ya-Salaam, I:257, XII:22
   ~ Yeshua Michael, I:255, XII:20
   ~ Yesu Christu, I:256, XII:21

M

mantras, (cont.)
    ~ YHWH, I:49, 254, XII:19
    ~ Yod Hay Vod Hay (or Yod Hay Wah Hay), I:49, 254,
      VII:106–7, XII:19
    ~ your name as, IV:199, IX:179–80
Manu, the, I:190, 192, 194, **I:199,** I:200, VII:19, X:236. *See also* Allah Gobi (Manu)
    ~ ashram of, VIII:127
    ~ and the first ray, I:189, 200–201
    ~ and Wesak, V:95, XII:78
manvantara (world cycle), I:3–4
Mao Tse Tung, I:119, V:106–7
MAP (Medical Assistance Program), I:38, 274, 283, 289, III:38–39,
    49, 57, 80, 97–98, 100, 192, 202. *See also* Great White Brotherhood
    Medical Unit; healing; Lorphan (doctor)
Marcarelli, Charles, IX:12
Marciniak, Barbara, IV:35
marijuana. *See* drugs
Marko, I:194
Marlowe, Christopher, V:240
marriage, III:118, IV:328, V:154, VIII:137, IX:149, XII:132, XIII:42,
    91–93, 123–24, 126–27, 140, 151, 175. *See also* relationships, romantic
    ~ arranged, IV:221, V:28, 159
    ~ of ascended masters, XI:16
    ~ and celibacy, XIII:132–33
    ~ divine, I:39, III:224, VI:164, VII:46, 53, VIII:47, X:117,
      XI:221, XIII:102–3
    ~ ending of, XIII:94–96
    ~ and friendship, XIII:40
    ~ and group consciousness, IX:94
    ~ homosexual unions, XIII:91–92
    ~ interracial, VII:150–51, IX:127, XIII:19, 172
    ~ and mission mates, X:66–67
    ~ open, IX:126–27, XIII:124, 162
    ~ and the prenuptial agreement, XIII:127–28, 153
    ~ recommitment to, XIII:95–98, 176
    ~ sexual intimacy in, XIII:96–98, 140–41, 167–68, 171–72,
      180–81
    ~ and walk-ins, IV:30, 32
Mars, IV:46–49
    ~ and Aries, **XI:176**
    ~ ascension seat of, VI:36
    ~ bases on, IV:17–18, 47, 53
    ~ colonization of, IV:7–8, 17–18

~ and color healing, **IV:212**
~ energy qualities of, I:94–96
~ face on, IV:8
~ and the Kabbalistic tree of life, **IV:302**
~ pyramids on, IV:8
~ and the rays, **I:131, 133, VI:83, XI:176**

martial arts, IX:101

Martians, IV:47–49. *See also* extraterrestrials

Martina, Roy, III:111, VIII:149–50

Mary Magdalene, I:176, V:45

masculine principle, III:199, 255, VI:56, 184, 197, VIII:15, 99, 112, 178, X:215, XI:40, XIII:2, 17–18, 55, 57, 100, 128, 177–78

Maslow, Abraham, I:106, XI:209

The Masters and the Path, V:224, 242. *See also* Leadbeater, C.W.

Master Universe, IV:113–14

masturbation, XIII:39–42

Mataji (Babaji's God-realized sister), I:161–62

materialism, I:8, 60, 76, III:2, 25, IV:3, V:180, **VI:63**, VI:140, 190, VIII:11, IX:110, 122, 135, 138, 141, 243, X:18, 48, 215–16, XI:29
~ and the church, IV:271, 274
~ in the media, IX:73, 75
~ in the police department, IX:70–71

materialization, I:277, III:255, VI:70, 123, IX:128, XI:57. *See also* ascended masters: advanced abilities of

material plane. *See* physical plane

material universe. *See* physical universe

mathmatikoi. *See* Pythagorean Mystery School

Matrix I, IV:75, 78

Matrix II, IV:75, 78

Matrix III, IV:75, 78

matsarya (jealousy), V:8

matter, I:2, 213, 266, IV:259, V:126, VI:181, 186, X:34, 145, 215, 217–19, 222
~ and the rays, I:115, VI:189–90
~ the spell of, I:222
~ as a vehicle for the soul, I:105

Matto Grosso Plains, IV:26

maya, I:57, 65, 271–72, III:71, 89, 230, IV:180, 189, 193, 220, 261–62, 273, V:11–12, 20–21, VI:59, 138, 212, 216, 245, VIII:6, 22, 92, IX:99, 132, X:8, 17, XII:96–97. *See also* glamour; illusion
~ dispelling of, I:66–67
~ and the etheric body, I:65
~ and the fourth ray, VI:190

~ and its remedy, inspiration, I:57, **I:58**–59, I:66

~ and the Lemurian root race, I:58, **I:59**

May 5, 2000 alignment, I:245

Mayan calendar, I:145, 220–21, 226, 240, IX:254–55

~ end of, I:35, VI:55, 222, IX:114, 133

Mayans, I:9, 231, IV:169

~ and extraterrestrials, VII:133

~ and the Ra, IV:93

~ and third-dimensional Sirians, IV:69

mayavarupa body, I:33, 35, 38, 140, III:28, VI:26, 53, 122, 193–94, 198, 208, 240, 243, VIII:183, XI:44, 55, 152, 154, XIII:68, 84. *See also* monadic blueprint body

~ anchoring of, III:142, VI:194, VIII:31, 60, XI:32, 50, 132, 182

McCarty, James Allen, IV:93

McClure, Janet, I:119, 178, 218, 242, 246, 275, III:14, 140, 144, 146, 151, 153, IV:16, 205–6, 309, 311, VI:7, 71, VII:148, VIII:164, 166, X:207, XI:19, 188

McMartin, Grace, VIII:xxv

Mead, G.R.S., V:175

Mecca, V:156, 158. *See also* Islam

media, I:225, VI:139, VII:28, 130, 134, IX:73–77, 160–61, X:33, XIII:6, 178. *See also* film industry

~ effects of, VII:97–98

~ and extraterrestrials, VII:130, 134

~ and the judicial system, IX:65–66, 148

~ and the negative ego, IX:73, 75–76, 148

~ and politics, IX:130, 147–48

~ and sex, IX:73–74, 138–39

Medical Assistance Program. *See* MAP (Medical Assistance Program)

medicine, bioenergetic, IX:86. *See also* healing

medicine, holistic, IX:57–58, 83. *See also* healing

medicine, New Age, IX:82, 84, 87. *See also* healing

medicine, oriental, VIII:89, 149, IX:58, 86. *See also* healing

medicine, Western, VIII:89, 143, 149, IX:55–58, 84, 86–90. *See also* health-care system

~ antibiotics, IX:56, 85

~ and chronic disease, VIII:33

~ and electroshock therapy, IX:147

~ and the fifth ray, VI:189, IX:62

~ and flu vaccinations, IX:58–60

~ and patient self-leadership, IX:61

~ plastic surgery, IX:107–8

~ prior to physical death, I:82–83

~ surgery, IX:57, 87, X:243

~ tools for handling for the lightworker, IX:34–36

~ *vs. preventive medicine, IX:56–57*

meditation, I:63, 92, 100, 164, 249, 264, 270, 282, III:16, 58, 190, IV:194, 227, 259, 262, 265, V:22, 25, 31–32, 42, 61, 85, 87, 90, 111, 114, 170, VI:4, 28, 33, 58, 158–60, 162–63, 168, 203, 220, 232, 244, VII:35–36, 54, VIII:38, 48, 69, 97–99, 110–11, 120, 136, 143, 170, IX:118, 261, X:7–9, 19–20, 49, 73, 232–33, XI:66–67, 149, 254, XII:103, XIII:31, 104–5, 162. *See also* ascension-activation meditations; ascension meditation treatment; Festival of the Christ; Wesak

~ ancestral mass karma clearing, III:100

~ for the animal kingdom, XII:68–69

~ and the antakarana, I:43, 49–50

~ and ascension, I:39, III:204–5, 211–15, VII:23–24, XI:25–34

~ and breath, I:255, XII:20

~ and building the light quotient, I:33, III:24, 32–33

~ and the chakras, III:19, 202, 211–15

~ and channeled dancing, III:192

~ for the core fear matrix removal program, III:201–2

~ corkscrew meditation, I:54–56

~ Cosmic-Cleansing Triangulation, VI:198–99

~ Cosmic Journey, III:207–11

~ Cosmic Meditation, XI:183–85

~ divine Mother and Father energies, III:247–49

~ elohim-scripture meditation, XI:114–15

~ for the environment, XII:67–69

~ of the Essenes, IV:293–94

~ and the evolution of Earth, VII:86

~ Festival of the Christ meditation, XII:86–87

~ fifty-point cosmic-cleansing meditation, XI:286–89

~ God Ascension-Seat Meditation, XI:276–79

~ Great Pyramid, III:250–53

~ and healing, IV:172, IX:61, 83

~ for healing faulty thinking, VII:45–46

~ Hong Sau, I:163, 165, VIII:101, XII:110

~ for imprinting humanity, III:129

~ and initiation, IV:180, 192, XI:25–34

~ and Jainism, V:16

~ Kabbalistic Tree of Life, III:187–89

~ with the keys of Enoch, IV:315

~ and the MAP, I:38

~ from Metatron, VI:258–59

~ the 1997 Wesak Ceremony, XI:279–81

~ and the ninth dimension, III:147

~ Om meditation, VII:105–6

~ of the rapture, I:38

~ and the rays, I:122, 124

meditation, (cont.)
- ~ for reprogramming the subconscious, VII:51–53
- ~ The Seamless Body of Golden Light, VI:210–12
- ~ and the second initiation, VII:25–26
- ~ self-love meditation, VII:41–42
- ~ the seven levels of initiation within the Great Pyramid meditation, XI:293–96
- ~ Seven-Terrace Meditation, VIII:100
- ~ So Ham meditation, I:163, 255, VIII:101, XII:20, 110 (*See also* breathing: So Ham; mantras: So Ham)
- ~ spiritual mudra exercise, VI:196–97
- ~ on spiritual occasions, I:283
- ~ spiritual whirlwind meditation, I:53–54
- ~ and the Synthesis Ashram, VII:144
- ~ as taught by Sai Baba, I:156
- ~ techniques of Kriya Yoga, I:163
- ~ the Three Seals of Creation, III:225
- ~ in Tibetan Buddhism, V:113–14
- ~ total-body alignment and integration, VII:163–64
- ~ triangulation meditation, I:52–53
- ~ Twelve Rays, III:203–4
- ~ Ultimate Cosmic-Ray Meditation, XI:263, 273–76
- ~ Ultimate Huna Prayer and Meditation, XI:121–26
- ~ Ultimate Kabbalistic Huna Prayer and Meditation, III:232–36
- ~ and union with God, XIII:103–5
- ~ Wesak Meditation, XI:284–86, 299–302, XII:81–83
- ~ working with pseudo-crystals, IV:60
- ~ and yoga, IV:244, 247

Medjugorje, Yugoslavia, V:183, 185–86

Meier, Billy, IV:35, 37–38, 91

Meishu-Sama, V:99–100

Melchior (Galactic Logos), **I:199,** I:202, 206, 234, 282, III:61, 132, 150, 174, **III:238,** III:246, 255–56, 258, VI:32, 43, 53, 77, 80, **VI:112,** VI:115, **VI:116,** VI:117, 230, IX:9, 179, XI:148, 192. *See also* Galactic Logos
- ~ ashram of, I:279, VI:225, VIII:127, IX:200
- ~ Chamber of, III:44, 187
- ~ crystals of, XI:257
- ~ and the galactic body, III:254
- ~ light rods of, XI:259
- ~ and the Mahatma, I:212
- ~ seed packets of, VIII:180, XI:257
- ~ silver-gold ray of, **VI:41**

Melchizedek, Age of, XI:5–6

Melchizedek Brotherhood, I:227–28, IV:26, 314. *See also* Order of Melchizedek

Melchizedek Church, I:229

Melchizedek energy, XI:4

Melchizedek (Eternal Lord of Light), I:227, 230, 234, **VI:111**

Melchizedek (galactic master), I:175, 207–8, 234, XI:1

Melchizedek Magnetizer, XI:102

Melchizedek (of Salem), I:207, 227, 229–30, 235–36, IV:280, 287–88, V:133–34
  ~ as an incarnation of Jesus, I:169, 171, IV:277, 287–88, V:174, VI:147, XI:1, 5

Melchizedek priesthood. *See* Melchizedek Brotherhood; Order of Melchizedek

Melchizedek, school of, VI:69, 71

Melchizedek (Source), III:144

Melchizedek Synthesis Light Academy, XI:250–51

Melchizedek Synthesis Light Ashram, XI:250–51

Melchizedek (Universal Logos), I:206–7, 232, 234, 274, 280–82, 285, III:46, 48, 64, 91, 102, 116–17, 122–23, 132, 148, 174, 194, 219, 222–24, 226–32, **III:238,** III:241, 246, 253, 255–58, VI:2, **VI:3,** VI:6, 9, 69, 75–78, 94, **VI:111,** VI:115, **VI:116,** VI:117, 125, 127, 130, 135, 163, 193–95, 202, 214–15, 219–20, 225, 230, 237, 239–43, VII:82, VIII:35, 42–43, 45–47, 49, 54–58, 60–64, 66, 68–69, 75, 86, 122, 128, 131, 135, 176–78, xxiii, IX:9–10, 133, 179, 200, 205, 235, 237, X:30, 91, 159–61, 214, 226, 238, XI:1, 3, 5–6, 27, 60, 74–75, 104, 130–31, 147–48, 151, 191, 241, 255, 257. *See also* Universal Logos
  ~ and the ascension ceremony, XI:86–87
  ~ ascension seat of in the center of the Earth, III:44
  ~ ashrams of, VI:224–25, VII:145, VIII:54, 99, 127, IX:17, 93, 200, 220
  ~ and building the light quotient, III:27, 34
  ~ cosmic ascension of, VI:9
  ~ cosmic computer of, III:205–6, VIII:56
  ~ crystal technology of, VI:231, VIII:56, XI:257
  ~ and the Godhead ascension seat, VI:31
  ~ Golden Book of, VIII:54–55
  ~ Golden Chamber of, I:279, 281, III:32, 44–46, 62–63, 85–86, 91, 128–29, 135, 148, 187, 198–99, 201, 255, 258–59, VI:31, 34, **VI:41,** VI:43, 54, 115, 124, 193, 195, 204, 235, VIII:41, 99, 102, 183, XI:74, 131, 199, XII:11 (*See also* ascension seats)
  ~ Golden Rod of, III:130
  ~ and the gong of time, XI:94
  ~ and healing, III:107, VIII:182
  ~ information disk of, III:128–29, XI:97
  ~ and the Kabbalah, III:217

~ light packets of information from, VIII:54–55
~ light rods of, XI:259
~ message from, XI:271–72
~ and the New Jerusalem energies, III:131
~ and Nikola Tesla, IV:10–11
~ and the Order of Melchizedek, XI:1–2
~ platinum ray of, **VI:41,** VI:42, VIII:50
~ and the rays, I:117, **VI:179**
~ sayings of, III:13, 21, 37, 237, VIII:126
~ scriptures of, VI:115
~ seed packets of, VIII:180, XI:257
~ silver-gold ray of, VIII:50
~ and Sirius, III:178
~ Star Codes of, III:226
~ and the Synthesis Ashram, VII:144–45
~ transmitting station of, III:128, XI:97–98
~ and the triple overlighting dispensation, III:101
~ and the universal body, III:254
~ and Wesak, III:266, VI:151, VIII:138, IX:93, 200, XI:174, 226, XII:78

Memphis, IV:175

Mencius, V:121. *See also* Confucius

Menendez brothers, IX:63, 130, 160

Men in Black, IV:48. *See also* extraterrestrials; UFOs

mental body, I:18, 45, 53, 59, 63, 109, 117, 213, III:21, **III:238,** III:239, 253, IV:206, 241, 258, V:129, 223, **VI:3,** VI:18, 61, 69, 72, 100, 194, 203, **VI:205,** VII:1, 3, 22–23, 138, 141, VIII:49, 59, IX:71, 79, 129, 140, X:4, 86, 88, 108, 120, 201, 220, 227, XI:150, XII:95, XIII:4, 62, 84, 103, 107. *See also* four-body system
~ and adultery, XIII:119–21
~ appearance of, VIII:4, XIII:7–8
~ and the Aryan root race, **VI:78**
~ clearing of, III:201, 228, IV:105, VI:45, 62, 240, VII:29, VIII:31, 46
~ death of, I:75, 97, 180
~ during dream time, IV:193
~ and the fifth dimension, III:142, 150
~ and the fourth dimension, **VI:205**
~ healing of, VIII:32, X:56
~ and integrating soul extensions, VI:93–94
~ integration of, VII:162, XI:17
~ and joy, X:86
~ light quotient of, VI:4
~ mastery of, I:23, 64, 66, 163, 197, 200, 265, III:2, 196, IV:183, 198, 253, 259, 270, VI:4, 60, 100, 193–94, 249, VII:27–30, VIII:24, 99, X:107, XI:154

~ and physical death, I:75, 81, 84–85

~ and the rays, I:122–23, VI:188–89, 191, X:39

~ and the repetition of the name of God, I:249, 251

~ and sex, XIII:39, 41–44, 47, 170

~ and the sleep state, VI:71

~ and the soul, I:106–8, 112

~ and the third initiation, I:23, 64, 66, III:2, IV:270, **VI:17,**
   VII:27–30

~ and the yoga sutras of Patanjali, IV:258

mental body, cosmic, **III:238,** III:259, **VI:3, 24, 205,** VI:206,
   XI:155

mental plane, I:16, 63, **I:184, 197,** I:215, III:139, **IV:195,**
   IV:196–97, **IV:267,** IV:269, V:126, **VI:8,** VI:56, 59–60, 167,
   207, VII:4, 10–12, 16, 104, IX:114, X:149, 167, 210, 232, XII:97,
   XIII:62–63

~ and illlusion, I:57, **I:58,** I:63

~ and the Kabbalistic tree of life, **IV:303, 307**

~ between lives, I:87–90, 92, 97, 99–101

~ lower, I:87, VI:18

~ mastery of, I:197, **III:139**

~ and physical death, I:75, 84

~ and the rays, **I:132,** VI:187

~ sexual expression on, XIII:62–63

~ and the third initiation, **III:4, 139, VI:17, XI:127**

~ upper, I:88, VI:18

mental plane, cosmic, I:17, **I:184,** I:198, **I:199,** III:167, 169–71,
   173, 181, **III:238,** III:240, **VI:3, 8, 24,** VI:206

mental ray, VI:186–87, X:11–13, 128. *See also* mind ray; rays, seven:
   configuration of

Merak, IV:314

Mercury (planet)

~ ascension seat of, VI:36

~ and color healing, **IV:212**

~ energy qualities of, I:95–96

~ and Gemini, **XI:177**

~ and the Kabbalistic tree of life, **IV:302**

~ and the rays, **I:131**–32, **VI:82, XI:177**

Mercury (Roman messenger god), V:124. *See also* Hermes-Thoth

merging, I:38, 213, XIII:57. *See also* attunement; soul merge

~ with angels, X:117

~ of the antakarana and the ascension column, III:92–93

~ with the ascended masters, III:257–58, VII:24, VIII:122,
   X:117, XIII:66–68, 101–3

~ of ascension seats, III:135, 192

~ with the clear light of God, III:8

~ of the conscious and superconscious minds, VI:58

~ of the Creator and cocreator levels, I:213

~ with the Eternal Self, IV:260, 263, 265, V:24

~ with the Father, X:116

~ of the feminine and masculine, VI:56, 197

~ with the fifth dimension, III:142

~ with the Galactic Core, III:61

~ with God, IV:269, VI:69, VIII:62–64, X:140, 236

~ with the Godhead, III:241

~ and group consciousness, IX:188

~ of the higher and lower minds, VI:58

~ with the higher self, I:23, 25, III:2, VI:19, VII:27

~ of the higher self and lower self, X:86–87

~ with light, I:31, 79–83, 267, III:8, 228, IV:180, 191, 259–60, V:87, 108, 114

~ with the logoic plane, I:200, 277

~ monadic, I:24, 27, 44–45, 64, 74, 110, 200, 212, 215, 277, III:2–4, 8–10, 52–53, 140, 146, **III:238,** III:242, IV:263, 269, V:128, **VI:3,** VI:7–8, 19, 56, 59, 62, 100, 222, VII:31–32, IX:70, 120, X:116–17, XIII:56, 64–65

~ with the Mother, X:116

~ with the nine dimensions, III:48

~ with the overself, III:259

~ with the oversoul, X:116–17

~ of the personality, soul and monad, I:36, 39, 45, 110, 200, 283, III:3, 52, 91, 242, VI:7–8, 58–59, VII:31, VIII:47

~ with the Planetary Logos, I:197, 200

~ with positive extraterrestrials, X:117

~ with Sanat Kumara and Shamballa, III:8, 177

~ and sex, XIII:64

~ with the sixth dimension of reality, III:10

~ with Source, VI:69, X:236

~ with the Spiritual Hierarchy, VIII:122

~ of the three energy cords, I:44–45

merkabah, I:37–38, 284, 290, III:28, 45, 61, 124, 137, VIII:60, XI:29, 57, 131, 149

~ group, XII:11

~ and soul travel, IV:201

~ and teleportation, III:43, 63

Merlin, VII:121

~ as an incarnation of Saint Germain, V:239, VI:148, X:240

mermaids, **IV:135,** IV:136. *See also* devas; elementals: undines (nature spirits of water); nature spirits

Mesmer, Anton, V:243

mesmerism, V:213, 243

Mesopotamia, I:230

Messiah (oratorio), IV:213, VII:97

Messiah, the, I:171–72, IV:280–81, 288–89, V:174, 237. *See also* Buddha Maitreya; Christ, the; Imam Mahdi; Maitreya (Planetary Christi)
~ Jewish, I:137, 141, 144, 243, IV:283
~ second coming of, I:137, IV:280–81, V:199

Metastronane, III:222

Metatron (archangel), I:36, 39, **I:199,** I:203, 227, 281–82, III:49, 62–63, 85–86, 122–23, 199–200, 217–32, **III:238,** III:243, 246, 250, 257, IV:197, 314–15, **VI:3,** VI:71, **VI:111,** VI:113, 115, 124–25, 127, 130, 230, 235, 239, 241–43, VII:82, VIII:35, 42, 45–47, 49, 54–61, 63–65, 86, 122, 135, 176, 178, IX:179, 262, X:159–61, 214, 232, 238, XI:27, 130–31, 151, 241–43, 250, 255
~ anchoring the lightbody of, VI:115
~ ascension seat of, VI:115
~ ashram of, VIII:54
~ and building the light quotient, III:25, 27–28, 30–31, 34, 108, 124, 132, 257, XI:26, 241
~ and the Great Pyramid, I:203, IV:174
~ and healing, III:38, 107, VIII:182
~ and the Kabbalistic tree of life, I:203, **IV:303,** X:159, 161, 232, XI:241–43
~ mantras of, I:255, XII:20
~ meditation from, VI:258–59
~ message from, VI:257–59
~ and the Microtron, I:280, III:28, 53, VI:115, VIII:58–59, XI:241
~ names of, III:225, 231, VIII:59
~ and the platinum ray, VI:42
~ platinum rod of, VIII:179
~ scriptures of, VI:115
~ shield of protection of, XI:131–33
~ super electrons of, III:221
~ and Wesak, XI:174

Mexico, VIII:148

Meyer, Ann, I:160

Miao Shan, **V:101**

Micah (prophet), IV:285, 288

Michael (archangel), **I:199,** I:227, III:49, 217, 220, 222–24, 226–30, 232, 246, V:189, **VI:111,** VI:115, 125, 127, 241–43, VII:18, 114, VIII:42, 46–47, 49, 56–58, 61, 64, 86, 122, IX:179, X:71, XI:32, XIII:11
~ ascension seat of, VI:115
~ and Commander Ashtar, IV:56
~ and the cords of negativity, III:50, 57, VIII:97
~ and the elohim computers, III:105, XI:51
~ and the first ray, **I:204, IV:121, 123, VII:115,** X:19, 29, 94

~ and the Kabbalistic tree of life, **IV:303,** VIII:55
~ message from, VI:254–56
~ protection by, I:284, III:98, 121, 132, 190, 198, 246,
   VII:111, 114, 118, VIII:97, IX:103, 262, XI:227, 241, XII:3,
   XIII:76, 109
~ Sword of Clarity and Vision of, VI:212
Michelangelo, VII:97, IX:52, X:24, 36
Microtron, I:280, III:53, VI:115, VIII:58–59, XI:31, 55, 241
microwave ovens, VIII:145
Middle East, I:173, 241, V:156, IX:3, 100, XII:57. *See also* Israel;
   Jerusalem; war
      ~ art of, X:93
      ~ predictions about, I:241
      ~ war in, V:156
middle self, IV:158–65. *See also* conscious mind
      ~ shadow body of, IV:159–60
Milanovich, Norma, III:78, IV:63, 68, VI:80
military, IX:100
      ~ and homosexuality, IX:147
military-industrial complex, IV:10–11. *See also* secret government
militia groups, IX:131
Milky Way galaxy, I:202, 205, IV:33, 66, 115, VI:80, 84
millennium, I:220, 222, 224, VII:110. *See also* 2000 (year)
mind control, IV:77
      ~ and Kriya yoga, I:163
mind-force-matter, IV:159
mind ray, I:116. *See also* mental ray; rays, seven: configuration of
      ~ of humanity, **VI:184**
mineral kingdom, **I:199,** I:270, **III:238,** IV:119, 122, **IV:130,**
   IV:140, 151–52, 154–56, 206, **VI:3,** VI:186, X:97, 235, 239. *See*
   also gemstones
      ~ and devas, IV:131, 139, X:96
      ~ evolution of, I:186, IV:153
      ~ and gnomes, IV:136, 153–54
      ~ hierarchy of, IV:153–54
      ~ and nature spirits, IV:131, 154
mini tornadoes, I:284, III:50–51, 206, VIII:66, 182–83, XI:131
Mintaka, IV:314
miscarriage, XIII:78, 83. *See also* abortion; death, physical
Mithra (Persian god of light), V:152
MJ12. *See* Majestic Twelve (MJ12)
Mnesarchus (son of Pythagoras), V:145
moha (attachment), V:8, 12

Mohammed, IV:278–79, 323, V:25, 155–61, VI:229, 248, VIII:xvii.
See also Islam; Moslems
~ and Archangel Gabriel, I:175, 236–37, IV:122, V:156–57,
159
~ initiations of, I:175
~ and Jesus, I:155, 236
~ other lives of, I:175, VI:148
~ prophecies of, I:153
~ and soul travel, IV:198
Mohammed, Mirza Ali, IV:327
Mojave Desert, IV:6
moksha (liberation), IV:219, V:12, 15, 21
monad, I:11, 13–15, 17, 37–38, 45, 50, 53, 109, 183, **I:184,** I:200,
211–13, 271, 274, 277, 285, III:2–3, 23, 28, 38, 44, 104, 126, 151,
219, **III:238,** III:243, 246, IV:61, 211, 270, 292, 319, V:8, 17,
127–28, VI:1, 8–9, 18, 25, 63–65, 73, 77, 85–88, **VI:89,**
VI:90–93, 95–97, 103–4, 123, 136, 170, 175, 198–200, 220, 222,
235, 238, 243–44, VII:4–6, 9, 13, 16, 22, 24, 27, 30–32, 39,
42–43, 77, 82, 120, 157, 161, VIII:39, 44, 47–49, 93, 133, 181,
IX:21, 55, 61, 78, 89, 91, 97, 100, 136, 143, 178, 221–22, 264,
X:1–2, 4, 7, 9, 16, 25, 48, 57, 70–71, 73, 75, 80, 85, 108–10, 114,
121, 127, 129, 134–36, 138, 146, 149, 154, 186, 188, 198–99,
201, 211, 232, 234, 244, XI:17, 29, 31, 51, 53, 157, 194, XIII:56,
59–60, 65, 80, 84, 92, 99, 165. *See also* I Am Presence; soul; spirit
~ anchoring of, I:16–17, 283, III:10, 53, 56, VII:32, VIII:47,
XI:32
~ and the antakarana, I:43–48, 51, 212, X:215
~ and the arts, IX:52
~ and ascension, I:28–30, VI:7, 216
~ aspects of, I:17, **I:106**
~ attunement to, I:56, VI:4, X:72, 133
~ and channeling, VI:228, VII:79
~ clearing of, VI:242, VIII:47
~ evolution of, I:15, 107, 109, VI:89
~ in the fifth initiation, I:25
~ in the fourth initiation, I:24–25, 200
~ as a guide/teacher for the soul, I:44, 105, 108–9, 200, III:2
~ and the Kabbalistic tree of life, IV:300–301
~ and relationships, XIII:4–5, 57–59
~ and self-actualization, I:18
~ and service work, XIII:59
~ in the sixth initiation, I:27, 78
~ and the soul, I:13–14, 105–6, 110
~ spiritual impressions from, I:113
monad, cosmic, I:183, **III:238,** III:242–43, 256, 259, **VI:3,** VI:8, 10,
42, 200–201, VIII:49, IX:222. *See also* I Am Presence, cosmic

monad, galactic-soul-extension, VI:96

monadic actualization, IX:121

"The Monadic Anchoring" (seminar), I:15–16

monadic blueprint body, I:35, III:55–57, VI:122, 194, 240, XI:44. *See also* mayavarupa body
   ~ anchoring of, I:283, III:56, 142, VI:194, VIII:31, XI:50, 132

monadic body, III:239, VI:203, **VI:205**, VII:4–5, 12, 64, XI:150, 159
   ~ anchoring of, VIII:59, XI:32, 154
   ~ and the fifth dimension, **VI:205**
   ~ and the sixth initiation, **VI:17**
   ~ and the sleep state, VI:71

monadic body, cosmic, **III:238**, III:259, **VI:3, 24, 205,** VI:206, XI:155

monadic braid, VI:136, VIII:48

monadic extensions, III:53, VI:87

monadic family, I:14, VI:64–65, 77, 85, 87–88, 90, 92, VIII:47–49

monadic group, VI:243, X:71–72

monadic plane, I:16–17, 127, **I:184, 197,** III:4, 8, 139, **VI:8,** VI:206, VII:4–5, 32–34, XIII:64–65
   ~ anchoring of, **III:139**
   ~ and the Kabbalistic tree of life, **IV:303, 307**
   ~ between lives, I:87–89, 92, 97
   ~ and the second ray, **I:132**
   ~ sexual expression on, XIII:64–65
   ~ and the sixth initiation (ascension), **III:4, 139, VI:17, XI:127**

monadic plane, cosmic, I:17, **I:184,** I:198, **I:199,** III:167, 181, **III:238,** III:240, 242, 256, **VI:3, 8, 24,** VI:206

monadic ray, I:116–17, VI:186–87, IX:200, X:11–14, 25, 127. *See also* rays, seven: configuration of

monadic realization, VI:99

monadic soul family, VI:64

monad, solar, VI:96

monad, ultimate cosmic, VI:202

monad, universal, VI:96

Mongolia, IV:171, 173, V:100, 107
   ~ legends of the inner Earth, IV:26

monotheism, V:133

Montaigne, V:240

Montana, Joe, IX:123

Montauk Army Base, IV:15

Monte, Woodrow, IV:14

Montgomery, Ruth, I:1, 95, 244, IV:31, 70, 81–82, 95, VIII:167

Moon, I:96, 134
  ~ ascension seat of, VI:36
  ~ bases on, IV:8, 53, 66, 74, XI:227
  ~ and Cancer, **XI:177**
  ~ colonization of, IV:7–8
  ~ and color healing, **IV:212**
  ~ and the Dark Brotherhood, XI:227
  ~ full moon celebrations, VI:149, 156, VIII:139, XI:174, 227–28, XII:91
  ~ and the Kabbalistic tree of life, **IV:302**
  ~ and the rays, **I:131**–32, **VI:83, XI:177**
Morgan, J.P., IV:11, IX:168
Mormon (prophet-historian), V:197
Mormon religion, V:197–99, XIII:128
Moroni (son of Mormon), V:197–99
Moses, I:172, 236, III:224, 226, IV:277–81, 283–86, 288, 327, VI:229, 248, VII:15–16, 147, XII:19
  ~ and the I Am Presence, IV:317, 319
  ~ and the Order of Melchizedek, I:228
  ~ as a walk-in, IV:31
Moses consciousness, IX:53
Moses of Granada, IV:286
Moslem calendar, V:156, 158
Moslem religion. *See* Islam
Moslems, IV:279, 281
Mother Earth, I:106, 266, 285, III:54, 200, **III:238,** III:249–50, IV:151–52, **VI:3,** VIII:40, 62, IX:110–11, 118, 121, 242. *See also* Earth
  ~ anchoring the lightbody of, I:126
  ~ and cremation, I:77
  ~ and Eco yoga, IV:250
  ~ and the New Age, I:224, 240–41
  ~ oneness with, VII:150
  ~ planetary kundalini of, VIII:43
  ~ removing fear from, III:202
Mother Mary. *See* Virgin Mary
Mother Teresa, V:72, 191–95, VIII:137, IX:39, X:119, XI:228
Mother, the, I:14, 159, 254, III:67–68, 246–49, IV:120, 218–19, 300–301, V:23–24, 28–29, 35, 40–41, 99, VI:2, VII:106, 148, VIII:178, xiv, IX:122, X:53, 76, 183, 197, 244, XI:242, XII:19, XIII:2, 16, 57, 65, 89, 101, 120
  ~ ascension seat of, VI:31, 35, VIII:179, XI:262
  ~ and Hinduism, IV:218–19
  ~ and the Kabbalistic tree of life, **IV:307**

~ merging with, X:116
~ rosary of, VIII:179

Mozart, Wolfgang Amadeus, I:121, III:148, VII:97, X:24, 36

Mu. *See* Lemuria (Mu)

mudras, IV:240. *See also* yoga
~ spiritual mudra exercise, VI:196–97
~ and yoga, I:163, IV:246

Mukherjee, Ramachandra, V:28

Muktananda, Baba, I:156, 163, V:85–91, VIII:136, X:74, XII:110
~ and divine sound, V:88
~ mantras of, I:219–20, 255–56, VIII:101, XII:20–21, 110
~ quotations from, V:89–91
~ teachings of, V:86–88

Multiplicity, IX:166

multiuniversal actualization, IX:121

multiuniversal body, VI:26, 205
~ and the dimensions, **VI:204**

Multiuniversal Council, VI:75

Multiuniversal Logos, III:256
~ crystals of, XI:257
~ seed packets of, XI:257

multiuniversal monadic group, **III:238**, III:256, **VI:3**

multiuniversal plane, VI:205

Munkar (angel), V:157, 160

murder, I:93, IX:64, 66–67, 72, 126, 128, 270
~ and abortion, XIII:77–78
~ and karma, I:93, V:142, VII:68–69
~ and the physical death process, I:85

Murphet, Howard, I:157, V:205–6, 208, 210, 214–16, 218–19, VII:55, VIII:xix, xxv

Murphy, Joseph, VIII:70

Muscida, IV:314

muses, X:24. *See also* arts, the

mushroom hat, VIII:58, XI:208–9, 228, 230

mushrooms. *See* drugs

music, IV:249, V:88, 140, VII:11, 79, 97, 133, VIII:96, 98, IX:51–52, X:37, XII:29. *See also* arts, the; devotional songs; sound
~ and the angelic kingdom, III:148, **IV:128**
~ and color, IV:205, 208, 213–15, X:36
~ diatonic musical scale, V:140
~ and dimensional shifting, III:148
~ and the fourth ray, I:193

~ and healing, IV:172, **IV:208,** IV:213–15, V:142, IX:83, X:36–37, 39
~ of mantras, I:252
~ and the negative ego, X:37
~ during physical death, I:82–83
~ and the Pleiadians, IV:39, VII:133
~ and Pythagoras, V:140–42
~ and Sanat Kumara, I:178
~ and the unborn child, XIII:79–80

Mussolini, Benito, IX:2, 7

mutilation
~ of animals, I:7, IV:6, 74–75
~ of humans, IV:7, 74–75

My Life for the Poor, V:192

The Mystery Rites Concerning Sacrifices, V:176. *See also* Apollonius of Tyana

mystery schools, I:233, V:242, VIII:161, IX:53–54, X:227
~ Astara, I:82, 166–67, 245, IV:192, VII:23, 148, VIII:164, IX:93, X:74
~ Earth as, I:11, III:12, 87, 198, IV:109, 262, 269, V:176, VI:23–24, 72, VII:130, VIII:12, 20–21, 94, 117–18, IX:37, 96, X:52
~ Eckancar, IV:195, 197, 249, V:168, VIII:167, IX:121
~ Egyptian, I:237, IV:167–77, V:135, XII:119
~ Greek Mystery School, I:237, V:135, 147
~ Heliopolis, IV:175
~ Orphic, V:135–36
~ Pythagorean, I:237, 272, V:139, 141, 143–45, 147, 174, VIII:98
~ Teachings of the Inner Christ, VIII:160–61

The Mystical Quabalah, IV:311

mysticism, III:95–97, VI:113, 187, VIII:135, X:40, 57, XI:148–49
~ and spiritual leadership, IX:16

mythology, I:3

N

nadis (etheric nervous system), I:85, 163, VI:37, 120, 212–13,
VIII:29, XI:49

NAFTA (North American Free Trade Agreement), IX:112

Nagarjuna, V:110

Nagasaki, Japan, IV:19–20, 27, 54, 56, VI:126, IX:245–46

Nag Hammadi codices, III:223

Nahum (prophet), IV:288

naiads, **IV:135**. *See also* devas; elementals: undines (nature spirits of
water); nature spirits

Nakir (angel), V:157, 160

Nam (repeating the name of God), V:168–71. *See also* chanting: repetition of the name of God; mantras

Nanak, Guru, IV:197, V:161
    ~ mantras of, I:257, XII:21
    ~ and soul travel, IV:198

Napoleon, I:118, V:240, IX:2–3

Nara, V:33

Narayana (Vishnu), V:33

NASA, IX:98, XI:227
    ~ photographs by, IV:8, 47

The National Enquirer, IX:73, 76, 138

National Geographic, IV:21

Native Americans, III:149, IV:109, 151, V:197, VII:134, 150,
VIII:191, IX:61, 112, 240, 242, X:96. *See also* Hopi Indians; Iroquois; Navajos; Pueblo Indians; Toltec Indians
    ~ and the animal kingdom, IV:151, VII:124, 150, IX:99, 167,
XIII:70
    ~ and the inner Earth, IV:25
    ~ and Yantra yoga, IV:247

NATO (North Atlantic Treaty Organization), IX:100

nature spirits, I:271, IV:122, 129, 131–32, 139–40, 142–45, 151–53,
VII:113, 118–20, VIII:130, IX:110, X:96–97, 213, XII:107. *See
also* brownies; devas; dryads; dwarves; elementals; elves; fairy folk;

fauns; goblins; hamadryads; nymphs; Pan (god of the nature spirits); pygmies; satyrs; sylvestres; trolls

~ clairvoyant sightings of, IV:140–42

~ evolution of, IV:133

~ and the human race, IV:134

~ and love, IV:136

~ and the mineral kingdom, IV:131, 154

~ and Native Americans, IV:151

~ and Wesak, X:152

naturopathy, V:140, VIII:149, IX:58, 86. *See also* healing

Navajos, IV:25. *See also* Native Americans

Nebadon (the local universe), IV:113–14, VI:73–74

negative ego, I:61, 63–64, 74, 88, 109, 180, 222–23, 269, III:25, 88–89, 193–94, 244, IV:258, 271, 281–82, V:51, 70, VI:2, 34, 58–61, 65, 100, 102–4, 108, 117, 130–31, 134, 136–41, 143, 172, 178, 180, 193, 207, 215–17, 220, 223, 239, VII:30, 40, 42–43, 47–48, 74–75, 101–2, VIII:11–12, 19, 72, 80, 112–13, 119, 128, 143, IX:16, 25, 45, 55, 72, 88, 92, 95, 97–98, 100, 102, 106–9, 117, 120, 132, 141, 150, 156, 230, 270–71, X:6, 16, 18–19, 47–48, 54, 69, 71, 75, 85, 113–15, 121, 134, 173, 175, 182, 187, 197, 210, 213, 215, 234, XI:158, 192, 216, XII:95, XIII:60, 74, 165. *See also* ego

~ and channeling, VI:132, 226, 228, VII:78, 80, IX:141–43

~ and the church, IV:271–75, 281–82, IX:53, 137, XII:108

~ clearing of, VI:57, 90, IX:183, X:4, 7, 51, 206, 237, XII:29, 121, 127–28

~ and communication, IX:201–2, 233, 272–74, XIII:26, 137–38, 148, 161

~ in the health-care system, IX:55, 88

~ and the Holy Spirit, XIII:144

~ and initiation, IV:187, IX:266, X:110–12, XI:21–22

~ in the judicial system, IX:64, 66–67

~ and leadership, IX:3–4, 20, 29, 44, 177, 187–88, 193, 202, 206–7, 209, 223, 228, 256

~ and the media, IX:73, 75–76, 148

~ and negative extraterrestrials, IV:17

~ and parental programming, XIII:72–73

~ in the police department, IX:69–71, 101

~ in the prison system, IX:69

~ and romantic relationships, XIII:24, 29–30, 32, 36–37, 50–51, 93–94, 123–24, 128–29, 137–38, 140, 144, 148, 153, 161–62, 166

~ and separateness, I:268, IV:102, VI:66, 93, 156, 219, VII:140, IX:127, XI:144

~ and sexuality, XIII:43–44, 122–23, 125, 130, 180

~ and sports, IX:123–24

~ transcendence of, I:74, 163–64, 220, 224, 226, 264, 273, 278, III:71, 195–96, IV:174, 187, 262, V:11, 21, 130, VI:4, 20, 51, 65, 83, 100–102, 108, 169, 190, 201, 249, VII:39, 86, 140–41, 153–54, 159, VIII:16, 22, 96, IX:5, 7, 175, 208, X:168, 185, XI:17, 234, 267, XII:124, 129, XIII:114–15, 140, 150

~ in the United States government, IX:44, 129–31, 135, 148, 162

~ *vs. Christ consciousness,* I:267, III:23, 69, 71, 88, VI:103, 138, 190, 218, 244, VII:27, 42, 75, 150, VIII:4, 13, IX:18, 64, 67, 69, 122, 259, 271, 278, X:44, 48, 70, 111, 128, 136, XI:35, XII:11, XIII:155

Nehemiah (prophet), I:170, IV:288

Nepal, I:173–74

Nephites, V:197

Neptune

~ ascension seat of, VI:36

~ and color healing, **IV:212**

~ energy qualities of, I:95, 97

~ and the Kabbalistic tree of life, **IV:302**

~ and the sixth ray, **I:131, VI:83**

nereids, **IV:135.** *See also* devas; elementals: undines (nature spirits of water); nature spirits

Neumann, Therese, V:55

~ as an incarnation of Mary Magdalene, I:176, V:45

New Age, I:124–25, 209, 222, 224, 226, 240–41, 253, III:3, 204, IV:16, 78, 109, 207, 275, 281, V:213, 239, VI:210, 218, 229, VII:92, VIII:187, IX:52–53, 114, 137, 143, **X:13,** X:20, 28–30, 39–40, 70, 95–97, 107, 123, 168, 176, 217, 219, 225, 234, 241, 246, XI:35

~ and extraterrestrials, IV:2, 71, 112

~ and group consciousness, IX:13, 132, 186, 221

~ and the negative ego, IX:187–88

~ political Light Party of, IX:46, 111

~ and the rays, I:123, 127–28, 194–96, VI:190

~ spiritual leadership in, IX:1–29, 256–58

New Age Journal, III:110

New Age Rosary, I:261–62, V:184, XII:7–8, 85, 89, 116–17. *See also* ascension rosary; prayers; Rosary

New Group of World Servers, I:60, 133, 143–44, 226, III:112, VI:155, 179, 182, 210, IX:39, X:68, 83, 178–83, 226, XI:174. *See also* Spiritual Hierarchy: externalization of

New Hampshire, IX:48

New Jerusalem, III:131

~ ascension seat in, III:131

~ and the second ray, **VI:179**

New Mexico, IV:4, 6–7, VI:127. *See also* Roswell, New Mexico

The New York Herald, V:36

New York, New York, IV:15, VI:185
    ~ blocked grid point in, IV:61
    ~ as Cancer, **VI:185**
    ~ and the rays, **VI:185**

The Next Dimension is Love, IV:101. *See also* Roeder, Dorothy

Nicaragua, IX:166

Nightmare on Elm Street, VII:97

Nikhilananda, Swami, V:28–29, 34

nine-body system, III:239–40, VI:194, 206. *See also* five-body system; four-body system; seven-body system; twelve-body system
    ~ anchoring of, VI:5, 17
    ~ and initiations, **VI:17**

Ninjas, IX:134

ninth ray, I:126, 129, **I:135**, III:203, **III:238, VI:3,** VI:39–40, **VI:41,** VIII:49, **X:13,** X:17, **XI:76.** *See also* rays, twelve
    ~ and color healing, **IV:210**
    ~ and the Kabbalistic tree of life, **IV:311**

nirvana, V:15, 93–95, 97, 100, 110, VII:34, 148. *See also* enlightenment; samadhi (enlightenment); wheel of rebirth: liberation from

Nityananda, Swami, V:77–84, 86
    ~ ashram of, V:78–80, 82–83
    ~ miracles of, V:78–82
    ~ quotations from, V:83–84

Nityananda, the Divine Presence, V:77, 79, 83–84. *See also* Hatengdi, M.U.

Nixon, Richard, IX:13, 144

Noah, I:228. *See also* Bible: and the story of Noah's ark

Nobel Peace Prize, V:105, 191

nonviolence, I:271, V:15, 17, 70, 73–74, 76, 253, VIII:13. *See also* ahimsa (nonviolence); harmlessness
    ~ and Hinduism, IV:221–22

Nordic races, IV:52

Nors, IV:52–53. *See also* extraterrestrials
    ~ Borealis, IV:51–52

North America, **I:5, VI:78**

North Pole, I:4
    ~ as an entrance to the inner Earth, IV:20–24, 28, VII:133
    ~ blocked grid point in, IV:61
    ~ vortexes of, III:149

Norway, IV:173

Nostradamus, VII:86, X:230

Notovitch, Nicholas, I:173–74

nuclear war, IV:74. *See also* war

nuclear waste, IV:152, IX:104, 110
  ~ disposal of, IX:167–68

nuclear weapons, IV:19–20, 27, 54, 56, 58, 89, 107, 152, VI:126–27, 191, IX:104, 245–46. *See also* war
  ~ destruction of, IX:163–64
  ~ and extraterrestrials, IV:5
  ~ and Maldek, IV:57

null zone, III:178

numerology, V:140, 148

Nutrasweet, IV:14

nutrition, I:270, 272, IV:14, VII:137, VIII:110, 142–43, 154, IX:5, 55, 58, 83, X:89, 199, XIII:4, 87

nymphs, IV:122, 134, 137, 141. *See also* devas; nature spirits

O

Oakland, California, V:37

Obadiah (prophet), IV:288

occultism, III:95–97, IV:312, VI:113, 187, VIII:135, IX:3, 16, X:20, 40, 57, XI:148–49
> ~ Eastern *vs.* Western, VI:186

The Occult World, V:224. *See also* Sinnett, A.P.

occupations, X:47–49, 54–57, 98, 104, 137, 218. *See also* service work
> ~ on Arcturus, IV:64–65
> ~ and karma, X:135–37
> ~ in Lemuria, I:6
> ~ between lives, I:90, 102
> ~ on Pleiades, IV:39
> ~ and the rays, I:118, 129, **I:130,** X:14, 16, 18–19, 22–24, 29, 104
> ~ and romantic relationships, XIII:36–37
> ~ and service work, I:90, 102, X:215, 217
> ~ on the spiritual path, X:82

oceanids, **IV:135,** IV:137. *See also* devas; elementals: undines (nature spirits of water); nature spirits

octaves, seven, IV:177, 180, V:154

Office of the Christ (World Teacher), I:201, X:30. *See also* Christ, the; Maitreya (Planetary Christ)

Ojas Shakti (brain illumination), I:270, IX:122

Olcott, Henry S., V:204–5, 207, 211, 213–21, 227. *See also* Theosophical Society; Theosophy
> ~ and the externalization of the Spiritual Hierarchy, I:142, V:213
> ~ healing powers of, V:213, 217

Olympians, IV:4. *See also* secret government

Olympic Games, the, IX:248–51

Omega Orion, IV:314

Omkar (ruler of the mental plane), **IV:195,** IV:197

Omnipotent Highness Krill, IV:6. *See also* extraterrestrials

Om, the, IV:226, 232, 234–35, 254, 257, VII:105–6

The One God, V:134. *See also* Akhenaton

oneness (unity), I:28, 48, 127, 145, 226, 268, III:59, 117, 171, 173–74, 180, IV:116, 231, 323, 327, V:12, 66, 76, 90, 112, 148–49, VI:28, 60, 156, 162, 197, 216, VII:12–13, 17, 33–34, 64, 68–69, 71–73, 83, 91–93, 101, 121, 130, 134, 136, 139–40, 145–46, 148, 150–51, VIII:2, 5–6, 76, 79, 107, viii, ix, IX:80, 106, 127, 201, 213, 236, 249, 265, 279, X:2, 4, 16, 44, 49, 74, 77, 86, 88, 92, 105, 111–17, 119, 123, 140, 145, 149, 175, 179–80, 183, 193, 202, 214, 218, 222, 226, 228, 239, 247, XI:4–5, 38, 44, XIII:19–20, 24, 31, 33–34, 55, 57, 63–65, 92, 109, 129, 138, 148, 154, 165, 181
   ~ and manifestation, VIII:75–78

Operation Victory, III:224

Ophanim, III:230

Ophanim Enoch (ascended master). *See* Enoch (ascended master)

opium. *See* drugs

Oracle of Delphi, V:139. *See also* prophecies

The Oracles Concerning Divination, V:176. *See also* Apollonius of Tyana

Orbito, Alex, VIII:162

Order of Melchizedek, I:207, 228, 230–31, 233, 235, 237, IV:26, 169–70, 174, 184, 188, 278, 288, 297, VI:6, 9, 76, VIII:63, IX:114, 133, X:161, 226–28, XI:2–6, 60, XII:105. *See also* Melchizedek Brotherhood
   ~ and Christianity, IV:277
   ~ cosmic order of, I:230, 232–33
   ~ and the Essene Brotherhood, I:231, 235–36, IV:287, 290
   ~ initiation into, I:207, 230–32, 236, 281, III:10, IV:157, 174–75, 181, 191, VI:215, VIII:64, XI:1–3, 5–6
   ~ and Judaism, IV:277

Order of Sonship, XI:147

Order of Sonship body, **III:238,** III:258, **VI:3,** VI:25, VIII:59, XI:147, 195

oreads, **IV:135.** *See also* devas; elementals: undines (nature spirits of water); nature spirits

original sin, IV:272

The Origin and Destiny of Man, IV:174

Orion, I:242, 246, **IV:33,** IV:38, 41–42, 58, 99, XI:227

Orions, IV:41–42. *See also* extraterrestrials

Ormazd, V:152, 154

Oronis, IV:314

Orpheus, V:135, 137, 148–49

~ as an incarnation of Gautama Buddha, I:237, V:135, 141, 147, 175, VI:148
~ and the Egyptian mysteries, V:135
~ and the Orphic mysteries, V:135–36

Orr, Miriam, V:49

Orvonton (the superuniverse), IV:113, 128, VI:73

Osiris, I:37, III:56, 101, 121, IV:170, 191, 198, VIII:41, XI:28. *See also* Egypt

Ossendowski, Ferdinand, IV:26

Our Father. *See* Lord's Prayer; prayers

out-of-body experiences, IV:199–200

overlighting, VI:24, VIII:122, X:236
~ of Mahatma energy, X:147–48
~ triple overlighting, III:101

Overseer, **I:199**

overself, III:259

overself body, III:218–20, **III:238, VI:3,** VI:25, XI:154, 194–95

overself body, cosmic, XI:194–95

overshadowing, I:25, 36, 138–43, 206, 216, III:257–58, IV:31, V:231, 236, XI:44, 102

oversoul, III:259, VI:65–66, 68, 85, 88–89, **VI:89,** VI:91–93, 96, 136, 199, 238, VII:4–5, 8, 11, 21–22, 25, 27, 30–31, 39, 42–43, 63, 154–55, VIII:47–48, IX:21, 61, 121, 178, X:7, 133, 136, 186, 232, XI:29, XII:97, XIII:55–56, 85, 165. *See also* higher self; soul family
~ attunement to, X:133
~ merging with, VII:32, X:116–17
~ relationships among members of, XIII:57–59
~ splitting of to form soul twins, XIII:68–69

oversoul family, VI:63–64, 85–88, **VI:89,** VI:90

ozone layer, IV:12, 152, IX:109–10, XII:73–74. *See also* pollution

O

P

Pacific Ocean, I:4, 7, IV:61

pacifism, V:16, 253

Padmasambhava (the Lotus-Born). *See* Rinpoche, Guru

Pallas Athena (Greek goddess of truth), **I:199,** III:156

Palmer, Ray, IV:20–21

Pan (god of the nature spirits), I:38, 271, III:38, 80, 97, **III:238,** IV:131–32, 134–35, 152, **VI:3,** VII:118–20, VIII:130, IX:110, X:96, XII:107. *See also* devas; nature spirits

pans, **IV:135.** *See also* devas; elementals: gnomes (nature spirits of earth); nature spirits

Paradise Sons, **I:199,** I:203, III:232, **VI:111,** VI:112, 115, XI:147, 195
    ~ ashrams of, VIII:127

Paradise Sons' body, **III:238,** III:258, **VI:3,** VI:25, 203, XI:195
    ~ anchoring of, VIII:59, XI:147
    ~ and the dimensions, **VI:204**

Paramatman (God), V:11–12

parenting, spiritual, VII:40, 47, 95, 152, XIII:71–76, 81, 85–87. *See also* relationships, parental
    ~ of your unborn child, XIII:76–77, 79–81

Parker, Janna, IX:11, 225

Parkinson's disease, IX:60

Parks, Rosa, IX:126, 274

Parlimentary Convocation of the World's Religions, V:36

Parsi religion, V:152. *See also* Zoroastrianism

Parthenon, IX:52

Parvati (Shiva's wife), IV:219, V:99

past lives, I:27, III:72, IV:109, V:45, 135, 141, VI:86, 198, 228, VII:31, 157, X:129–31, 216, 227–28, XIII:83–85. *See also* reincarnation
    ~ of ascended masters, I:9, 118, 138, 142, 169–72, 175–76, 207, 217, 227, 234–38, 244–45, III:130, IV:168, 171–74, 194, 198, 218–19, 223–24, 251, 277, 284, 287–88, 290, V:1,

P

8, 20, 71, 108, 119, 123, 128, 133–35, 139, 141–42, 147,
151, 153, 160, 163, 173–75, 203, 226, 239, 241–43, 245,
VI:145, 147–48, 154, 243, VII:19, 106, VIII:98, 163, 165,
xv, xx, IX:115, X:42, 240, XI:1, 5, 225, XII:80, 131, XIII:21,
101
~ clearing and mastery of, I:283, VI:60, 238
~ and the etheric body, VI:126–27
~ karma of, IV:262, V:50, VI:18, 55, X:128, 131–39, XI:29
~ between lives, I:92–93
~ and the physical body, IV:2
~ and physical death, I:75
~ and the rays, X:15
~ and the Theosophical Society, V:227, 232–33
~ and twin souls (flames), XIII:56–57

Patanjali, III:55, IV:257, 260, 264, VIII:64. *See also* Hinduism; yoga;
The Yoga Sutras of Patanjali
~ and yoga, I:160, 163, IV:253
~ yoga sutras of (the Eightfold Path), IV:242, 253–70, VIII:164,
XII:120

The Path, VI:162

The Path of Bliss, V:111, 113. *See also* Dalai Lama

patriotism, IX:120

Patton, George, I:118

Paul, Saint, I:160, 191

Paul the Venetian (ascended master), I:142, III:48, **III:238, VI:3,
112,** VII:79, 116, IX:9
~ ashram of, I:284, **VI:204,** VI:225, VIII:127
~ as Chohan of the fourth ray, I:192–93, **I:199,** I:201, III:257,
IV:121, VI:144, 163, 214, 241, **VII:19,** VII:116, **VII:117,**
X:14, 35–37, 152, XI:70–71
~ divine mission of, X:37
~ and Wesak, X:152

peace, I:62, 64, 93, 139, 265, 267, III:115, 205, 224, IV:15, 81, 153,
173, 224, 233–35, 241, 258–59, 289, 294, 327, V:11, 32, 50, 53,
58, 65, 75, 90, 97, 105, 110, 116, 128, 156, 169, 172, 185,
249–54, VI:4, 60, 101, 124, 139, 158, 173, 178, 193, 223, 232,
244, VII:12, 20, 27, 30, 33–34, 45, 47, 71–72, 93, 107, 140, 161,
VIII:2, 4, 9–10, 16, 25, 72, 84, 92, 99, 116, 190, IX:8, 21, 99, 104,
170, 181, 270, X:95, 98, 105, 116, 158, 218, 222, 231, 242, XI:36,
83, 168, 225, XIII:136, 140, 164–65, 172
~ gospel of, IV:292–93

Peace, Elana Marti, IX:11

Peace Pilgrim, V:249–54, VIII:136–37
~ philosophy of, V:253–54

Peace Pilgrim: Her Life and Work in Her Own Words, V:254

Pearl Harbor, VI:129

Pentagon, IV:13, 47. *See also* United States government

Perelandra garden, Virginia, IV:142–44, 148–49, VII:119

Peripatetic. *See* Aristotle

Perls, Fritz, VIII:112

permanent atoms, I:81, 271, VII:59, 62–64, 66, 68, X:129, 133
    ~ astral seed atom, I:81, 83
    ~ destruction of, I:111
    ~ exit of, I:81, 83
    ~ heart seed atom, I:81–83
    ~ and karma, XIII:84
    ~ mental seed atom, I:81, 83
    ~ and the prebirth bardo experience, I:92

Perot, Ross, IX:131

Persia, I:173–74, IV:327, V:151

personality, I:5, 11, 13, 18, 45, 66, 109–10, 181, 212, III:2, **III:238,**
    III:243, IV:32, 257, 261, **VI:3,** VI:57, 86, **VI:89,** VI:90–91, 166,
    169, 174–75, 181, 189, VII:5, 25, VIII:44, 49, 116, IX:96, 190,
    193, 221, 230, 264, X:72, 133–34, 146, 188, 192, 198, 208–9. *See*
    also soul extensions
    ~ and the antakarana, I:43–47, 51, 110
    ~ and the ascended masters, I:111, X:207–8
    ~ and ascension, I:28–30
    ~ aspects of, **I:106**
    ~ and channeling, VI:226, 228
    ~ clearing and integration of, I:17–18, VI:167, IX:208, X:206–9
    ~ creation of, I:13–14, 47, VI:77
    ~ death of, I:74
    ~ evolution of, I:109, 112
    ~ and initiation, I:21, 23
    ~ and the Kabbalistic tree of life, IV:301, 309–10
    ~ and the Meruvian root race, **VI:78**
    ~ and physical death, I:80–81
    ~ and the soul, I:13–14, 105–6, 108–9, 112

personality ray, I:116–18, VI:186–87, X:11, 13, 25. *See also* rays,
    seven: configuration of
    ~ of cities, I:118, VI:185, **VI:185**
    ~ of countries, I:118, VI:182, **VI:182,** VI:183, **VI:183,**
    VI:184
    ~ of humanity, **VI:184**

Peru, IV:23, 173, 175

Peter, Saint, V:194
    ~ as an incarnation of Zoroaster, I:217, V:133–34
    ~ other lives of, I:176

Phaedrus, V:149. *See also* Plato

pharmacies. *See* health-care system: pharmacies

Philadelphia Experiment, III:42, IV:14–15, VI:128–29. *See also* extra-terrestrials; secret government

Philadelphia, Pennsylvania, IV:15

Philippine healers, VIII:162. *See also* healing

Philo (Jewish philosopher), IV:289–90

philosophy, I:92

Philostratus, Flavius, V:173, 175–76

Phoenix, Arizona, VIII:103

photon belt, III:103

physical body, I:1, 18, 45, 58, 63, 67, 126, 156, 213, 268–69, III:102, 201, 205, 227, **III:238,** III:239, IV:129, 160, 164–65, 224, 292, 301, 305, V:21, **V:21,** V:61, 87, 128–29, 150, **VI:3,** VI:4, 18, 22–23, 48, 56, 61, 71–72, 85, 87, 100, 118–22, 126, 128, 162, 194–95, 203, **VI:205,** VI:209, 221, 231, VII:1–3, 6, 8, 23, 105, 138, 141, VIII:2, 12, 14, 31, 40, 43, 49, 77, 82, 143, 147–48, 154, IX:79, 96, 101, 110, 114, 121, 127, 129, 188, X:4, 56, 86, 198–99, 220, 227, 243, XI:42, 150–52, 194, XII:95, XIII:4. *See also* four-body system

  ~ Adam Kadmon type, I:8, III:223, IV:2, 37, 55, 102, VII:146, X:205

  ~ anchoring the twelve strands of DNA in, III:19, 50, 128, 194, 241, 257, 266, VI:27, VIII:45, XI:32, 94, 268

  ~ of angels, IV:122

  ~ and ascension, I:27, 30–31, 35, 79, III:3, 64, XI:214

  ~ and the astral plane, VII:9–10

  ~ attractiveness/appearance of, VIII:4, 115, XIII:5–8, 40, 165–67, 178–79

  ~ and the chakras, III:17, 21

  ~ clearing and integration of, III:201, IV:105, VI:45, 62, 193–94, 240, VII:158–60, VIII:28–29, 31, 35, 149, IX:71, X:89, XI:48, 154, XIII:107–8

  ~ death of, I:73–76, 84–85, 180

  ~ and the dimensions, III:142, 150, **VI:205**

  ~ and the ego, I:222–23

  ~ and the etheric body, III:192, 201, 206, 245

  ~ of extraterrestrials, IV:37, **IV:74**

  ~ healing of, VI:118, VIII:31–32 (*See also* healing)

  ~ and the Hyperborean root race, **VI:78**

  ~ and initiation, I:22–24, 27, 64, III:1, 3, 193, IV:176, 270, **VI:17,** VII:24–25

  ~ and integrating soul extensions, VI:93–94

  ~ and joy, X:88

  ~ and karma, IV:220, XIII:84

  ~ and the Lemurian root race, **VI:78**

~ of Lemurians, I:7

~ mastery of, I:64, 66, 163, 197, 200, 265, III:1–2, 152, 196,
III:238, IV:183, 240, 259, **VI:3,** VI:4, 60, 100, 249,
VII:24–25, VIII:24, X:107, XIII:5

~ of a Planetary Logos, I:179

~ and the Polarian root race, **VI:78**

~ and the rays, I:117, 119–20, VI:189

~ and the repetition of the name of God, I:249, 251, 253

~ and self-love, X:198–99

~ and sex, XIII:39–40, 44–45, 47, 170

~ and the shadow body, IV:159, 165

~ and the soul, I:106–7, 112

~ during soul travel, IV:193, 199

~ during walk-ins, IV:30–32

~ and Western medicine, IX:84, 108

~ during yoga, IV:240–41

~ and the yoga sutras of Patanjali, IV:258

physical body, cosmic, **III:238,** III:259, **VI:3, 24,** XI:155

physical plane, I:16–17, 27, 78, **I:184,** I:185, **I:197,** I:212, III:139,
IV:116, **IV:195, 267,** IV:269, **VI:8,** VI:59–60, 171, 181, 206–7,
VII:4, 6–7, 9, 25, 62, 104, 131, IX:137, X:149, 167, 206, 210,
215–16, 232, XI:195. *See also* physical universe

~ and the Cosmic Night, VI:67, 70

~ and the dweller on the threshold, **I:58**

~ and the first initiation, **III:4, 139, VI:17, XI:127**

~ and the Kabbalistic tree of life, **IV:303, 307**

~ and the Mahatma energy, I:212, 215

~ mastery of, I:197, **III:139**

~ and the supersenses, **I:71**

~ and the third initiation, **XI:127**

physical plane, cosmic, I:17, 31, 40, 132, 183, **I:184,** I:198, **I:199,**
I:200, 212, III:4, 139, 146–47, 167, 169, 181, 218, **III:238,**
III:239–40, **VI:3,** VI:8, **VI:8, 24,** VI:206–7

physical ray, I:116, VI:186–87, X:11–13, 128. *See also* rays, seven:
configuration of

~ of humanity, **VI:184**

physical universe, I:1–2, 13, 90, III:141, 198, IV:114–16, V:169,
VI:72, VII:1, 84, VIII:78–79. *See also* physical plane

~ organization of, IV:113–14

Picasso, Pablo, I:121–22

Pietà, the, VII:97

pilgrimages, I:163, VIII:159–60, X:227

~ Hindu, IV:221

~ to Lourdes, V:179

~ to Mecca, V:156, 158

~ of Peace Pilgrim, V:249–53

P

~ to Sai Baba, I:153

Pillar of Light, I:38, III:226

pineal gland, I:43, 47, 77, 81, 83, VIII:45, XI:52. *See also* chakra:
third-eye (sixth); death hormone; life hormone

Pippin, Scotty, XI:68

Piscean Age, I:139, 141, 172, 240, IV:54, 112, 240, 281, 286, VI:6,
180, 217, VIII:127, IX:133, 143, 169, 274, X:24–25, 30, 40, 83,
120, 225

Pisces. *See also* astrology
~ and color healing, **IV:212**

pituitary gland, I:83, 274, XI:52. *See also* death hormone; life hormone

planes, cosmic, I:17, 132, 183, 215, III:4, 139, 146–47, 151–52, 169,
181, 218, 240, **VI:8,** VI:24, 84, 206

Planetary Christ, I:201, VII:19. *See also* Maitreya (Planetary Christ)
~ Kuthumi as, I:243, III:169, VI:35, XI:102, 111, 210, 218

Planetary Logos, I:6, 40, 78, 131, 178–79, 183, **I:184,** I:185–89,
191, 197, **I:199,** I:201, 212, III:10–11, 172–75, 180–81, **III:238,**
IV:33, 205, **VI:3,** VI:77, 125, VII:19, 116, 130, 133, 149,
VIII:161, 181, IX:7–8, X:52, XI:30, 168. *See also* Sanat Kumara
(Planetary Logos)
~ and the ascension ceremony, I:29, XI:87
~ Buddha as, VI:86, 125, 220, 243, VII:19, 116, 133, 149,
VIII:50, 127, 181, IX:7–9, 115, X:115, 152, XI:18, 30–31,
168, 225–26, 242, XII:84
~ and initiation, I:24, 200, 277, XI:168
~ and the rays, I:116, 126
~ training of, I:179–82, 208, III:173
~ of Venus, VI:32
~ will aspect of, I:191, 200

Planetary Spirits, the three, **I:199,** I:201

planet M, XI:205

planet R, XI:205

plant kingdom, I:105, **I:199,** I:270, III:119, **III:238,** IV:119, 122,
IV:130, IV:133, 140, 151–52, 154, **VI:3,** VI:186, VII:7, 113, 119,
IX:110, X:235. *See also* devas; nature spirits; trees
~ and building angels, X:97
~ and devas, IV:129, 131, 139–40, X:96
~ evolution of, I:186
~ physical death of, IV:145
~ and telepathy, X:239

platinum net, XI:255–56

platinum ray, **VI:41,** VI:42, 194, VIII:50, XI:256

platinum rod, VIII:179

platinum screen, XI:255–56

Plato, I:10, IV:184, V:147–50
~ philosophy of, V:148–50
Playfoot, Janet N., V:192
Play of Consciousness, V:87. *See also* Muktananda, Baba
Pleiades, the (seven sisters), I:242–43, 246, III:176, **IV:33,**
IV:35–39, 168
~ ascension seat on, VI:32
~ Erra, IV:35–36, 39
Pleiadians, IV:35–39, VI:224, VII:131–33, IX:105, XI:205. *See also*
extraterrestrials
~ healing center of, III:99–100
~ spacecraft of, IV:36–37, XI:205
Pliny (Roman), IV:290
Pluto
~ ascension seat of, VI:36
~ and color healing, **IV:212**
~ energy qualities of, I:95, 97
~ and the first ray, **I:131, VI:83**
~ and the Kabbalistic tree of life, **IV:302**
polarity, III:171, V:126–29, VI:59, 137–40, 175, VIII:15, 79–80
~ and color, IV:206–7
~ and the Path of Magnetic Work, III:171
pole shift, I:8, 224, 245, IV:23, V:127
political system (U.S.), VII:28, 98–99, IX:39, 44–45, 48–49, 91, 108,
112–13, 130–31, 144–45, 147–48, 159, 244, X:29, 56–57, 70. *See
also* United States government
~ and campaigning, IX:46, 130, 144–45
~ and the Dark Brotherhood, IX:113, 148
~ and drug manufacturers, IX:84
~ and gun control, IX:102
~ isolationalism *vs.* internationalism, IX:108
~ and the media, IX:130, 147–48
~ and polls, IX:48–49
~ and term limits, IX:135–36
~ tools for handling for the lightworker, VIII:154–55, IX:32–33,
112–15, 170
~ and voting, VIII:155, IX:47–49, 112, 170
pollution, III:34–35, IV:8, 11–13, 61, 152, VIII:130, 149, IX:56, 104,
109–11, X:213–14, XII:73–74. *See also* Earth; environment; greenhouse effect; ozone layer
~ clearing of, I:243
~ and disease, IX:86
~ electromagnetic, VIII:145
~ in the fourth dimension, III:150
~ and Nikola Tesla, IV:11

P

~ and the Pleiadians, IV:37

poltergeists, I:90

polygamy, XIII:128–29. *See also* marriage

Ponder on This, VI:149, 153, VII:34, 107, XII:8, 79. *See also* Bailey, Alice A.

Poole, Eileen, VIII:142, 151, IX:27

Pope, the, V:107, 181, 186, IX:53, 137–38

pornography, I:269, VIII:114, IX:75, 122, XIII:42–43, 46, 149

The Portable Romantic, XIII:181

Portia (goddess of justice), **I:199,** III:156

Poseidia, I:10. *See also* Atlantis

Posid (underground city), IV:26

possession, I:98–99, IV:30

potamides, **IV:135.** *See also* devas; elementals: undines (nature spirits of water); nature spirits

Powder, IX:122

Powell, Colin, IX:18–19, 131

The Power of Your Subconscious Mind, VIII:70

Power Rangers, IX:134

powers (heavenly governors), **IV:123,** IV:124. *See also* angelic kingdom

The Practice of Yoga, IV:240. *See also* Sivananda, Swami

Practicing the Presence, VIII:3

prana, I:65, IV:130, 258, 264–65, VI:212–13, XI:42

pranava, IV:257

pranayama, I:163, 166, IV:259, 264. *See also* breathing

prasad (consecrated food), V:5

pratyahara, IV:240, 242

Prayer of Saint Francis, VII:106, XII:5–6, 87, 89. *See also* prayers

Prayer of Thanksgiving, XII:12. *See also* prayers

prayers, I:92, 124, 216, 264, 266, 270, III:24, 62, 155, IV:138, 202, 205, 314, 323, V:25, 31, 50, 61, 184–85, VI:216, 219, VII:86, 107, VIII:16, 20, 70–73, 77–78, 81–85, 98, 110, 136, IX:83, 137, X:142, 239, XI:66, XII:5, 11–12, XIII:2, 139, 141, 146, 173. *See also* affirmations; visualization; individual prayers

~ The Affirmation of the Disciple, XII:5, 8–9, 77, 87, 91

~ Apostles' Creed, V:184

~ ascension rosary, XI:206

~ "Dear God" letters, VIII:111

~ and death, I:82, 97

~ of the Essenes, IV:293–95

~ to Ganesha, VIII:69

~ The Great Invocation, I:55–56, 140, 250, 259–60, VI:190, VII:107, XII:3–5, 12, 85, 87, 89, 91
~ Hail Mary, I:258, V:184, VII:107, XII:23
~ Holy Grail Benediction and Blessing, III:260–61
~ Huna prayers, III:21–22, 27, 82, 155–66, 232–36, IV:161–64, VI:23, VIII:68–69, IX:214–16, XI:10, 66, 68–69, 83, 93–96, 102–3, 105, 109–10, 121–26, 128, 141, 182–83, 193–94, 203–4, 259–60, XII:108–9, XIII:2
~ I Am Presence prayers, IV:319–21, XII:112–14
~ invocation and prayer for leadership, IX:237
~ Invocation of the Yod Spectrum, VI:195–96
~ of Islam, V:157
~ language of, VIII:70
~ Lord's Prayer, I:140, 250, 255, 258, **IV:305,** V:184, VII:107, XII:5, 20, 23, 85, 89
~ for manifestation, III:165–66, VIII:68–69
~ New Age Rosary, I:261–62, V:184, XII:7–8, 85, 89, 116–17
~ for opening the chakras, III:19, 21–22
~ over- and underpraying, VIII:70–71
~ Prayer of Saint Francis, VII:106, XII:5–6, 87, 89
~ Prayer of Thanksgiving, XII:12
~ of protection, VIII:96–97
~ relationship prayer, XIII:179
~ Rosary, I:250, 260–61, V:179, 184–85, XI:206, XII:5–7, 85, 89, 116–17
~ Shinto, IV:326
~ and Sufism, IV:324
~ Ultimate Huna Prayer and Meditation, XI:121–26
~ Ultimate Kabbalistic Huna Prayer and Meditation, III:232–36
~ Ultimate Monadic Merger Prayer, VI:88
~ in Zoroastrianism, V:152
prejudice, VII:149–51
Prema Sai Baba, I:149–50, III:243, V:8, VIII:xv, xx, X:74, 139. *See also* Sathya Sai Baba (Cosmic Christ)
premonitions, IV:159, VII:84–86
Price, John Randolph, III:29
PrimeTime Live, VIII:157, IX:68, 77, 89
principalities (heavenly messengers), **IV:123,** IV:124. *See also* angelic kingdom
The Prism of Lyra, IV:41–42, 70–71, 75, 83, 85, 101, 107
prison system (U.S.), IX:67–69, 71–73, 144, 151. *See also* crime; Los Angeles, California
~ tools for handling for the lightworker, IX:36–37
Problems of Humanity, IV:271. *See also* Bailey, Alice A.
Procyon, IV:79

Procyonians ("the Swedes"), IV:79. *See also* extraterrestrials

Prodigal Son, **VI:179**

Project Signa, IV:5

promiscuity, XIII:40, 46. *See also* sex; sexuality

prophecies, I:239–47, IV:287, IX:142, X:229–32, 245, XII:105. *See also* prophets
> ~ about the antichrist, I:241
> ~ in the Bible, I:215, 240, IV:275, VII:86, 147
> ~ of the coming of Sathya Sai Baba, I:148, V:8
> ~ for the economy, III:99
> ~ by Edgar Cayce, I:215, 240, VI:217
> ~ Egyptian, I:35, IV:174
> ~ by the Hopi Indians, I:153
> ~ millennium and doomsday, I:224, VII:85, X:229–31, 233, 245
> ~ by Mohammed, I:153
> ~ by Nostradamus, VII:86, X:230
> ~ positive, X:231–32
> ~ by Saint Germain, V:241
> ~ by the Virgin Mary, I:240, V:181–82

Prophet, Elizabeth Clare, I:30, VI:227, IX:141

prophets, I:238–39, IV:285, 288, 290, V:160, VII:85. *See also* prophecies; individual prophets

prostitution, IX:154–55

Proxima Centauri, IV:91. *See also* extraterrestrials

psychedelics. *See* drugs

psychiatry, IX:58, 62. *See also* psychology

psychic powers, I:33, 83, 100, III:97, 104, IV:41, **IV:267,** IV:287, V:201–4, VI:51, 113, 123, 132, IX:55, 83, X:20, 57, XI:6
> ~ development of, VII:75–77
> ~ of Madam Blavatsky, V:201–11, 214, 216–18

psychic senses. *See* psychic powers; supersenses

psychic surgeons. *See* Philippine healers

psychological ray, X:11. *See also* rays, seven: configuration of

psychology, I:92, 106, 236, VI:57, VII:154, VIII:16, 115–16, 158–59, IX:54–55, 58, 62, 78, 86, 150, X:19, XII:95
> ~ of animals, VII:126–27
> ~ art therapy, XIII:75
> ~ of ascension, VII:39–56, 139
> ~ behaviorism, IX:55
> ~ blank-slate theory, XIII:85
> ~ child, XIII:75
> ~ clinical, IX:55
> ~ and electroshock therapy, IX:147

~ esoteric, I:115, 118, 129
~ Gestalt, VIII:112
~ Jungian, VIII:159
~ psychosynthesis, VIII:159
~ and the rays, I:117–18, VI:189, IX:62
~ soul, I:106, VI:60, XII:95
~ spiritual, I:118, V:125, VI:60, 90, IX:6, 39–40, 58
~ transpersonal, I:106, 118, VI:90

psychometry, **I:71**, IV:165, **IV:267**, VII:2

psychotronics, IV:13, 170. *See also* radionics

Ptah Melchizedek, XI:26

Public Health Service, IX:60

Pueblo Indians, IV:25, VII:134. *See also* Native Americans

puja, IV:217, V:7, 231

Puranas, IV:219. *See also* Hinduism

purgatory, I:87, 89, IV:165

Puri, India, IV:221

purity, **I:96,** I:122, 124, 163, 172, 270, III:100, IV:206, 209, 226,
    228–29, 245, 264, 269, 324–25, V:32, 37–38, 65–66, 95, 136,
    154, 169, **VI:17,** VI:83, 141, VII:32, 36, 59, 65, 68, 76, 139,
    VIII:9, 24, X:24, 124, 139, 179, XIII:91, 121

Purple Positive Energy Plate, III:120–21, VIII:142, 144, 151

Putaparti, India, III:130, VII:54

pygmies, **IV:135,** IV:136. *See also* devas; elementals: gnomes (nature
    spirits of earth); nature spirits

Pyle, Howard, V:252

pyramids, I:9–10, IV:23, VIII:102. *See also* Great Pyramid
    ~ building of, I:173, 242, 245, IV:23, 70, 93, 167–71, 174,
      VII:133
    ~ Egyptian, I:9–10, 242, 245, IV:70, 167–70, V:242, X:226–27
    ~ Incan, IV:169
    ~ on Mars, IV:8
    ~ Mayans, IV:169
    ~ at Mount Shasta, I:36
    ~ at Saqqara, IV:175
    ~ as temples of initiation, I:9, 173, 231, 236

Pythagoras, I:272, V:139–40, 144–45, 203, VIII:98. *See also* Pythagorean mystery school
    ~ as an incarnation of Kuthumi, I:237, V:139, 147, VI:148,
      VIII:98
    ~ and conscious death (mahasamadi), IV:198
    ~ educational system of, V:140–42
    ~ philosophy of, V:142–43, 173–74, 176

Q

Quan Yin (Bodhisattva of Compassion), **I:199,** III:156, 198,
    V:98–100, 102–3, 105, 113, **VI:112,** VII:15, VIII:75, 97, 168,
    178, XI:106, 242, XII:116. *See also* Avalokitesvara (Avalokita);
    Tara
        ~ and Avalokitesvara, V:99–100
        ~ genesis of, **V:101**
        ~ personality of, X:207
        ~ sacred garden ascension seat of, III:191
Quatrini, Rosa, V:186–87
Quetzalcoatl (avatar), IV:26
        ~ as a walk-in, IV:31
The Quiet Mind, VIII:99. *See also* White Eagle
Qumran, I:171, 228, IV:288, 290–91

R

Raai, King, IV:171

races, five, I:3, 8. *See also* root races
~ "black root race," I:3
~ "brown root race," I:3
~ "red root race," I:3
~ "white root race," I:3
~ "yellow root race," I:3

racism, VII:149–51, IX:45, 152, 159–60, 272
~ in the judicial system, IX:63–66, 156, 158–61
~ in the police department, IX:70
~ in the United States government, IX:130

Radha (wife of Krishna), V:24, 99

radionics, IV:13, VIII:144–45, IX:58. *See also* psychotronics

Ra (Egyptian sun god), I:173, V:134. *See also* Egypt

Ra (extraterrestrials), IV:93–94. *See also* extraterrestrials

Raiders of the Lost Ark, I:245, IV:169

The Rainbow Bridge, Phase 1: The Link with the Soul, I:52

Raincloud of Knowable Things, III:55

rain forests, IV:152

Rainier, Mount, XI:207

rajas (activity), I:121, IV:256

Rakoczy, Prince
~ as an incarnation of Saint Germain, V:239, 242, VI:148

Rama (avatar), I:119, IV:20, 218, 241, V:2, 4, 9–11, 23–24, 27, 36, 74, VIII:160, IX:240
~ quotations from, V:11–13

Ramadan, V:156–58. *See also* Islam

Ramakrishna, IV:219, V:23–25, 27–28, 32, 37, 45, 49, VI:248, VIII:166
~ and Mother Sarada, V:28–30
~ quotations from, V:25–26
~ and Swami Vivekananda, V:25, 27, 33–36

Ramanand. *See* Kabir (the poet-saint)

The Ra Material: An Ancient Astronaut Speaks, IV:93

Rama (underground city), IV:26

Ramayana, IV:20, 218–19, V:9–11, VIII:160. *See also* Hinduism;
  Valmiki (poet-saint)
    ~ quotations from, V:11–13

Ramkar (ruler of the causal plane), **IV:195**

Raphael (archangel), **I:199,** I:220, 222, III:199, IV:122, VII:115, 118
    ~ and the fifth ray, **I:204, IV:121, 124, VII:115,** X:95, 153
    ~ and healing, VII:114, IX:35
    ~ and the Kabbalistic tree of life, **IV:304**

Ra-Ta (prophet), IV:171–74, 192. *See also* Cayce, Edgar
    ~ as an incarnation of Edgar Cayce, V:245, VI:171–74
    ~ and Hept-Supht, IV:172–73

Ratziel (archangel), **IV:303**

The Rays and Initiations II, XII:79. *See also* Bailey, Alice A.

The Rays and the Initiations, I:41, 47, 135, 177, III:180–85, VI:17,
  81–83, 153, 190, VII:32, IX:264. *See also* Bailey, Alice A.

rays, seven, I:40, 63, 115–17, **I:132,** I:133, 188–89, III:179, 244,
  257, IV:120, VI:39, 144, 149, 156, 163, 184, 214, VII:19, **VII:19,**
  VII:65, 81, **VII:115,** VII:116–17, **VII:117,** VII:138, 144–45,
  156–57, VIII:13, 61, 123, 127, IX:185–86, X:1, 14–16, 27–28,
  39–40, 74, 82–83, 92, 152, XI:70, 76, XII:127. *See also* rays,
  twelve; individual rays
    ~ and the archangels, **I:204, IV:121, 123**–24, X:94–95
    ~ ashrams of, VI:171, X:201
    ~ and astrology, **XI:176**–77
    ~ and the chakras, I:118, 130
    ~ clearing of, VI:125, 241
    ~ and color, **XI:176**–77
    ~ configuration of, I:116–18, 128, 271, III:132, 244, VI:65,
      186–87, 228, 241, VII:156–57, VIII:122, 125, IX:108, 176,
      184–85, X:3, 5, 14–19, 25–26, 127–28, XI:70, 75
    ~ configuration of for nations, VI:177, 182, **VI:182,** VI:183,
      VI:183, VI:184
    ~ dates of manifestation of, VI:185
    ~ and the dimensions, I:131–32
    ~ and the elohim, I:203, III:199–200
    ~ glamour of, I:61–63, X:15–21
    ~ and the Great Bear constellation, I:131, 202
    ~ and initiation, XI:73, **XI:127**
    ~ and karma, X:127–28
    ~ and the Olympics, IX:249–50
    ~ and the planets, I:131, VI:82, **VI:82,** VI:83, **VI:83,**
      XI:176–77

~ and professions, I:118, 129, **I:130,** X:14, 16, 18–19, 22–24, 29, 104
~ qualities of, I:118–25, 129
~ rays of aspect, I:116, X:28
~ rays of attribute, I:116, X:28
~ and the solar system, I:130–31, VI:82, **VI:82,** VI:83, **VI:83**
~ and spiritual leadership, IX:43, 182, 185–86
rays, twelve, I:115, 128–29, 268, III:68, 172, 192–94, 242, IV:211, VI:39–40, 44, 79, 113, VIII:49–50, 96, 161–62, IX:4, X:12–13, 43, 92, 140, XI:73, **XI:75**–76, XI:133, XII:94. *See also* rays, seven; individual rays
~ chohans of the five higher rays, XI:210
~ and color, I:134–35, **VI:41, X:12**–13
~ configuration of, I:128, X:11–13, 47, 140
~ and healing, III:107–8, IV:210, **IV:210**
~ integration of, VI:57, 59
~ and the Kabbalistic tree of life, IV:309, **IV:311**
~ and the Mahatma, I:212–13
~ meditation for, III:203–4
~ qualities of, I:118–27
rays, twelve (cosmic), I:118, 131, III:259, IV:11, VI:39–41, **VI:41,** VI:42–43, 45, 65, 78–80, 83, 201, VIII:50, X:26, XI:133, XII:122
~ cosmology of, **VI:41**
~ at the Godhead level, VI:41, **VI:41**
~ at the multiuniversal level, **VI:41,** VI:42
~ at the universal level, **VI:41,** VI:43
Reach for Us, Your Cosmic Teachers and Friends, I:209. *See also* Roeder, Dorothy
Readers Digest, VIII:25
Reagan, Ronald, IV:11, IX:13
The Reappearance of the Christ, I:142. *See also* Bailey, Alice A.
Rebazar Tarz, IV:197
rebirth, I:75
recording angels. *See* angels: recording angels
Redfield, James, III:110–11
Red Sea, IV:283
The Refusal. *See* initiation: ninth (the refusal)
regeneration, I:97
Reiki, III:107, VIII:168, X:89
reincarnation, I:3, 8, 14, 74, 88, 94, 97, 243, 267, III:2–3, 88, IV:53, 186, 219, 265, 287, V:15, 135, VI:70, VII:1, 4–6, 11, 21–22, 62–63, 141, IX:114, 134, 239–40, 264, X:128–31, XI:267–68, XIII:77–78, 95, 157. *See also* death, physical; past lives
~ of animals, I:101, IV:148

~ astral, VI:69
~ in the Bible, IV:273
~ and the Cosmic Night, VI:67
~ and the Essene Brotherhood, IV:290
~ and the Hindu caste system, IV:220
~ and Jainism, V:15–16
~ and Judaism, IV:284
~ and karma, VII:66
~ new patterns of, IX:8–9
~ and past-life trauma, X:130
~ process of, I:91–92
~ and the Second Council of Constantinople, I:73, 174
~ and Tibetan Buddhism, V:97

relationships, I:110, 145, V:120, VI:190, VIII:10, IX:26, 75, 229, X:59, 208–9, XI:222, XIII:2
~ and ascension lineage, X:74–76
~ familial, I:60, VII:95–96, 152–55, X:132–35, XIII:2, 161, 171
~ friendship, VIII:136, 156, IX:27, 225, X:208–9, XI:228, XIII:2, 40, 143, 171
~ with God, VIII:10, X:76–77, XI:267, XIII:2, 20, 99–110, 135–36, 181
~ group, X:67–72
~ group monadic mates, XIII:60
~ mission mates, X:60–63
~ and the monadic group, X:71–72
~ monadic mission mates, XIII:59
~ to oneself, VIII:10, XI:267, XIII:5, 9, 13, 135–36, 164–65, 181
~ parental, III:109, 118, VII:95–96, X:133, XIII:71–73, 87 (*See also* parenting, spiritual)
~ and the soul group, X:71–72
~ spiritual, X:68–70

relationships, romantic, III:171, VI:187, VII:94–96, VIII:9–10, 137, X:59, 63–65, 138–39, XI:222, XII:98, 102, XIII:105. *See also* homosexuality; marriage; soul mates; twin souls (flames)
~ balance within, XIII:9–20, 111–17, 137, 142, 146, 151, 162, 165
~ and commitment, XIII:27–28, 95–98, 116, 120, 123–24, 126, 136–37, 176
~ and communication, VII:95, VIII:113, 137, IX:27, XIII:12, 17–18, 23–24, 26–27, 29, 45, 47, 53, 118–20, 126–27, 136, 138–39, 141, 144–45, 159, 161–62, 164, 168–69, 172–73, 176, 178
~ and compatibility, XIII:165–67
~ competition within, XIII:31–33, 35–37
~ and the differing elevator syndrome, XIII:49–53, 94, 153

~ and emotional appearance, XIII:7

~ equality within, XIII:34–35, 145, 161

~ and fame, XIII:32–33

~ and forgiveness, XIII:27–30, 52, 133–34, 136, 156

~ and the four-body system, XIII:4–5, 8–9, 15, 144

~ golden keys of, XIII:135–81

~ interracial, VII:150–51, IX:127, XIII:19, 172

~ intimacy in, X:219–21

~ and life's challenges, XIII:115–17, 180

~ living together, XIII:123–26

~ male/female needs, XIII:177

~ and mental appearance, XIII:7

~ mission mates, X:60–61, 63–66, XIII:13, 58, 154, 165

~ monadic mates, XIII:59, 122, 165

~ and the negative ego, XIII:24, 29–30, 32, 36–37, 50–51, 94, 124, 137–38, 140, 144, 148, 161–62, 166

~ and physical appearance, XIII:5–7, 40, 165–67, 178–79

~ relationship paradigms, XIII:3, 10–19, 143–44, 152, 154–55

~ search for, III:151, VIII:138, XIII:1–4, 141–42, 177

~ and spiritual evolution, III:109, XIII:49–51, 53, 57–58, 113–15, 143, 146–47, 150, 155, 162, 166

~ and the spiritual path, X:59–77

~ and trust, XIII:27, 94, 116–17, 120, 143–44

~ and unconditional love, XIII:21–28, 52–53, 116, 125–26, 135, 150, 152, 156, 166–67, 170–71, 176

~ and unresolved parent/child scenarios, XIII:88, 136, 152

religion, I:101, 155, 236, 240–41, IV:35, 281–83, 329, V:25, 36, 38, 76, 107–8, 121, 128, IX:53–54, 240, X:20, XII:103. *See also* individual religions

~ evolution of, IV:280–82, 284

~ integration of, I:124, 194

~ and the negative ego, IV:271, 282–83, IX:53

~ and science, VI:186, IX:136–37

~ survey about, IV:111–12

~ unification of, V:176–77

~ universality of, I:144, 173, 195, 235–38, 268–69, IV:161, 223, 227, 275, 282, 284, 327–29, V:96, 108, 128, 155, VII:145–49, IX:17, 53–54 (*See also* Baha'i)

renunciation, I:24, 164, 268, III:2, IV:219, 225, 232, 242, 244, 263, V:12, 21, 30–31, 61, 82, 88–89, VI:159–60, 189–90, VIII:10, X:217. *See also* initiation: fourth (crucifixion)

~ vow of, VIII:24–25

Reptilians, IV:5, 7, 9, 42, 77–79, VII:134. *See also* extraterrestrials

Republicans, IX:44, 47, 49, 81, 89, 95, 107, 128, 147–48. *See also* political system (U.S.)

Requiem (mass), VII:97

resurrection, I:40, 278, III:199, 223, IV:191, 285, V:117, 158, VI:150, XI:82, **XI:127,** XI:143, 152. *See also* initiation: seventh (resurrection)
~ a personal experience of, XI:85–91, 93–155
Revelations of Things to Come, IV:23, 169–70, V:181, 187. *See also* Chaney, Earlyne
Ribera, Antonio, IV:43–44
The Rider on the White Horse, I:176, V:133–34. *See also* Grattan, Brian
Rigel, IV:73–74
Rigelians, IV:74. *See also* extraterrestrials; Grays
Rinpoche, Guru, V:105
Rishabha (jinah), V:17
rishis (sages), I:250, IV:220, 231, V:34, 53
The Rite of the Girdle, V:135–36. *See also* Orpheus
Robbins, John, IV:149–50
Robinson, Lytle, IV:174
Rockefeller, Nelson, IV:5, IX:168
Rock of Salvation, III:227
rod of initiation, VI:1, 144, 215, 220, XI:3, 10–12, 30, 87, 173, 186
Roeder, Dorothy, I:209, IV:101
Roerich, Nicholas, I:125, 174, IV:19, 250
Roger, John, IV:195
Rogo, Scott, IV:201
Rome, Italy, V:182, VII:79
Roosevelt, Eleanor, I:121
root races, I:3–5, **I:5,** I:134, 162, 189, 191, IV:196, 281, **VI:78,** VI:81–82, 187, 189, VII:152. *See also* races, five
   ~ Aryan, I:3–4, **I:5,** I:58, **I:59,** I:63, 133–34, IV:196, 239, 241–42, 253, 257, VI:77, **VI:78,** VI:135, 180, 182, 189, VII:151
   ~ Atlantean, **I:5,** I:7–9, 58, **I:59,** I:60, 63, 133–34, 191, IV:196, 239–40, VI:77, **VI:78,** VI:134–35, 182, 189, 193, VII:151 (*See also* Atlantis)
   ~ and the chakras, VI:72, 77, **VI:78**
   ~ Hyperborean, I:4, **I:5,** IV:239, **VI:78**
   ~ Lemurian, I:4, **I:5,** I:7, 58, **I:59,** I:60, 133–34, IV:196, 239–40, **VI:78,** VI:134–35, VII:151 (*See also* Lemuria (Mu))
   ~ Meruvian, I:3, **I:5, 59,** I:133, IV:196, 239, 249, VI:77, **VI:78,** VI:182, VII:151
   ~ Paradisian, I:4, **I:5, 59,** IV:239, **VI:78,** VII:151
   ~ Polarian ("archetypal race"), I:4, **I:5,** IV:239, **VI:78**
   ~ pre-Lemurian, I:4

~ and the problem of delusion, I:58, **I:59**
~ and yoga, IV:239–42, 249, 257, **VI:78**
Rosales, Mary, IX:11
Rosary, I:250, 260–61, V:179, 184–85, XI:206, XII:5–7, 85, 89, 116–17. *See also* ascension rosary; New Age Rosary; prayers
Rosicrucianism, V:241, 243
Roswell, New Mexico, I:247, IV:4–5, 17
Rothchild, Nathan Meyer, IX:168
Royal, Lyssa, IV:41–42, 69–71, 75, 83, 85, 97, 101, 107
Rubens, Peter Paul, I:121
rudraksha seeds, I:252
Rueckert, Carla, IV:93
Russak, Marie, V:219–21
Russia, V:180, IX:107, XII:57. *See also* Soviet Union
    ~ blocked grid point in, IV:61
    ~ and the feminine principle, VI:184
    ~ leadership role of, IX:243–44
    ~ and the rays, **VI:182,** VI:183

S

Sabda Brahma. *See* Vedas

sacred geometries, I:280, III:19, 55, 122–23, 205, IV:247, VI:66, 207, 213, VIII:55–56, X:227, XI:228
> ~ anchoring of, I:284, VI:115, X:225, XI:94

Sacred Paths, IV:247, 251

The Sacred Vesture, V:135. *See also* Orpheus

Saddharma Pundarika Sutra, V:100

Sadducees, I:171

sadhana (spiritual practice), V:50–51, 60, 67, VI:216, 232, VIII:2, 9, X:220

sadru (spiritual seeker), V:26

Sagittarius, I:205. *See also* astrology
> ~ and color healing, **IV:212**
> ~ and Jupiter, **XI:177**
> ~ and the second ray, **XI:177**

sahaj (the natural state of the soul), V:172

Sai Baba, Avatar, I:157, VIII:xix, xxv. *See also* Murphet, Howard

Sai Baba, Man of Miracles, I:157, VIII:xxv. *See also* Murphet, Howard

Saint Germain (ascended master), I:28, 78, 118, 138, 142, 172, 203, 237, III:46–48, 94–95, 131, **III:238,** IV:224, 285, 317, V:201, 230, 239, 241–44, **VI:3, 112,** VI:248, VII:18, 84, 112, VIII:42, 74–75, 123, 163, IX:9, 176, 274, X:25, 45, 71, 240–43, XI:20, 61, XII:117, XIII:11, 67. *See also* violet transmuting flame
> ~ ascension of, V:239–40, VI:6
> ~ ashram of, I:284, **VI:204,** VI:225, VIII:127
> ~ and the Atomic Accelerator, I:280, VI:37
> ~ as Chohan of the seventh ray, I:125, 192, 195–96, **I:199,** I:201, III:257, **IV:121,** V:239, VI:144, 163, 214, 241, **VII:19, 117,** X:14, 21, 25, 33, 42–43, 152, 240, XI:70–71
> ~ and the color violet, IV:207
> ~ divine mission of, X:43
> ~ and the I Am teachings, IV:317–21, XII:111–12
> ~ Lemurian ascension seat of, III:30

~ as the Mahachohan, I:192, **I:199,** I:201, **III:238,** V:239,
VI:3, VI:151, X:21, 33–34, 43–44, 46, XI:210, XII:78

~ other lives of, I:171, 237, 245, IV:290, V:239–43, VI:148,
VIII:163, 165, X:240, XIII:21

~ and Wesak, VI:151, X:152, XI:174, XII:78

Saint Mary Coptic Orthodox Church, V:187

saints, I:195, V:17, 168, 170, VIII:24, 166. *See also* individual saints

salamanders. *See* elementals: salamanders (nature spirits of fire)

Salem, Palestine. *See* Jerusalem

samadhi (enlightenment), IV:236, 256, 260, 266, V:7, 24, 28–29, 34,
42–43, 47, 83, 87, VI:157–59, 161–64, VII:34, 148. *See also* enlightenment; nirvana; wheel of rebirth: liberation from

~ isasam-prajnam, VI:160

~ and Mantra yoga, IV:245

~ nine stages of, VI:157–60

~ nirbikalpa, V:21, 24, 35, 64, VI:162–63

~ sabikalpa, VI:162–63

~ sahaja, VI:162

~ samprajna, VI:160

~ soruba, VI:162–63

samsara, V:12

samskaras, VI:160

Samuel (prophet), IV:285, 288, 290

~ as an incarnation of Saint Germain, I:237, IV:290, V:239,
VI:148

Sanaka Kumara, I:187, 189

Sananda, I:176, III:194, **III:238,** IV:57, **VI:3, 112, VII:19,**
VII:82, 111, 147, IX:2, 9, 262, X:30, 40, XI:1, 90, XIII:1, 67. *See*
also Jesus

~ ascension seat of, VI:32

~ ashram of, **VI:204,** VI:225, VIII:127

~ and the Atomic Accelerator, VI:37

~ as Chohan of the sixth ray, III:257, VI:144, 241, X:40–41,
152

~ divine mission of, X:40

~ and healing, X:141

~ necklace of rejuvenation of, XI:90

~ and Wesak, X:152

San Andreas fault, IX:104

Sanat Kumara (Planetary Logos), I:3, 6, 29, 32–33, 35, 39, 78, 162,
182, 185–90, 192, 195, **I:199,** I:201, 206, 208–9, 214, 216, 280,
282–83, III:3, 38, 46, 51, 56, 62, 77, 83–84, 100, 105, 116–17,
125, 128–29, 132, 148, 169, 172, 176, 180–82, 187, 195–96,
III:238, III:246, 255–56, 258, IV:51–52, 206–7, V:233, VI:1,
VI:3, VI:43, 73, 86, **VI:112,** VI:125, 149, 163, 207, 214, 222,

VII:19, 116, 121, 130, VIII:46, IX:7–9, 84, 97, 114, 179, 235–36,
X:34, XI:18, 30, 32, 48, 64–65, 68–69, 174, 226, 242. *See also*
Planetary Logos
    ~ and the ascension ceremony, I:29, III:4, XI:10–12, 86, 173,
      186
    ~ ascension of, I:278
    ~ ascension seat of, III:32, 44, 62
    ~ ashram of, IX:200
    ~ and building the light quotient, III:26
    ~ divine plan of, III:170
    ~ evolution of, I:178
    ~ Golden Medallions of, III:127
    ~ on group consciousness, III:111–15
    ~ and initiation, I:24–25, III:8, 10, 177, VI:144, XI:168
    ~ initiations of, I:178, 186, 205, III:11–12
    ~ and the kingdoms of Earth, III:116, 173
    ~ other lives of, IV:33
    ~ and the Path of Earth Service, III:168
    ~ and the Path of Training for Planetary Logos, III:172–73,
      175–77
    ~ and the Ray Path, III:179
    ~ and the rays, I:116, 126, **VI:179,** XI:45
    ~ and the Shamballa ascension seat, VI:32, 43
    ~ Shield of the Sun, III:122
    ~ and the six kumaras, I:185–88, 191, **I:199,** I:201, III:182,
      III:238, VI:3, IX:9
    ~ training of, I:177–83
    ~ and Vywamus, I:178, 188, 202, 207, III:52, 243, VI:243,
      XI:17, 164, 208
    ~ and Wesak, III:266, VI:125, IX:7, XI:174–75, XII:78
    ~ white ray of, **VI:41,** VIII:50
Sandalphon (archangel), I:217, 285, III:53, 200, **III:238,** III:257,
VI:3, VIII:40, 62, XI:26
    ~ and the Kabbalistic tree of life, **IV:304**
sandalwood, I:81, 252
San Damiano, Italy, V:186–87
San Francisco, California, V:37
sangha (spiritual community), V:96, VIII:160
Sanhedrin, IV:280
Sankaracharya (Sri Sankara), V:19–22, 64–65, VIII:166
    ~ and Integral yoga, IV:251
    ~ philosophy of, V:20–21
    ~ quotations from, V:21–22
Sankara, Sri. *See* Sankaracharya (Sri Sankara)
Sankey, Mikio, IX:10, 12, 16, 225

S

sankirtan, IV:249. *See also* devotional songs

sanobim, IV:125

Sanskrit, V:17, 19, 41, 48, 99

Santa Clara, California, V:37

sanyasin(i) (renunciate), IV:226, V:20, 24, 64–65, 85

Saqqara, IV:175

Sarada, Mother (the Holy Mother), V:27–31
    ~ quotations from, V:31–32

Saraswathi, Paramahansa Viswananda, V:64

Saraswati (Hindu goddess of wisdom), IV:219

sarcophagus, IV:179–81, 186, 189–90, VI:69

Sarvajit, V:164–65

sat (absolute existence), V:20

Satan, I:8, IV:273, V:160, 182, VI:58, **VI:179,** IX:53, 137

Satchidananda, Swami, V:64

satellites, I:246

Sathya Sai Baba (Cosmic Christ), I:147–57, 217, 240, 250, III:51, 55,
    130, 151, 182, 193–94, **III:238,** III:252–54, IV:149, 198, 220,
    223, 231, 255, 260, V:8–10, 37, 58, **VI:3,** VI:7, 14, 27, 69,
    VI:111, VI:114, 161, 218–19, VII:82, 148, VIII:9, 16, 68–69, 73,
    80, 92, 127–29, 131, 135, 165, 177–78, 187–92, vii, viii, ix, xiii,
    xiv, xv, xvii, xviii, xix, xx, xxi, xxii, xxiii, xxiv, xxv, xxvi, xxvii,
    IX:3–4, 93, 103, 262, XI:4, 17, 20, 26, 32, 36, 98, 104–6, 169–71,
    208, 219, 226, 238, 241–43, 249, 253, 267, XII:29, XIII:101, 110.
    See also Cosmic Christ; virbhuti ash
        ~ advanced abilities of, III:16, 41, IV:143, V:78, 125–26, 128,
            VI:12, 160, VIII:78, 183
        ~ ashram of, I:149–51, 153–54, III:130, IV:197, VI:124,
            VII:143, VIII:127, xviii, xix, xxiii, xxiv, xxvi, XI:30
        ~ birthday of, XII:77, 90
        ~ childhood stories of, I:148–49
        ~ current life of, I:76, 141–43, 150–54, 206, 215, 226, III:51,
            102, 242–43, IV:218, 227, VI:6, 208, 248, VII:16, 18,
            VIII:129, IX:114–16, 133, 143, 175, XIII:67
        ~ and the higher dimensions, III:148
        ~ light quotient level of, III:31, 241, VI:5, 17, 44, 207,
            VIII:128, XI:187
        ~ love seat of, III:130, VI:36, 124, VIII:41, XI:105
        ~ mantras of, I:163, 219–20, 255–56, VIII:101, XII:20–21, 110
        ~ miracles of, I:147, 150–55, IV:199, VII:54–55, VIII:xxi, xxii,
            xxiii, xxiv
        ~ other lives of, I:149, III:243, IV:194, 251, V:1, 8, 160, 163,
            VI:147, VIII:5–6, 165, xv, xx, X:74, 139
        ~ Sai Bita, IV:147

~ Sai Ram, I:156, V:9
~ sayings of, I:147, 155–56, 235, 253, 263–64, III:24, 60, 70–71, 88, 108, 242, IV:205, 242, 261, VI:23, 49, 66, 102, 218, VII:28, 63, 101, 140, VIII:19, 93, 95, 99, 126, xxv, IX:6, 39, 54, X:41, 108, 201, XI:35, XIII:7, 103, 115
~ teachings of, I:155–57, III:103, VI:104, 138, 216, VIII:2, 160, IX:150
~ and Wesak, VI:19, X:153, XI:174
~ and yoga, IV:241, 244–45, 249

Satir, Virginia, IX:27, XIII:136

Sat Nam (ruler of the Atma Lok dimension), **IV:196,** IV:197–98, V:168

satsang (company), I:272

sattva (rhythm or harmony), IV:256

Saturn
~ ascension seat of, VI:36
~ and color healing, **IV:212**
~ energy qualities of, I:96
~ and the Kabbalistic tree of life, **IV:302**
~ and the rays, **I:131**–32, **VI:83**

Saturnian Council, IV:93–94

Satyagraha, V:70–74, 76. *See also* Gandhi, Mahatma

satyrs, I:2, IV:122, 131, **IV:135.** *See also* devas; elementals: gnomes (nature spirits of earth); nature spirits

Schindler's List, VII:97

Schwarzenegger, Arnold, IX:93, 134

science, I:9, VI:40, IX:54–55, 61–62, 68, 78, 137, 165–66, X:38–39, 57
~ and the fifth ray, VI:188–89, X:20
~ and religion, VI:186, IX:136–37
~ tools for handling for the lightworker, IX:34–36

Science of Mind, VIII:78, 161

Scientology, IX:141

Scopes of Dimensions, III:140, 144, 146, 151, 153. *See also* McClure, Janet

Scorpio. *See also* astrology
~ and color healing, **IV:212**
~ and Darjeeling, India, **VI:185**

Scorpius, IV:87

Scotland, VII:109

sea maids, **IV:135.** *See also* devas; elementals: undines (nature spirits of water); nature spirits

seances, IV:165

Seattle, Washington, XI:205

S

Second Council of Constantinople, I:73, 174, IV:273

second ray (of Love/Wisdom), I:11, 116, 119–20, 126–28, 130, 132, **I:134,** I:166, 190, 192, **I:199,** I:201, III:108, 203, **III:238, IV:121, VI:3,** VI:35, 39, **VI:41,** VI:177, **VI:184,** VI:185–86, **VII:19, 117,** VIII:7, 49, IX:49–50, 185, **X:12,** X:13–14, 16–19, 21–23, 27, 30, 33, 91, 93, 141, XI:45, 70, **XI:75,** XI:111, 218. *See also* rays, seven; rays, twelve

~ and Apollo and Lumina, **I:203,** III:199

~ and Archangel Christine, **I:204, IV:123, VII:115,** X:94

~ and Archangel Jophiel, **I:204, IV:121, 123, VII:115,** X:94

~ and Brazil, VI:183, **VI:183**

~ and the Christ, **VI:179**

~ and color healing, **IV:210**

~ corresponding professions, **I:130**

~ and Darjeeling, India, **VI:185**

~ Djwhal Khul as Chohan, III:257, VI:241, **VII:19,** X:14, 32–33, 140

~ and the fifth ray, VI:189

~ and the fourth ray, VI:190

~ and Geneva, Switzerland, **VI:185**

~ glamour of, I:61–62, X:17

~ and the Goddess of Liberty, III:156

~ and Great Britain, **VI:182,** VI:183–84

~ and the heart chakra, **I:130**

~ and Jupiter, **XI:177**

~ and the Kabbalistic tree of life, **IV:311**

~ Kuthumi as Chohan, I:166, 190, **I:199,** I:201, III:67, 257, **IV:121,** VI:144, 163, 214, **VII:19, 117,** X:14, 30, 140, 149, 152, XI:45, 70–71, 111, 218

~ and the light quotient building program, I:283

~ and Lord Maitreya (Planetary Christ), I:190, 201, VI:184

~ and the monadic plane, **I:132**

~ and New Jerusalem, **VI:179**

~ and New York, NY, **VI:185**

~ and the Olympics, IX:249

~ and the planet Jupiter, **I:131, VI:82**

~ and the planet Mercury, **I:132**

~ qualities of, I:120, **I:129,** X:22–23

~ and Raja Yoga, **I:132**

~ as a ray of aspect, I:116, X:28

~ and the Ray Path, III:180

~ and Sagittarius, **XI:177**

~ and the seventh initiation, **XI:127**

~ and the Solar Logos (Helios), I:116–17, 120

~ and the Spiritual Hierarchy, VI:178, **VI:179**

~ and spiritual leadership, IX:2–3, 43, 51, 185

~ and the Sun, **I:131, VI:83**

~ and the Synthesis Ashram, VII:145, X:149

~ three-tier structure of, X:30

~ and the United States, **VI:182,** VI:183

~ and Wesak, VI:151, X:152, XII:78

~ in the world today, VI:178–79

The Secret Doctrine, IV:38, V:201, 208–11. *See also* Blavatsky, Madam

secret government, I:246, IV:3, 5, 10, 16, 77–78, VII:130–31, IX:45, 74, 130–31. *See also* extraterrestrials; Tesla, Nikola

~ and Agartha, IV:20–21

~ Alternative 1, IV:8

~ Alternative 2, IV:7–8

~ Alternative 3, IV:7–8, 18

~ and assassinations, IV:3, 9, 16

~ cover-ups of, IV:4–28, IX:104, 130, 162–63, 165–66

~ and depopulation, IV:8–9

~ and drugs, IV:4, 9, 17, IX:166

~ and the environment, IV:13

~ and human health, IV:12–14

~ and the media, IX:74

~ and negative extraterrestrials, IV:10, 16–17, VII:135, IX:162

~ solution to, IV:14

~ and a staged alien invasion, IV:15–16

The Secret Life of Plants, VII:119

Secret of the Siddhas, V:89. *See also* Muktananda, Baba

Secrets from the Lives of Trees, IV:153

Sedona, Arizona, III:35, 149

Sedona Journal of Emergence!, I:247, IV:16, IX:213, XI:177

Sedona Project, VIII:167–68

Seichim, III:107

Seles, Monica, IX:63

self-actualization, VIII:10, 22, 126, IX:55, 92, 96, 121, XIII:136, 162

~ at a monadic level, I:18, IX:94

~ at a personality level, I:18, IX:94

~ at a soul level, I:18, IX:94

self-hypnosis, IV:262, VIII:110–11, XII:103. *See also* hypnotism

self-inquiry, XI:36

self-integration, VII:158–65

selfishness, I:2, 25, 121, 124, 155, 169, 208, 222–23, 268, III:25, IV:3, 152, 228, 261, 275, V:117, 180, VI:101, 142, 173, 175, VII:140, VIII:15–16, IX:15, 95, 108, 243, X:16, 138, 216, XI:144, XIII:111, 142

~ transcendence of, I:220, 273, III:2, V:51, 67, 88, 105, 117, VIII:11, XIII:179

S

selflessness, I:120, 122, 155, V:71, 108, VI:169, 173, VIII:15–16, 156, IX:231, X:44, 138, 240, XIII:111, 142
~ and discipleship, VI:169–70
~ and spiritual leadership, IX:3–4

self-love, I:267, III:72, VII:40–42, 44–45, 158–59, VIII:105, 110, 124, 147–48, X:71, 86, 132, 196–200, 210, XIII:21–22, 30, 74, 146, 150, 175, 181. *See also* love
~ and the emotional body, X:199–200
~ and manifestation, VIII:83
~ and the mental body, X:201
~ and the physical body, X:198–99

self-mastery, I:23, 46, 64–65, 116, IV:139, 246, 255, 263, 266, V:70, VI:13, 23, 104–5, 110, 118, 122, 158, VII:4, 9, 24, 26, 62, 136, VIII:12, 44, 72, 82, IX:1, 5, 22, 75, 100, 139, 198, 219, 222, 225, 234, 236, X:42, 210, 212, XI:198, XIII:154

self-parenting, VI:100, 249, VIII:110–11, IX:4, XI:267, XIII:73–75, 79, 151, 153. *See also* inner child

self-realization, I:46, 100, 147–48, 264–65, IV:225, 232–36, 253, 256–57, 262–63, V:30–31, 51, 57–60, 63, 65–67, 69–70, 88–89, 110, VI:4, 60, 66, 99–105, 133, 158, 236–37, VII:21, 96, 148, VIII:78, 86, 110, 166, X:116, XI:42, 195, XII:123, XIII:114–15, 143

Self-Realization Fellowship, I:159–61, 163–65, V:39, 46, VI:247, VII:148, VIII:164, IX:54, 143, X:74, 139, XIII:132. *See also* Babaji, the Yogi Christ; Yogananda, Paramahansa
~ address of, I:165

self-worth, VIII:11

Senate Foreign Relations Committee, V:107

senses, inner, VIII:70

senses, physical, I:70, **I:71,** III:150, IV:165, 235, 240, **IV:267**–68, V:169, VI:51, VII:1, IX:62
~ hearing, **IV:267**
~ and science, IX:54, 136
~ sight, **IV:267**–68
~ smell, **IV:267**–68
~ and soul travel, IV:200
~ taste, **IV:267**–68
~ touch/feeling, **IV:267**

separateness, I:2, 46, 117, 155, 206, 220, 222–23, 278, III:25, 89, IV:46, 233, 235–36, 261, V:20, 52, 89, 95, 250, VI:66, 97, 101–2, 104, 156, 173–74, 193, 216, 218–19, 244, VII:92, 140, VIII:76, 113, 154, X:111, 114, 116, 118, 123, 145, 149, 218–19, XI:37, 144

seraphim (heavenly counselors), I:233, III:199, 231, **IV:123,** IV:125. *See also* angelic kingdom
~ cosmic hierarchy of, IV:126, **IV:127**–28

~ and the Kabbalistic tree of life, **IV:304**
~ twelve master seraphim, IV:125–26

Serapis Bey (ascended master), I:30, 37, 193, III:38, 48, 56, 131, **III:238,** IV:224, **VI:3, 112,** VII:116, IX:9, X:33, 35, XI:129–30
~ ascension retreat of, V:214
~ ashram of, I:284, **VI:204,** VI:225
~ as Chohan of the third ray, I:191–93, **I:199,** I:201, III:257, **IV:121,** VI:144, 163, 214, 241, **VII:19,** VII:116, **VII:117,** X:14, 33–34, 152–53, XI:70–71
~ divine mission of, X:33–34
~ Luxor ascension retreat of, I:30–31, 36, 279, III:25, 32, 43, 56, VI:32–33, VIII:126, X:34, XI:27, 29, 31
~ and Wesak, X:152–53

Sermon on the Mount, V:75

service work, I:39, 46, 111, 128, 266, 269–70, 277, III:60, 129, 265, IV:197, 227, **IV:267,** V:8, 51, 66, VI:12–13, 17, 20, 22, 28–29, 56, 69, 84, 108–10, 114, 133–34, 141, 202, 207, 209, 233, 235, 245, VII:9–10, 19, 23, 33, 35, 139, VIII:16–19, 23, 25, 64, 82, 86, 94, 110, 126, 129, 156, IX:129, 199, 205, 210–13, X:1, 12, 16, 23, 46–47, 49–50, 54–55, 59, 69, 76, 80, 82–84, 112, 114–15, 118–19, 121, 128, 163, 171, 186, 195, 197, 216, 218, 228–29, XII:123, XIII:103
~ and ascension, III:205, IX:199, 234, XI:186, 190–91
~ and ascension lineage, X:141–42
~ and building the light quotient, III:24
~ and discipleship, I:112, VI:168–69, 172–74
~ global, III:67–68, 129, VI:107–9, 232, VIII:20, 129, X:52, 168, 193, 241, XI:206–7, XII:56–76
~ and group monadic mates, XIII:60
~ on the inner plane, VIII:183
~ between lives, I:90, 102
~ misconceptions about, X:82–83
~ of monadic mission mates, XIII:59
~ and occupations, IX:50, X:215, 217
~ and the rays, VI:187, 191
~ and romantic relationships, X:138, XIII:15
~ and the second initiation, VII:26
~ and spiritual evolution, III:86, IX:12
~ and yoga, I:163, IV:241–42

Serving Humanity, VI:149, 155, XII:88. *See also* Bailey, Alice A.

Set, IV:188. *See also* Egypt

Seth, VIII:167, XI:28

Sethi, V.F., V:165–66, 168

seva (selfless service), V:82

S

seven-body system, III:21, VI:203. *See also* five-body system; four-body system; nine-body system; twelve-body system

Seven Rishis of the Great Bear, **I:184**

Seven Sisters. *See* Pleiades, the (seven sisters)

Seventeen Point Agreement, V:107

seventh-dimensional frequency, IV:65

Seventh Heaven, V:160

seventh ray (of Ceremonial Order and Magic), I:116, 123–26, 128, 132, **I:135,** I:192–93, 195–96, III:104, 108, 203, **III:238, IV:121,** V:239, **VI:3,** VI:39–40, **VI:41,** VI:177, **VI:184,** VI:185–87, **VII:19, 117,** IX:114, 132, 169, 185, 245, X:13, **X:13,** X:17, 20–21, 24–25, 30, 42, 44–46, 93, 120, 164, 226, 228, 241–43, XI:70, **XI:76,** XI:111. *See also* rays, seven; rays, twelve
   ~ and the Age of Aquarius, X:83
   ~ and Archangel Amethyst, **I:204, IV:124, VII:115,** X:95
   ~ and Archangel Zadkiel, **I:204, IV:121, 124, VII:115,** X:95
   ~ and Arcturus and Victoria, **I:203,** III:200
   ~ and Atlantis, VI:182
   ~ and the business world, IX:50–51
   ~ and ceremony, **I:133**
   ~ and color healing, **IV:210**
   ~ corresponding professions, **I:130**
   ~ and the Earth, IX:38, **XI:177**
   ~ and Earth's kingdoms, VI:186
   ~ and the first initiation, VI:187, **XI:127**
   ~ glamour of, I:63, X:20–21
   ~ and the Kabbalistic tree of life, **IV:311**
   ~ and London, England, **VI:185**
   ~ and the New Age, I:195–96, X:20
   ~ and the Olympics, IX:249
   ~ and the physical plane, **I:132**
   ~ and the planet Jupiter, **I:133**
   ~ and the planet Uranus, **I:131, VI:83**
   ~ and Portia, Goddess of Justice, III:156
   ~ qualities of, I:125, **I:129,** X:25
   ~ as a ray of attribute, I:116, X:28
   ~ and Russia, **VI:182,** VI:183
   ~ and the sacral center, **I:130**
   ~ Saint Germain as Chohan, I:125, 192, 195–96, **I:199,** I:201, III:257, **IV:121,** V:239, VI:144, 163, 214, 241, **VII:19, 117,** X:14, 21, 25, 33, 42–43, 152, 240, XI:70–71
   ~ and Spain, **VI:183**
   ~ and spiritual leadership, I:192, IX:43, 185
   ~ and the Synthesis Ashram, VII:145
   ~ and Taurus, **XI:177**

~ and Wesak, X:153

~ in the world today, VI:180–82, 184, 210, X:45

seventh seal, XI:83–84

Severus, Emporer Alexander, V:175

sex, XIII:39, 45–46, 48, 61, 149, 180–81. *See also* sexuality

~ abstinence from, XIII:126

~ and ascended masters, XIII:68

~ on the astral plane, XIII:61–62

~ on the atmic plane, XIII:64–65

~ on the Buddhic plane, XIII:64

~ on the causal plane, XIII:64

~ and the emotional body, XIII:39, 41, 44, 47, 170

~ and the etheric body, XIII:170

~ on the inner plane, XIII:60–61

~ on the logoic plane, XIII:65

~ and the media, IX:73–74, 138–39

~ ménage à trois, XIII:124–25

~ and the mental body, XIII:39, 41–44, 47, 170

~ on the mental plane, XIII:62–63

~ on the monadic plane, XIII:64–65

~ and the physical body, XIII:39–40, 44–45, 47, 170

~ premarital, XIII:124, 126

~ and the second chakra, XIII:98

~ and the spiritual body, XIII:39, 44, 47, 170

~ as a weapon, XIII:23

sexual fantasy, XIII:42–44, 149

~ outside a commited relationship, XIII:119–21

sexual harassment, IX:122–23

sexuality, I:269–70, VI:4, VIII:9, 12–13, 20, 110, 114, 134, IX:18, 122, 155, XII:101, XIII:39–40, 43, 118, 120, 140–41, 151, 162–63, 170, 177. *See also* sex

~ of ascended masters, XI:112

~ and the four-body system, XIII:39, 44, 46–47

~ and the lightworker, XIII:46–47

~ lower-self *vs.* higher-self, XIII:43, 180

~ male/female needs, XIII:39–40, 44–45, 141, 180–81

~ in marriage/committed relationships, XIII:96–98, 140–41, 167–68, 171–72, 180–81

~ and the negative ego, XIII:43–44, 122–23, 125, 130, 180

~ physical attraction, XIII:40, 166–67

~ and STDs and AIDS, XIII:129–32

~ tantric, IV:246–47, V:24, VIII:12, 114, XIII:23, 97, 141, 177

Shabd (the holy word or sound), V:168–70

shadow body, IV:159–61, 163–65

Sha, Jahan Gasht, V:165

S

Shakespeare, William, VII:97, IX:28
   ~ quotations from, III:118, VI:227, IX:181, X:15, 56, XIII:21
   ~ and Saint Germain, V:239–41, 243, VI:148, XIII:21
Shakti, V:99
Shakti energy, I:150, IV:218–19, V:1, 8, VIII:vii, xiii, xiv, xx, XIII:57, 100
shaktipat, V:85, XIII:108
Shakyamuni, Buddha, V:113
Shamballa, I:29, 40–41, 45, 143, 182, 185–86, 232, III:10, 62, 101, 125, 175–76, IV:19, 23, 26, V:95, **VI:41,** VI:43, 74, 155, 168, 175, 185, 194, 204, 208–9, VII:133, VIII:54, 107, 127, IX:220, **XI:127,** XII:87
   ~ ascension seat in, I:279, III:21, 30, 32, 44, 46, 85, 135, 187, VI:32, 43–44
   ~ council chamber at, III:173, VIII:126
   ~ and the Great White Lodge on Sirius, III:178–79
   ~ and Lhasa, Tibet, IV:19–20
   ~ and the rays, I:195, VI:178, **VI:179,** VI:191
   ~ and the seventh initiation, I:277–78, III:8, 10, 177
   ~ and Wesak, XI:175
   ~ and will, I:186, XII:87
Shambhavimudra, IV:247
Shan [Earth], IV:56
Shang-ti, V:118
Shankara, IV:247
   ~ as a walk-in, IV:31
Shankaracharya, I:160
shapeshifting, III:41. *See also* ascended masters: advanced abilities of
Shasta, Mount, III:35, V:242, VI:29, 151, 154, 242, IX:94, XI:207
   ~ ascension seat at, I:279, III:25, 32, 43–44, 94, VI:32–33, VIII:41, XI:26–27
   ~ and Telos (underground city), I:36, 230, 237, III:25, 32, 43, IV:24, 26, VI:32, XI:27–28
Shekinah (Holy Spirit), III:220, 222, 224, 226, VIII:61, XI:195
Shiites. *See* Islam
Shingwa (underground city), IV:26
Shintoism, IV:325–26
Shirdi, India, V:1
Shirdi Sai Baba, I:149–50, IV:260, V:1–2, 8, 163, VI:147, VIII:189, xv, xx, X:74, 139, XII:116. *See also* Sathya Sai Baba (Cosmic Christ)
   ~ miracles of, V:2–7, VIII:5
Shiva, I:142, 153, 256, IV:217–18, 221–22, 250, V:8–9, 85–90, VIII:190, xx, IX:240, X:71, XII:21, 119

Shiva Babaji. *See* Babaji, the Yogi Christ

Shiva energy, I:150, V:1, 8, VI:223, VIII:vii, xiii, xiv, xx, XIII:57, 100

Shonshe (underground city), IV:26

Shree Shree Anandamayee Charitable Society, V:52

Siberia, III:149, XI:205

Siddhaloka, V:88

Siddha path. *See* yoga: Siddha yoga

Siddharudha Swami, V:85

siddhis (powers), IV:269, VIII:188, IX:129

Sightings, VI:127

Sikhism, IV:249, V:160–61. *See also* Hinduism; Islam

Sikhs, IV:197
        ~ mantras of, I:257, XII:21

silver cord, I:43–44, 51, III:23, 91, IV:159. *See also* life thread;
    sutratma
        ~ during the physical death process, I:77, 81, 83
        ~ and the soul, I:113, VII:8

Simonton, Carl, VIII:88

Simpson, Nicole Brown, IX:156

Simpson, O.J., IX:36, 63–64, 67, 74, 130, 156–61

simran (repeating the name of God), V:170. *See also* chanting: repeti-
    tion of the name of God; mantras

sin, I:272, IV:272
        ~ and Hinduism, IV:221
        ~ and the Huna teachings, IV:162

Sinai, Mount, IV:278–79, 288, 317

Singh, Govind (the tenth Guru), V:161

singing waters, I:99–100

Sinnett, A.P., V:206–7, 214, 219, 224

Sirian Brotherhood, VII:32

Sirian Lodge. *See* Sirius

Sirians, IV:69–70, 83, VII:133, XI:205. *See also* extraterrestrials

Sirius, I:242, III:176–79, 183, **IV:33**, IV:38, 69–70, 99, 168–69,
    VI:41, VI:43, 53, 125, XI:41
        ~ higher university on, I:41, 282, III:61, 83, 101, 147, 176–78,
            IV:69–70, XI:41, 91
        ~ initiations on, III:178
        ~ light information packets from, III:61, 100–101, 176, VIII:54

Sirius, inner-plane. *See* Great White Lodge; Sirius

The Sirius Mystery, IV:69–70

Sistine Chapel, III:148, VII:97, IX:52

Sita (Rama's wife), IV:219, V:10–11, 24, 99, VIII:160

S

Siva (God), V:37–38

Sivaguru. *See* Sankaracharya (Sri Sankara)

Sivananda Ayurvedic Pharmacy, V:65

Sivananda Eye Hospital, V:65

Sivananda General Hospital, V:65

Sivananda, Swami, IV:239–40, V:63–66, VIII:165–66
    ~ ashram of, V:65
    ~ and the Divine Life Society, V:64–66
    ~ mantras of, I:256, XII:21
    ~ quotations from, IV:239
    ~ teachings of, V:65–67

six enemies of man, the, V:8

sixth ray (of Abstract Idealism or Devotion), I:116, 123–24, 127–28, 132, **I:132, 134,** I:192–95, **I:199,** I:201, III:104, 156, 203, **III:238, IV:121,** V:239, **VI:3,** VI:39–40, **VI:41,** VI:177, **VI:184,** VI:185–88, **VII:19,** VII:79, **VII:117,** VII:156, IX:38, 114, 132, 169, 185, 249, **X:12,** X:13, 19–20, 24–25, 30, 40–42, 45, 120, 141, XI:70, **XI:75,** XI:111. *See also* rays, seven; rays, twelve
    ~ and Archangel Aurora, **I:204, IV:124, VII:115,** X:95
    ~ and Archangel Uriel, **I:204, IV:121, 124, VII:115,** X:95
    ~ and the Aryan race, VI:180
    ~ and the astral plane, **I:132**
    ~ and Bhakti Yoga, **I:133**
    ~ and Cancer, **XI:177**
    ~ and color healing, **IV:210**
    ~ corresponding professions, **I:130**
    ~ glamour of, I:62–63, X:20
    ~ and Italy, **VI:182**
    ~ Jesus as Chohan, I:192, 194–95, **I:199,** I:201, III:48, 257, **IV:121,** VI:163, 214, **VII:19,** VII:79, **VII:117,** XI:70–71
    ~ and the Kabbalistic tree of life, **IV:311**
    ~ and the Moon, **XI:177**
    ~ and Peace and Aloha, **I:203,** III:200
    ~ and the Piscean Age, X:83
    ~ and the planet Mars, **I:131, 133, VI:83**
    ~ and the planet Neptune, **I:131, VI:83**
    ~ qualities of, I:124, **I:129,** I:195, X:24–25
    ~ as a ray of attribute, I:116, X:28
    ~ and Russia, **VI:182,** VI:183
    ~ Sananda as Chohan, III:257, VI:144, 241, X:40–41, 152
    ~ and the second initiation, VI:188, **XI:127**
    ~ and the solar plexus, **I:130**
    ~ and Spain, **VI:183**
    ~ and spiritual leadership, I:192, 194, IX:43, 185
    ~ and the Synthesis Ashram, VII:145

~ and Tokyo, Japan, **VI:185**
~ and the United States, **VI:182,** VI:183
~ and Wesak, X:153
~ in the world today, VI:180–82, 210

60 Minutes, VIII:157, IX:76, 89

Skarin, Analee, I:31–32, VIII:167

sleep state, I:33, 35, 76, 91, 251, 269, III:128, 146, 189, 197, 202, 205, VI:69, 71, 94, 236, 244, VII:8, 35–36, 84, VIII:69, 106, 185, XI:4. *See also* dreams; dream state
~ and the dimensions, III:143–44, 147
~ and physical death, I:74, 98
~ and the Synthesis Ashram, VII:144
~ and the university at Sirius, III:176–77

Smith, Joseph, V:197–99

"smoky god," IV:22. *See also* Sun, inner

The Smoky God, IV:22–23

The Society of Friends of Space, IV:43

Society of Psychical Research, V:209–10

Society of Rosicrusse Freemasons, V:241

sociology, IX:53

Socrates, V:148, 150

So Hang (ruler of the etheric plane), **IV:195,** IV:197

Solara, I:233, VIII:166

solar activation, VI:51–52

solar actualization, IX:121

solar body (10th), **III:238,** III:240, 254, **VI:3,** VI:12, 34, 51–52, 87, 194, 203, 206, XI:28, 136, 150
~ anchoring of, VI:13–14, 19, 23, 44, 52, **VI:62,** VI:117, XI:120, 148, 154, 187, 192, 252
~ and the tenth dimension, **VI:204**

Solar Core, I:206, III:44, 187, **VI:41,** VI:52
~ ascension seat in, III:32, 44, 258, VI:32, 43, 115, XI:59

Solar Councils, I:188

Solar Hierarchy, I:187, 189, 192

Solar Logos, I:40, 126, 181, 187, 192, **I:199,** I:201–2, 212, **III:238,** IV:129, 206–7, 315, **VI:3,** VI:77, 230, VII:19, X:52, 236. *See also* Helios (Solar Logos); Vesta
~ ashram of, VI:225
~ causal body of, **I:184**
~ cosmic evolution of, I:183, **I:184**
~ and the second ray, I:116–17, 120
~ seed packets of, VIII:179
~ training of, III:180–82

S

solar monadic group, III:256

solar plane, VI:206

solar spirits, **IV:130**

solar system (Earth's), I:246, III:177, 182, IV:2, VI:77, VII:39,
X:91–92. *See also* individual planets
>   ~ chakras of, XI:42
>   ~ energy qualities of, I:94
>   ~ evolution of, I:202
>   ~ and the rays, I:130–31, VI:82, **VI:82,** VI:83, **VI:83,** VI:188
>   ~ and the second ray, VI:177, X:14, 17, 21, 212
>   ~ seven planes/dimensions of, I:16–17

solar systems
>   ~ fourth, VI:72
>   ~ and the occult century, **I:11, VI:68,** VI:81
>   ~ and the rays, I:130–31
>   ~ third, VI:72

Solomon, King, IV:288

Solomon, Paul, I:9, 142, 236, 241, 243, 245, 251, III:155, IV:120,
157, 167, 199, 202, V:156, VI:49, VIII:21, 68, 93, 100, 117,
IX:110, XI:86

Soltec, III:28

Son of the Morning, **VI:179**

Son principle, I:17

Sons of Belial, I:8–9, IV:23, 41, 59–60, 169, 172–73, VI:178, XI:154.
See also Dark Brotherhood
>   ~ and pseudo-crystals, IV:59–60

sons of fire, VII:130

Soruba Samadhi, I:160. *See also* ascension

Soubirous, Bernadette, V:179

soul, I:17, 38, 50, 53–54, 66, 90, 106–8, 110–11, 189, 211, 213–14,
221, 224, III:23, 28, 104, 126, **III:238,** IV:61, 119, 163, 175,
207, 292, V:11–12, 17, 20–22, 127, 149, 175, VI:1, **VI:3,** VI:57,
61, 75, 103–4, 121, 167, 181, 186, 199, 218, 220, 222, 228, 244,
VII:1, 4, 6, 8, 10, 21–22, 25, 27, 30, 32, 64, 82, 120, VIII:44, 93,
IX:52, 55, 79, 81, 91–92, 97, 100, 108, 121, 136, 149, 221, 264,
X:1–2, 4, 7, 55–57, 73, 75, 80–82, 84–85, 108–10, 114, 133–34,
149, 154, 157, 198–99, 201, 211, 222, 227, 232, 234, 244, XI:157,
XII:97, XIII:55–56. *See also* higher mind; higher self;
superconscious mind
>   ~ and abortion, IX:96, XIII:77–78
>   ~ anchoring of, I:17–18, VIII:47, IX:78
>   ~ from another planet, I:134, VI:134–35
>   ~ and the antakarana, I:43–47, 110, 212, 271, VI:170, VIII:39
>   ~ Aryan, VI:135

~ and ascension, I:28–29, VI:7, 216, VII:24

~ Atlantean, I:134, VI:134–35

~ attunement to, **I:5,** I:56, III:153, VI:4, **VI:78,** VI:172, X:70–72

~ in Baha'i, IV:329

~ on the buddhic realm, VII:11–12

~ characteristics of, **I:106,** I:108

~ and childbirth, IX:96, XIII:82–83

~ creation of, I:13, 47

~ and death, I:73–74, 76

~ and discipleship, I:112, VI:172–75

~ evolution of, I:15, 92, 107, 109, 112, VI:67, 69, VII:12, 14, 22, VIII:47–48, XI:29

~ five groups of, I:133–34, VI:134–35

~ in Hinduism, IV:219

~ and initiation, I:23–25, 200, IV:181, 189–91

~ as intermediary/guide between the personality and monad, I:105, 200, 212, III:2, VI:9, X:146

~ and the Kabbalistic tree of life, IV:300–301

~ Lemurian, I:134, VI:134–35

~ between lives, I:90–91

~ and the monad, I:13–14, 105–6, 110

~ Moon-chain, I:134, VI:134–35

~ and the Paradisian root race, **VI:78**

~ and the personality, I:13–14, 105–6, 109, 112, 200, III:2

~ and the prebirth bardo experience, I:91–92

~ and the rays, VI:187–88, X:16, 25

~ rehabilitation of, I:93, IX:71

~ and relationships, I:110, XII:102, XIII:4–5

~ and soul extensions, I:11, 13–15, III:243, VI:113, 136, 166, XI:28

~ souls awaiting incarnations, I:134, VI:135

~ and the Spiritual Hierarchy, I:45, 108–9

~ spiritual impressions from, I:113

~ three aspects of, I:17–18

~ and walk-ins, IV:29–32, X:147

soul actualization, IX:121

soul body, I:21, 200, IV:130, VI:18, 71, VII:5, XI:32. *See also* causal body

~ and the fourth initiation, I:24, 44, 74, 105, 108, 110, 200, III:2

~ during soul travel, IV:194, 197–99

soul braid, VI:53, 89, 136, VIII:48

soul, cosmic, VI:8

soul extensions, I:11, 13, 15, 45–46, 51, 68, 80, 181, 198, 223, III:39–40, 53, 219, VI:64, 68, 87–88, 90, 136, 166, 238,

S

VIII:48–49, 181–82, IX:21, 178, X:186, XI:28–29, 194, XIII:56, 92, 165. *See also* personality
~ and ascension, I:28–30, 37
~ clearing and integration of, I:17, III:218, VI:65, 85–86, 91–98, 238, VIII:47, XII:130
~ creation of, I:13–14, 47
~ evolution of, I:15, 74, 109
~ and the four-body system, I:18
~ between lives, I:87–103
~ and physical death, I:74–76, 78–83, 85
~ and the rays, I:116–18, 126
~ and the soul, I:13–14, 200
~ and walk-ins, IV:29–32, VI:89

soul family, I:14, VI:64, 88, 92, VII:5, 26–27, VIII:47, XIII:56. *See also* oversoul

soul fragments, VIII:48

soul group, X:71–72

soul infusion, III:2. *See also* initiation: third

soul liberation, V:169

soul mates, IV:187, VIII:134, XIII:56–58, 147, 165. *See also* relationships, romantic; twin souls (flames)
~ karma of, X:138–39
~ search for, XIII:55–56, 141

soul merge, I:23, 32, 64, 66, 106, 121, 126, 200, 211, 265, 271, III:2–3, 146, **III:238,** IV:269, **VI:3,** VI:8, 56, 59, 77, 82, 188–89, 222, VII:25, 27, 31, X:13, 186, 229, XI:227. *See also* initiation: third; merging
~ and fundamentalist Christians, VI:130
~ and spiritual leadership, IX:183–84

soul plane, IV:193, 197

soul ray, I:116–18, VI:186–87, IX:200, X:11–13, 25, 127, 140. *See also* rays, seven: configuration of
~ of cities, I:118, VI:185
~ of countries, I:118, VI:182, **VI:182,** VI:183, **VI:183,** VI:184
~ of humanity, **VI:184**
~ of organizations, I:118

soul-realization, I:66, IV:255, 257, 262–63, V:94

soul star, I:50–51, **I:52,** I:53–55

soul travel, I:37, 271, 290, III:41–43, 146, IV:187, 193–99, 287, V:88, 163, 168, VI:80, 118, VIII:60, 106–7, 167, XI:28–29, XII:119. *See also* ascended masters: advanced abilities of; astral travel
~ and the Ataiens, IV:102
~ and color, **IV:195**–96

~ mantras for, **IV:195,** IV:196, **IV:196**
~ potential dangers of, IV:198–99
~ and Rebazar Tarz, IV:197
~ and sound, **IV:195,** IV:196, **IV:196,** IV:198
~ techniques for, IV:198–203

sound, I:8, 242, III:172–73, IV:89, 140, 249, V:88, 169, VIII:80, 96, IX:60, 260. *See also* chanting; mantras; music; words of power
~ and building the light quotient, III:24
~ channeling of, III:192
~ and color, **IV:208,** X:36
~ and dimensions, **IV:195,** IV:196, **IV:196,** IV:197, 249
~ of flowers, IV:140
~ and healing, I:246, 250, IV:205, **IV:208,** VII:105, 107–8, X:36–37, 39, XII:107
~ and the Path of Training for Planetary Logos, III:173
~ and soul travel, **IV:195**–96, IV:198
~ and world service, III:68, VIII:20

Source, I:7, 11, 202–3, 212–13, 234, III:23, 91, **III:238,** III:242, 256, IV:206, V:36, 78, 156, VI:2, **VI:3,** VI:23, 41, 50, 59, 65, 72, 84, 96–97, 213, VIII:40, 184, X:40, 42, 99, 135, 140, 143, 152, 211, 222, 237, XI:17, XIII:10, 64–65
~ ascension seat of, VI:35, 37
~ attunement to, I:234, X:219
~ merger with another Source, III:144
~ merging with, VI:69, X:236
~ will aspect of, I:209

Source, multiuniversal, VI:75

Source of our Cosmic Day, III:143–45, 201, 243, VI:2, 6, 9, 34, 44, 75–77, 79–80, **VI:116,** VI:127, VIII:65, XI:106

South Africa, V:69, 71, 74, XI:116. *See also* apartheid
~ blocked grid point in, IV:61
~ end of apartheid in, III:141
~ rods of power in, I:206

South America, IV:60, 93, 152, 169, VIII:148, XI:207
~ vortexes of, III:149

South Pole
~ as an entrance to the inner Earth, IV:20–22, 24, VII:133
~ blocked grid point in, IV:61
~ vortexes of, III:149

Soviet Union, I:224, 240, III:141, IV:13–14, VI:6, IX:106, 131, 133, 244, XI:116. *See also* Russia
~ and the Ashtar Command, IV:57
~ entrance to the inner Earth in, IV:25
~ and extraterrestrials, IV:5, 7–8
~ leadership role of, IX:243
~ and religion, I:240

Soylent Green, IX:122

space, I:224, IV:113–14, VI:74

spacecraft, I:7, 243, 246, IV:5, 7, 11, 15, VII:132, IX:130, 162. *See also* extraterrestrials; UFOs
   ~ of the Arcturians, III:25, 27, 43, IV:64, 66–67, VI:212–13, 231, VII:132, VIII:28, IX:224, XI:28, 205, 239
   ~ of the Ashtar Command, III:25, 30, 189–90, IV:55, 57, 59, VI:32, XI:205
   ~ of the Cessnans, IV:81
   ~ of the Grays, IV:75, VI:71
   ~ of the Iargans, IV:46
   ~ of the Kantarians, IV:70
   ~ of the Martians, IV:48
   ~ of negative extraterrestrials, IV:3, 58
   ~ of the Pleiadians, IV:36–37, XI:205
   ~ of the Sirians, XI:205
   ~ of the Ummites, IV:44
   ~ of the Venusians, IV:51–53

space, outer
   ~ four levels of, VI:74

space-time continuum, IV:44, X:230

Spain, IV:43–44, V:188–89
   ~ and the rays, **VI:183**

Spalding, Baird, VIII:163

Spangler, David, III:119, IV:132

Spenser, Edmund, V:240

Sphinx, I:142, IV:170, 189, X:93, 227. *See also* Egypt; Great Pyramid; Hall of Records
   ~ building of, IV:169, 171, 173–74

Spiderman, IX:134

spirit, I:13, 105, 200, 211, 221, 224–25, III:2–3, IV:64, 155, 191, 257, 270, V:126, VI:57, 89, 139–40, 166, 172, 174, 181, 186, 189–90, 203, VII:1, 4, 6, 31, IX:149, X:34, 55, 57, 71–72, 77, 81–85, 88, 104–5, 108–9, 157, 199, 206, 215, 217, 219–20, 222, 227, 236. *See also* I Am Presence; monad

spirit actualization, IX:121

spirit guides, I:91, 97–98, IV:29, V:202, IX:52
   ~ and walk-ins, IV:30–31

Spirit of Peace and Equilibrium, I:141–42, 211

spirit travel, VI:80

spiritual alignment, I:36

spiritual body, I:1, 28, 30, 63, 213, 251, III:59–60, 142, **III:238,** III:239, IV:183, 241, **VI:3,** VI:61–62, 135, 194, 203, 212, X:113, 120, 129. *See also* four-body system

~ appearance of, XIII:8

~ clearing and mastery of, I:163, III:201, VI:45, 194, VIII:31

~ and color, IV:207

~ during dream time, IV:193

~ and the etheric nervous system, III:21

~ and integrating soul extensions, VI:93–94

~ light quotient of, VI:4

~ nine bodies of, III:239–40

~ and physical death, I:74, 84–85

~ and sex, XIII:39, 44, 47, 170

spiritual government, I:30, 138, 182, 185–86, 192–94, 275, III:197, V:239, VI:224, VII:17, 149. *See also* Great White Brotherhood of the Spiritual Hierarchy; Spiritual Hierarchy

~ hierarchy of, I:189–91, 200–201, 205–6, IX:9

spiritual harvesting, I:29, 146. *See also* ascension: mass

Spiritual Hierarchy, I:16–17, 23–24, 27, 29–30, 79, 133, 142, 145–46, 185–87, 191, 197, 200–201, 205, III:3, 10, 84, 128, 148, 176, 196–97, IV:51, 58, 121, 283, V:72, 201, 223, VI:43, 114, 133, 154–55, 168, 171, 175, 178, 185, 208, VII:15–19, 35–36, 90, 136, VIII:155, IX:146, 175, 178–79, 192, 194, X:6, 16, 41–42, 71, 179, 246, XI:41, 48, 52–53, 64–65, 71, **XI:127,** XI:174, 186, 197, XII:79–80, 88, 104. *See also* Great White Brotherhood of the Spiritual Hierarchy; spiritual government

~ and the Arcturians, III:26, 77

~ and the core fear matrix removal program, I:281, III:69–70, 72

~ externalization of, I:56, 137–46, 215–16, 225–26, 228, 233, 240, III:194, IV:10, V:213, 221, VI:6, 27, 29, 149–50, 174, 223–26, VIII:92, IX:43, 114–15, 133, 174, 219–20, X:160, XI:71 (*See also* New Group of World Servers)

~ goals of, VI:56, VII:146

~ holy days of, I:283, III:29, VI:149–56, VIII:138–39, XI:175, 228, XII:77–91

~ Kuthumi as future head of, I:146, 243, III:197

~ Lord Maitreya as head of, I:137, 139, 147, 170, III:2, 176, IV:223, VI:9, 114, 150, VIII:xvii

~ "Manual on Death," I:79

~ merging with, VIII:122

~ and the rays, VI:178, **VI:179,** VI:190, X:18

~ and the soul, I:108–9, 111

~ spiritual leadership in, IX:9–10

~ structure of, VII:19–20

~ three types of hierarchical workers, I:108–9

~ and war, IX:99–100

spiritual integration, I:36

spiritual masters. *See* ascended masters

spiritual mind, III:23

spiritual path, I:17, 51, 61, 112, 117, 263–65, 268, 275, III:1, 85, 87–88, 97, 107, 121, 126, 139, 151, 205–6, IV:105, 193, 241, 250, 259–60, 265, 268, 273, 312, V:83, 90, 125, 130, 167, VI:13, 36, 60, 85, 104, 117–18, 142–43, 173, 197–98, 200, 203, 219–20, 222–23, 237, 245, VII:29, 145–49, VIII:3, 11–12, 14–15, 19–22, 24–25, 35, 40, 44, 79–81, 86, 103, 105, 124, 131, 137, 149, 154–55, 159–61, 188, xvii, IX:6, 20, 39, 46, 100, 113, 118, 129, 136, 190, 211, 222, 277, X:52, 57, 82–83, 109, 118, 121, 128, 174, 177, 196, 198, 200, 206, 212, 217, 219, XI:36, 158, 200, 209, XIII:31–32, 48, 85, 116, 139, 142, 162, 180. *See also* dharma (life path)
    ~ loneliness on, VI:123–24, VIII:124
    ~ and mystic vision, III:95–97, VIII:135, XI:148–49
    ~ and occultist vision, III:95–97, VIII:135, XI:148–49
    ~ path of discipleship, VI:175
    ~ path of evolution and probation, VI:175
    ~ path of initiation, VI:175
    ~ tests of, VIII:131, IX:4, 25, XII:121–22
    ~ three stages of, I:18–19, 264, 275, VI:175
    ~ universality of, IX:17
spiritual plane, I:16, **I:184,** VI:218, IX:114. *See also* atmic plane
spiritual realization, VI:99
The Spiritual Science of Kriya Yoga, VI:164
The Spiritual Teaching of Ramana Maharshi, V:59–60. *See also* Maharshi, Ramana
spiritual triad, I:25, 77, 109–10, 112–13, **I:184,** I:223, 271, III:63, 81, 175, **III:238,** IV:300–301, **VI:3,** VI:188, VII:54, VIII:133. *See also* higher mind; intuition; will: spiritual
    ~ and the antakarana, I:43–48
spiritual world, I:90, 93, 99–102, 270, V:111, VII:84. *See also* inner plane
spontaneous combustion, XI:133
sports, III:149–50, IX:123–25
    ~ and competition, IX:123–24
Sri Yantra (Auspicious Wheel), IV:248, **IV:248**
Stacy-Judd, Robert, IV:24
Stalin, Joseph, IX:2, 7
Stallone, Sylvester, IX:93, 134
The Star, IX:73, 76, 138
starborn. *See* star people
Starborn, IV:109–12
Star Master, III:49
Star of David, VI:58, XI:12
star people, IV:109–12

starseeds, X:214

Starseed: The Third Millennium, I:225

The Starseed Transmissions, I:220, 222, 225, IV:122, VIII:166. *See also* Carey, Ken

Starship Athena, IV:64. *See also* Arcturians: spacecraft of

Star Trek, III:43, 149, IV:37, 58, 67, VII:15, 135, IX:107, 188
    ~ "Data," IV:36
    ~ Prime Directive, III:26, IV:3, 68

Star Wars, III:71, IV:38, X:181
    ~ and the Orion conflict, IV:41

Star Wars project, IX:97

Stationary Isle of Paradise, IV:113–14

Steac, W.T., V:209

Steckling, Fred, IV:8

Steiger, Brad, IV:109–12

Steiger, Sherry Hansen, IV:109–12

Steiner, Rudolph, IV:120, 194, V:229

Stevens, Wendelle C., IV:39, 45–46, 90

stigmata, I:176, V:45, 55

The Story of Sanat Kumara—Training a Planetary Logos, I:178. *See also* McClure, Janet

Stranger at the Pentagon, IV:47–49

Stranges, Frank, IV:47–49

Strauss, Richard, I:121

Subba Row, V:230

subconscious mind, I:64, 78, 92, 180, 269, 273, III:69–70, 104, IV:254, 258, VI:86, 93, 108–9, 140, 221, 239, 245, VII:39–41, 50, 74–75, VIII:11, 15, 68–70, 72, 77, 79–81, 84, 90, 110–11, 114, 116–17, 159, IX:34, 83, 129, 224, X:7, 108, 113, 216, XII:95, XIII:73, 76, 104, 143, 155. *See also* lower self
    ~ and channeling, VI:227–28, VII:77
    ~ clearing and integration of, I:207, 281, III:24, VI:60, 100, 103, 249, X:4, XI:267
    ~ and the Huna teachings, IV:158–65
    ~ and the Kabbalistic tree of life, IV:301
    ~ and Kriya yoga, I:163
    ~ and the rays, I:123, 126
    ~ and repetition of the name of God, I:251–54
    ~ reprogramming of, IV:262, VII:30, 42, 45, 47–48, 50–51, 53, 140, 161, VIII:111, XII:96, XIII:4, 11, 73–75, 153

Submad Purusha (ruler of the Sugmad Lok dimension), **IV:196**

subpersonality, I:68, V:234, VI:86, 93

subtle body, **V:21**, V:87

Sudan
　～ and the "black root race," I:3
Sufi dancing, IV:323
Sufism, IV:323–24, 327, V:25, 160, X:36. *See also* Islam
Sufism, IV:324. *See also* Haeri, Shaykh F.
Sugmad (ruler of the Sugmad dimension), **IV:196,** IV:197
suicide, I:85, 91, III:125, IV:31, V:50. *See also* bardo experience;
　death, physical
Sun, III:174, IV:2, VI:117, 230, XI:28
　～ and color healing, **IV:212**
　～ energy qualities of, I:96
　～ galactic, VI:117
　～ and the Kabbalistic tree of life, **IV:302**
　～ and Leo, **XI:177**
　～ and the Path of Magnetic Work, III:171
　～ and the Ray Path, III:179
　～ and the rays, **I:131, VI:83, XI:177**
　～ universal, VI:117
　～ vibrational frequencies of, IX:254–55
sun crystals. *See* crystals
Sundari, Nirmala. *See* Anandamayi Ma (Joy-Permeated Mother)
Sun, inner, IV:21–23, 25, VII:133
Sunnites. *See* Islam
superconscious mind, I:13, 17, 269, IV:234, VI:58, 86, 158,
　VII:74–75, 155, 161, VIII:15, 84, 111, 159, X:129–30, XII:95. *See*
　also higher mind; higher self; soul
　　～ clearing and integration of, VI:60, 100, 103, X:4
　　～ and the Huna teachings, IV:158–65
Super Cosmic-Clearing Invocation, VI:242–43
superelectron, VIII:59
Superman, IX:134
supersenses, I:70, **I:71,** VI:51, VII:71–88, IX:136, XII:125
superstition, IX:252–54
superuniverses, VI:73
supracausal body, V:87
Supreme Self, V:11
surrogate mothers, IX:109
Surya (Sun god), IV:219
sushumna, I:83. *See also* chakras: chakra column
Sutra of the Lotus Flower, V:102
sutratma, I:43–47, 51, 77, 113. *See also* life thread; silver cord
Swedenborg, Emanuel, IV:31

Swiss Alps, IV:39

sylphs. *See* elementals: sylphs (nature spirits of air)

sylvestres, **IV:135**. *See also* devas; elementals: gnomes (nature spirits of earth); nature spirits

synthesis, VI:174–75, 189, VII:91–92, 99, 109, 139–41, 143–45, 158, 165, X:145, 149–52, 154–58, 199, 202, 205, 230, XII:12, 132
~ anchoring of, X:149–50
~ and integration, X:155–57, 161

Syria, I:173, 241. *See also* Middle East

Szekeley, Edmond Bordeaux, IV:292–96

T

Table Mountain, Wyoming, XI:207
~ and the Atomic Accelerator, I:279, III:43, 47, 94, VI:32, 37, VIII:42, XI:205, 224
Tablets of Creation, VIII:54
Tadd Pan. *See* Logos of the Great Bear
Tai Chi, VI:49–50, VIII:68
Taj Mahal, VI:148, IX:52, X:93
talisman, IV:185
Talmud, IV:284–85
tamas (inertia), I:121, IV:256
tankas, IV:247
tantra, IV:246–47, V:24, VIII:12, 114, XIII:23, 97, 141, 177
Taoism, I:237, V:115–18. *See also* Lao-tzu
~ and Buddhism, V:117–18
~ and Confucianism, V:117, 121
~ wu-wei (non-action), V:115, 117
Tao Te Ching, V:115–17
Tao, the, I:266, III:15, 109, V:115–17, VI:23, VIII:14, 157, X:56, 67, 84, 86, 98, 100, 111, 150, 155, 173, 177, 187, 195, 217, 239, XI:3, 87, 200, XIII:165, 176
Tara, I:4, **I:5,** V:100, **V:101, VI:78.** *See also* Avalokitesvara (Avalokita); Chenrezi; Quan Yin (Bodhisattva of Compassion)
tarot, VIII:161–62, 168
~ and the Kabbalistic tree of life, IV:305, **IV:306, 308**–9
Tashih-Chih (bodhisattva master), V:100
Taurus, IV:35, VII:133. *See also* astrology
~ and color healing, **IV:212**
~ full moon in, III:6, V:95, VI:149, 152, 243, VII:116, 149, VIII:138, IX:7, 94, 201, XI:30, 173–74, 226, 228, 242, 262, 264, XII:77, 83, 115 (*See also* Wesak)
~ and the Moon, **XI:177**
~ and the seventh ray, **XI:177**

Teachings of the Inner Christ mystery school, I:160, VIII:161. *See also* Babaji, the Yogi Christ

technology, IV:15, IX:121–22
    ~ of Agartha, IV:22–23, 26
    ~ of the Arcturians, III:26, 37, 75–84, 122, IV:66–67, VI:119, 213–14, 231, VII:132, VIII:28–30, 34, XI:28, 90, XII:109, XIII:174
    ~ of Atlantis, I:8, 244–45
    ~ of crystals, I:8–9, 242, 244, IV:1, 66, VI:231, VIII:29, XIII:174
    ~ of extraterrestrials, I:242, IV:6–7, 10, 15, 36–38, 45–46, 48, 102, VI:119, 129, XI:29
    ~ of light, I:8, VI:58
    ~ New Age, VIII:144–45
    ~ of sound, I:8

Telano, Rolf, IV:51–52

telepathy, **I:71,** I:102, 221, III:41, 81, 170, IV:105, 160, **IV:267,** V:45, VI:114, 171, VII:16, 35, 77–81, 83, VIII:105, 170, vii, IX:55, X:238–39, XIII:102–3. *See also* ascended masters: advanced abilities of
    ~ of the Alabramians, IV:95
    ~ of the Alpha Centaurians, IV:83
    ~ of animals, IX:125, X:239
    ~ of the Arcturians, IV:64, 66, 68, VII:132, XIII:102
    ~ of the Ataiens, IV:102
    ~ and extraterrestrials, VII:132, XIII:102
    ~ of the Grays, IV:74
    ~ and spiritual etiquette, X:170–71
    ~ of the Ummites, IV:43
    ~ of the Venusians, IV:53

teleportation, I:33, 206, 274, 277, 283, III:16, 19, 42, 61, 63, 81, 149–50, 206, 227, 245, 255, VI:12, 14, 20, 23, 25, 54, 123, 134, 208, VII:17, VIII:80, IX:128, XI:48, 56–57, 131, 187, 195. *See also* ascended masters: advanced abilities of
    ~ light quotient level for, III:43
    ~ *vs. death,* III:106

Teleshift Light Field, III:220

television, III:148, IV:12, VII:130, IX:73–75, 135, 152, X:33. *See also* media
    ~ and sex, IX:138–39
    ~ talk shows, IX:76–77
    ~ and violence, IV:13, VIII:13

Telos (underground city), I:36, 230, IV:24, 26
    ~ ascension seat in, I:279, III:25, 30, 32, 43, 47, VI:32, XI:27–28
    ~ and Shield and Sharula, I:230, 232, 237, IV:24

Temple Beautiful. *See* Ra-Ta (prophet)

Temple of Sacrifice. *See* Ra-Ta (prophet)

Temple of the Seven Spheres, I:100

Temple on the Mount, I:241–42

Temple, Robert, IV:69–70

temples of wisdom, I:92

Ten Commandments, III:221, IV:279, 285, 288, IX:98, 270, 275–77
~ cosmic, VI:115

The Ten Commandments, XI:261

tenth ray, I:126–29, **I:135,** III:204, **III:238,** III:239, **VI:3,** VI:39,
VI:41, X:13, XI:76, XI:158–59. *See also* rays, twelve
~ and color healing, **IV:210**
~ and the Kabbalistic tree of life, **IV:311**

Teresa, Mother. *See* Mother Teresa

terrorism, IX:247–48, 250

Tesla, Nikola, I:234, IV:10–13, V:247, VI:127, IX:104, 111, 168
~ inventions of, I:242–43, IV:10–13, VIII:145
~ and the Philadelphia Experiment, IV:14–15

Teslar watch, IV:13, VIII:145

Tetragrammaton (Hayavah), III:229, VIII:57

Thanksgiving, IX:91, XII:77, 89–90

Theosophical Society, I:139, 142, 144, 183, 275, IV:130, 194, 197,
317, V:141, 201, 206, 209–11, 213, 215–20, 223–24, 229–36,
242–43, VI:228, VII:84, IX:6, 53, X:31, 74, XI:19, XII:117. *See
also* Besant, Annie; Blavatsky, Madam; Krishnamurti; Leadbeater,
C.W.; Olcott, Henry S.; Theosophy
~ at Adyar, V:207–8, 216, 224–25, 229–30
~ founding of, V:204, 213

The Theosophist, V:216

Theosophy, I:134, 243, III:95, V:205, 210–11, 219–20, 223–24, VI:6,
229, VII:148, VIII:164, IX:53, X:82, XI:20, 39. *See also* Theosophical Society

Therese of Lisieux, Saint, V:45

Think and Grow Rich, IX:51

The Third Millennium, VIII:166. *See also* Carey, Ken

third ray (of Active, Creative Intelligence), I:11, 116, 120–21, 123,
126, 130, 132, **I:134,** I:191–93, **I:199,** I:201, III:203, **III:238,**
IV:121, V:239, **VI:3,** VI:39, **VI:41,** VI:177, **VI:184,** VI:185–86,
VII:19, VII:116, **VII:117,** IX:185, **X:12,** X:13–14, 18–20, 23,
27, 33–35, 74, XI:70, **XI:75,** XI:111. *See also* rays, seven; rays,
twelve
~ and the angelic kingdom, X:34–35

~ and Archangel Chamuel, **I:204, IV:121, 123, VII:115,** X:95
~ and Archangel Charity, **I:204, IV:123, VII:115,** X:95
~ and the atmic plane, **I:132**
~ and the business world, IX:50–51
~ and China, **VI:182**
~ and color healing, **IV:210**
~ corresponding professions, **I:130**
~ and the devic kingdom, X:34
~ and Earth, **I:131**
~ and France, **VI:182,** VI:183
~ glamour of, I:62, X:18
~ and Heros and Amora, **I:203,** III:199
~ and the Kabbalistic tree of life, **IV:311**
~ and Lady Nada, III:156
~ and Leo, **XI:177**
~ and Lucifer, **VI:179**
~ and New York City, **VI:185**
~ and the Olympics, IX:249
~ and the planet Saturn, **I:131, VI:83**
~ and the planet Venus, **I:132**
~ and the Prodigal Son, **VI:179**
~ qualities of, I:121, **I:129,** X:23
~ as a ray of aspect, I:116, X:28
~ and the Ray Path, III:179
~ and Sanat Kumara (Planetary Logos), I:116
~ Serapis Bey as Chohan, I:191–93, **I:199,** I:201, III:257, **IV:121,** VI:144, 163, 214, 241, **VII:19,** VII:116, **VII:117,** X:14, 33–34, 152–53, XI:70–71
~ and the sixth initiation, **XI:127**
~ and the Son of the Morning, **VI:179**
~ and spiritual leadership, I:191, 193, IX:43, 185
~ and the Sun, **XI:177**
~ and the Synthesis Ashram, VII:145
~ and thought, **I:132**
~ and the throat chakra, **I:130**
~ and Wesak, X:153
~ in the world today, VI:179

Third World, IX:163

Thoth-Hermes. *See* Hermes-Thoth

thought forms, I:2–3, 266, IV:160, 165, VI:50, 86, 203, VII:10, 27, 75, 101, 105, 111, VIII:4, 98, IX:252–53, X:54, 71, 237, XI:35, 222, XIII:43
~ appearance of in the physical body, XIII:7–8
~ attack thoughts, VI:101, VIII:2, XI:41
~ and channeling, VI:227
~ and devas, IV:140

~ and elementals, IV:138
~ and the fairy folk, IV:133
~ and manifestation, IV:145, VII:3, 104, VIII:73, 77–78, 80
~ mastery of, VII:27–30, 101–8, 162, VIII:16, X:238
~ negative, I:34, 53, VI:60, 101, VII:28–29, 42–43, 48, 75, 93, 102–5, 111–12, 155, VIII:3, 11, 13, 16, 92–93, X:215, XIII:7, 75, 95
~ positive, VII:30, 86
~ and prayer, IV:162–64
~ protection from, VII:111–12
~ and the rays, VI:188–89, 191
thought transference, IV:47
threefold flame, III:55, XI:40
~ cosmic, III:246
The Threefold Lotus Sutra, V:102
threefold personality, I:23, 64, 106
~ mastery of, I:64, 66, 200
Three Veils of Light, III:223
three wise men, I:175
~ Balthazar as an incarnation of El Morya, I:171, VI:148
~ Caspar as an incarnation of Djwhal Khul, I:171, VI:147
~ Melchior as an incarnation of Kuthumi, I:171, VI:148
Throne of Grace, III:62, 222, 228, 232, **III:238**, III:243, **VI:3**, VIII:127. *See also* Twenty-Four Elders of Light
thrones (heavenly counselors), **IV:123**, IV:124. *See also* angelic kingdom
Tibet, I:173, IV:23, 169, V:100, 105, 107
~ and Agartha, IV:19–20
~ entrance to the inner Earth in, IV:25
~ invasion of by China, V:105–7
~ vortexes of, III:149
The Tibetan Book of the Dead, V:98. *See also* Tibetan Buddhism
Tibetan Buddhism, V:97–98, 100, 105, 107–13, VIII:160, IX:239. *See also* Buddhism; Dalai Lama; *The Tibetan Book of the Dead*
~ and Djwhal Khul, I:237
~ and the Four Ripening Factors, V:113
~ mantras of, V:97
~ meditation of, V:113–14
~ the Six Perfections, V:108
~ teachings of, V:107–13
~ and the Three Jewels, V:108, 114
Tibetan Foundation, I:1, 4, 182, 202, 207, 218, 275, IV:10, 16, 59, 153, 167–68, 177, 196, 205, 223, 309, 319, VI:6, 228–29, VIII:164, 166, IX:121, XI:19–20, 188
~ mantras of, I:258, XII:23

Tillet, Gregory, V:226, 228–30

time, IV:113–14, 257, VI:23, 26, 71, 74, 142, IX:132, 254
~ acceleration of, I:35, III:106–7, VI:208, X:198
~ alone time, XIII:103–5, 162
~ divine use of, I:272, III:44, 109, IV:242, 258, VI:4, 14, 37, 141, VIII:24, 92, 115, 148–49, 184–85, IX:62, 150, 160, 211, 226–27, 229, X:21, 172, 205, XI:66, XIII:140
~ on the inner plane, I:110, III:173, VI:71, VIII:85, XI:94
~ null time, I:219–21, 225, 274, IV:36
~ transcendence of, I:28, 222, 224, III:19, 229, 253, IV:93, 257
~ veil of, III:229, VIII:58

time travel, III:227, VI:25, 71, XI:196
~ by Arcturians, IV:66
~ by Pleiadians, IV:36
~ by Procyonians, IV:79

Tiravalla (yogi), V:205–6

tithing, IV:291, VIII:86, IX:50, 209

tobacco industry, IX:118

Tokyo, Japan, VI:185
~ as Cancer, **VI:185**
~ and the rays, **VI:185**

Toltec Indians, IV:26. *See also* Native Americans

The Tonight Show, XI:164

Torah (of YHWH), III:217, 223–24

Torah Or, VI:115

Torah, the, III:217, IV:284. *See also* Judaism

Toronto Globe and Mail, IV:23

Totapuri, V:24, 28

transfiguration, I:24, 33, III:41, VI:51, XI:152. *See also* initiation: third

Trans-Himalayan Brotherhood, IV:197–98, V:207, 242

transmutation, VIII:79, X:240–41, 244. *See also* violet transmuting flame

Treasury of Light, III:223, VIII:54

A Treatise on White Magic, VI:187

tree of life. *See* Kabbalistic tree of life

trees, **IV:130**, IV:134, 153, IX:110, X:101. *See also* devas; nature spirits
~ etheric trees, IV:153
~ vibrational frequencies of, IV:153

Trilateral Commission, I:246, IV:4, 10, 12, 17. *See also* secret government

trilocation, XI:57. *See also* ascended masters: advanced abilities; bilocation

trinity, IV:161
~ Buddhist, V:100
~ Christian, IV:161
~ cosmic, VI:9
~ God as, IX:222
~ Hindu, I:147, 153, 255, IV:161, 218, 250, VIII:xx, XII:20–21, 119
~ Huna, IV:161
~ of love, will and light, VII:53–55
~ of the Mahatma, Melchizedek and Metatron, X:159–61, 238
~ of the monad, soul and personality, VI:9
~ of Sanat Kumara, Vywamus and Lenduce, III:243
~ of three cosmic ascension paths, VI:80
~ of three cosmic rays, VI:80

trolls, IV:131. *See also* devas; nature spirits

Truman, Harry S, IV:5

Tsewant, Tsedrung Lobang, V:106

Tudor, Francis, V:240

Tuella, IV:56, 58, 61

tulkus, V:97–98

Tulobra, III:178

tunnels, underground, I:246, IV:23–26, 168

Turiya, IV:234. *See also* superconscious mind

twelfth ray, I:127–29, **I:135,** I:274, 290, III:104, 204, **III:238,** IV:309, **VI:3,** VI:39–40, **VI:41,** VI:43, **X:13,** XI:45, **XI:76.** *See also* rays, twelve
~ and color healing, **IV:210**
~ and the Kabbalistic tree of life, **IV:311**

12:12, I:283, III:29, 196, 201, IX:7, XI:49, 64, 72, 115–16, 173

twelve-body system, III:190, 192–94, 219, 227, 237, 239–41, 246, 258, VI:17, 27, 34, 54, 90, 203–4, 230, VIII:58, 63, X:147, XI:136, 150, 187–88. *See also* five-body system; four-body system; nine-body system; seven-body system
~ anchoring of, III:218, 239, 257, VI:63, 87, 95, 122, VIII:56, 59, XI:154–55, 185–87, 209
~ and chakras, VI:205–6
~ clearing and integration of, III:253, VI:241, VIII:35, X:155–56
~ and dimensions, VI:205–6
~ and initiations, VI:205–6
~ and light quotient, VI:205–6

Twelve-Lesson Huna Correspondence Course, IV:158

Twenty-Four Elders of Light, III:222, 232, **III:238,** III:243, 250, **VI:3,** XI:60. *See also* Throne of Grace
~ ashram of, VIII:127

20/20, VIII:157, IX:89

twilight masters, VI:130, 143, VIII:97, IX:142, XII:125

Twilight Zone, VI:70

twin souls (flames), I:171, IV:182–83, 187, 189–91, XIII:56–58, 68–69, 141, 147, 165. *See also* relationships, romantic; soul mates

Twitchell, Paul, IV:195, 197, 200, VIII:167

Two Disciples, I:52

2000 (year), I:6, 29, 32, VI:6, 55, 217, IX:133, X:246. *See also* millennium

2012 (year), I:35, 145, 220, 224–26, 240, VI:55–56, 222, 224, IX:8, 133

Tzadkiel (archangel), **IV:303**

Tzaphkiel (archangel), **IV:303**

U

UFO: Contact from Andromeda, IV:90. *See also* Stevens, Wendelle C.

UFO: Contact from Planet Iarga, IV:45–46. *See also* Denaerde, Stefan; Stevens, Wendelle C.

UFO: Contact from Planet Ummo, IV:43–44. *See also* Ribera, Antonio

UFO: Contact from the Pleiades, IV:39. *See also* Stevens, Wendelle C.

UFOs, III:125, IV:11, 15, 21, 23, 112, VII:133, IX:161, XI:29. *See also* extraterrestrials; spacecraft
  ~ crashes of, IV:4–5, VII:133
  ~ sightings of, IV:1–2, 21

Uighur culture, IV:26

Ultimate Divine Dispensation, VI:243–44

Ummites, IV:43–44. *See also* extraterrestrials

Ummo, IV:43–44

undines. *See* elementals: undines (nature spirits of water)

unicorns, I:2

United Nations, III:141, IV:58, V:106, VI:155, 185, IX:100, 106–7, 115, XI:116, XII:88

United States, I:8, 244, IV:3, 17, 20, 48, 60, V:36, 44, 107, 243, VI:184, IX:56, 79, 241
  ~ divine mission of, III:131
  ~ and the feminine principle, VI:184
  ~ group consciousness of, IX:156
  ~ initiations of, IX:158
  ~ leadership role of, IX:241–42
  ~ and nuclear weapon testing, VI:126
  ~ and the rays, **VI:182,** VI:183, X:93
  ~ rods of power in, I:206

United States Air Force, IV:4, 28

United States Congress, IV:5, IX:89, 129, 135–36, 186–87

United States Constitution, V:242, IX:48, 101, 186–87

United States government, III:125, IV:67, V:107, VII:133, IX:1, 46–49, 78, 101, 119. *See also* political system (U.S.)
  ~ and AIDS, IV:8–9, 89, IX:117
  ~ corruption of, IX:129–31

U

~ cover-ups by, IV:14–15, 21, 25, 28, IX:105, 129–30, 161–63
~ employees of, IX:78
~ and the environment, IV:152
~ and extraterrestrials, IV:5–7, 33, 57, 78–79, VI:127,
    VII:130–31, 133, IX:162
~ and the flat tax, IX:143–44
~ foreign aid by, IX:106
~ and the national debt, IX:130, 135, 168–69
~ and the negative ego, IX:44, 129–31, 135, 148, 162
~ and the Philadelphia Experiment, III:42
~ Postal Service, IX:78
~ and psychotronics, IV:13
~ racism in, IX:130
~ and the secret government, IV:3–4
~ and the space program, IX:97–98
~ and the Star Wars project, IX:97
~ treaty with the Grays, IV:6, 67, 73–74
~ and the U.S. trade agreement, IX:164–65
~ and Valiant Thor (Martian visitor), IV:47–48

United States Navy
    ~ and the Philadelphia experiment, IV:14–15

United States Senate, IX:186–87

universal activation, VI:54

universal actualization, IX:121

universal body (12th), **III:238,** III:240, 254, 258, **VI:3,** VI:12, 54,
    87, 161, 194, 203, 206, XI:136, 150, 154, 194. *See also*
    twelve-body system
    ~ and advanced ascended master abilities, VI:14, 123
    ~ anchoring of, VI:13–14, 19–20, 23, 44, 54, **VI:62,** VIII:59,
        XI:120, 148, 187, 192, 252, 266, 268
    ~ and the twelfth dimension, **VI:204**

Universal Core, III:128, 178, **VI:116**
    ~ ascension seat in, III:258

Universal Hierarchy, I:187, 189

Universal Logos, I:117, 181, **I:199,** I:202, 234, III:178, 194, VI:71,
    75, X:146, 236. *See also* Melchizedek (Universal Logos)

universal masters, I:206, VI:72. *See also* ascended masters; cosmic
    masters; galactic masters

Universal Mind, the, I:1, 174–75, 235–36, 251, III:155, IV:157, 291,
    V:125, 129, 156, 169, 245–47, VI:188
    ~ mantras of, I:257, XII:22

universal monadic group, **III:238,** III:243, 256, **VI:3**

universal plane, VI:205–6

universal transmitting system, VIII:43

University of Chicago, IV:112

Unnameable One, IV:52–53

Unveiled Mysteries, III:47. *See also* King, Godfré Ray

Upanishads, IV:217, 219, 223, 232, V:9, 20, 47. *See also* Hinduism; Vedas
    ~ quotations from, IV:233–37, 242–43
    ~ and the yoga sutras of Patanjali, IV:254

The Upanishads, IV:233. *See also* Easwaran, Eknath

upayas (spiritual techniques), V:85, 89

Ur
    ~ as an incarnation of Jesus, I:169, VI:147

The Urantia Book, I:228–30, 232–34, IV:113–14, 125–26, 128, VI:73–74, 228, VIII:164–65, XII:114

Urantia (Earth), IV:113. *See also* Earth; Mother Earth

The Urantia Foundation. *See The Urantia Book*

Uranus
    ~ ascension seat of, VI:36
    ~ and color healing, **IV:212**
    ~ energy qualities of, I:95–96
    ~ and the Kabbalistic tree of life, **IV:302**
    ~ and the rays, **I:131**–32, **VI:83**

Uriel (archangel), **I:199**, III:199
    ~ and the sixth ray, **I:204, IV:121, 124, VII:115**, X:95

Ursa Major, IV:73

USSR. *See* Soviet Union

Uversa (capital of Orvonton), IV:113, 128

U

V

vaccination, IV:12–13

vairgya, V:82

Valerian, Valdimar, IV:75, 78

Valiant Thor (Martian visitor), IV:47–48. *See also* extraterrestrials

Valley Forge, I:244

"valley of judgment." *See* bardo experience: third phase (Valley of Judgment)

Valmiki (poet-saint), V:9, 11. *See also* Ramayana

Van Gogh, Vincent, I:121–22

Vanos, Lucky, IX:74

van Tassel, George, IV:56

vasanaksaya, V:59

Vatican, V:181, 183
    ~ secret libraries of, IV:274, 292

Vedanta, IV:232, 324, V:13, 20, 22, 24, 37, 65, 67
    ~ and yoga, IV:243–44, 247

Vedas, IV:217, 219–20, 223, 232, V:9, 17, 19–20, 22, 47, 60, 66, VIII:160, 166, XII:120. *See also* Hinduism; Upanishads; Vedanta
    ~ Aranyakas, IV:232
    ~ Athaarva-Veda, IV:232
    ~ Brahmanas, IV:232
    ~ and Jnana yoga, IV:243
    ~ Mantra-Samhitas, IV:232
    ~ quotations from, IV:231
    ~ Rig-Veda, IV:232
    ~ Sama-Veda, IV:232
    ~ Yajur-Veda, IV:232

Vega, I:242, **IV:33,** IV:38, 99

Vegans, IV:38, 99. *See also* extraterrestrials

Venkataraman, T.N., V:57–59

Venkusa, V:2

Venus, I:179, 185, III:173–74, 182, IV:51–55, VII:121, 130–31, IX:97, X:91

V

~ ascension of, VI:77
~ ascension seat on, VI:32
~ bases on, IV:53
~ and color healing, **IV:212**
~ energy qualities of, I:94, 96
~ as Eysmnje, I:179
~ and the Kabbalistic tree of life, **IV:302**
~ and Libra, **XI:177**
~ Mother Temple, IV:52
~ Planetary Logos of, I:180
~ and the rays, **I:131**–32, **VI:82, XI:177**
~ school of, I:179–81, 208

Venusians, IV:51–54, VII:131. *See also* extraterrestrials

Vermont, IV:81

Verne, Jules, IV:20

Vesta, III:255, VI:51–52, 117, IX:179, XI:116. *See also* Helios (Solar
   Logos); Solar Logos
~ ashram of, VI:225, VIII:127, IX:200
~ copper-gold ray of, VIII:50
~ crystals of, XI:257
~ Golden Chamber of, VI:230, 234
~ light rods of, XI:259
~ seed packets of, VIII:179, XI:257

vibhuti. *See* virbhuti ash

vibrational frequencies, V:125–26, VI:74, 171, VII:81, 83, 85, IX:52,
   XI:29
~ and ascension, I:37–38
~ of devas, VII:110
~ of the Earth, IX:254–55, X:237, XIII:81–82
~ and the four-body system, XIII:106
~ of love, VI:74
~ and music, I:178, IV:172
~ of the permanent atoms, XIII:84
~ rising, I:28, XIII:105–7
~ seven octaves of, **IV:177,** IV:180, 189
~ of the Sun, IX:254–55
~ of the third dimension, III:141
~ of trees, IV:153
~ and the unborn child, XIII:79–81

Vietnam War, IX:108, 153–54. *See also* war

violence, XIII:22–23, 159
~ and sports, IX:123
~ and television, IV:13, IX:152

violet transmuting flame, I:125, 128, III:50, 100, 190, V:239, VII:112,

VIII:61, IX:256, X:17, 25, 43–46, 153, 217, 240–44, XI:53, XIII:11. *See also* Saint Germain (ascended master)

virbhuti ash, I:153–54, III:55, V:2, 5–6, VII:54, VIII:178, IX:118, XI:74. *See also* Sathya Sai Baba (Cosmic Christ)

Virgin Mary, I:171–72, **I:199,** I:250, 260–61, III:199, IV:277, 288, V:99, 179, 192, 239, **VI:112,** VII:15, 18, 111, 115, VIII:178, IX:240, XI:242, XII:116–17, XIII:101, 109
    ~ appearances of, V:179–83, 185–89, XIII:67
    ~ and Archangel Gabriel, I:172, 175, 237, IV:122
    ~ ascension of, I:175
    ~ and the fifth ray, **I:204, IV:124, VII:115,** X:95, 153
    ~ and healing, V:179, 186, VII:114
    ~ messages of, I:240, V:180–83, 185–86, 188–89
    ~ and the Miracle of the Sun, V:180–82
    ~ other children of, I:174–75
    ~ personality of, X:207

Virgo. *See also* astrology
    ~ and color healing, **IV:212**

virtues (heavenly governors), **IV:123,** IV:124. *See also* angelic kingdom

Vishnu, I:142, 147, 153, IV:217–18, 221–22, 250, V:8–10, 33, 36, VIII:190, xx, IX:240, XII:21, 119
    ~ mantras of, I:256

Vision, VIII:166. *See also* Carey, Ken

The Vision of Hermes, IV:198

The Visitors Within, IV:97. *See also* Royal, Lyssa

Vista, **I:199**

visualization, I:266, III:24, 73, IV:138, 205, 262, V:98, VII:26, 30, 86, VIII:20, 70–73, 80–84, 90, 96, 104–5, X:49, 185, XIII:173. *See also* affirmations; prayers
    ~ of Avalokitesvara (Quan Yin), V:113
    ~ of Buddha Shakyamuni, V:113–14
    ~ in the building of the antakarana, I:46, 48, 53–54
    ~ with color, IV:210
    ~ of the form of God, I:155, 249–50, 265, V:51
    ~ and healing, VI:117, IX:83
    ~ and the Huna prayer method, IV:163
    ~ and the inner senses, VIII:70
    ~ of Manjushri, V:113
    ~ during soul travel, IV:200

Vivekananda: A Biography, V:34. *See also* Nikhilananda, Swami

Vivekananda, Swami, V:11, 25, 27, 33–37, VIII:166
    ~ quotations from, V:37–38

The Voice of Silence, V:210. *See also* Blavatsky, Madam

Voice of the Avatar, VII:28, VIII:xxv. *See also* Sathya Sai Baba (Cosmic Christ)

V

von Lamberg, Count, V:241

vortexes, I:10, III:149

vows, spiritual, I:272, III:85–87, IV:227, V:111, VIII:23–25, 77, 87, 120, 133–34, 143, 156–57, IX:237
  ~ of Avalokitesvara, V:100
  ~ bodhisattva, V:112–13, VIII:23, 160, IX:218, 234, 237, XI:42
  ~ the Bramacharya vow, I:270, V:70, VIII:24
  ~ of celibacy, XIII:132
  ~ of commitment, XIII:92–93, 124, 136, 144, 160
  ~ of C.W. Leadbeater, V:225
  ~ of the Essenes, IV:290, 294–96
  ~ Five Great Vows of the yati (ascetic), V:16
  ~ of Gautama Buddha, V:93
  ~ of harmonic living, VI:223
  ~ of immortality, I:270
  ~ of the Missionaries of Charity, V:192
  ~ of nonviolence, I:271, VIII:13
  ~ of renunciation, VIII:24–25
  ~ restating, XIII:96–98, 176
  ~ of sainthood, VIII:24
  ~ of service work, VIII:25
  ~ Sevenfold Vow, IV:295–96
  ~ of silence, I:272, VIII:98
  ~ Twelve Great Vows of Jainism, V:16

vrittis, IV:259

Vulcan
  ~ and the first ray, **I:131, VI:82**

Vywamus (ascended master), I:6, 34, 39, 182, 186, **I:199,** I:207–8, 213, 234, 280–85, III:17, 38, 48–49, 52, 56, 62, 64, 69–70, 98–101, 172, 191–92, 195, 201–2, **III:238,** IV:16–17, 153, 205–6, VI:7, 52–53, **VI:112,** VI:115, 119, 126, 194, 207, 214, 239, 241–42, VII:112, 148, VIII:35, 46–48, 97, 164, 180, X:151, 156, XI:17–18, 29, 32, 48, 52, 100, 148, 188, 192
  ~ ascension of, I:178
  ~ ashram of, VIII:127
  ~ Heaven on Earth mantra of, III:105–6
  ~ initiations of, III:191, XI:116
  ~ and Lenduce, I:207, III:243, XI:208
  ~ prophecies of, I:246–47, III:99
  ~ quotations from, I:211, 219, 287, III:167, IV:1
  ~ and Sanat Kumara, I:178, 188, 202, 207, III:52, 243, VI:243, XI:17, 164, 208
  ~ teachings of, I:211–18
  ~ and the Tibetan Foundation, I:202, 207

W

walk-ins, I:276, IV:29–32, XI:78
    ~ Adolf Hitler as, IV:30, IX:3
    ~ cosmic, I:36, 214, 216
    ~ for the Mahatma energy, X:147–49
    ~ and soul extensions, VI:89

Wallace, Mike, IX:76

Wallace, W.B., V:173, 175

Walters, Barbara, IX:18

war, I:6–7, 241–42, IV:8, 13, 74, V:182, IX:98–101, 276. *See also* individual wars
    ~ and animals, IV:148
    ~ and the Ashtar Command, IV:56
    ~ in the *Bhagavad-Gita*, IV:224
    ~ egotistical, IX:99
    ~ Electrical, I:6–7, 182, IV:1
    ~ and karma, VII:68–69, VIII:21, IX:99–101
    ~ and physical death, I:85
    ~ and the rays, I:119, 123, VI:190
    ~ spiritual, VIII:21–22, IX:99
    ~ and spiritual law, IX:126
    ~ veterans of, IX:90, 153–54

Warburg family, IX:168

Washington, George, I:244
    ~ other lives of, I:244–45, V:242, VI:147, VIII:163

Watergate, IV:3

water spirits, **IV:135**. *See also* devas; elementals: undines (nature spirits of water); nature spirits

We Discovered Alien Bases on the Moon, IV:8

Weintraub, Pamela, IV:203

welfare. *See* economics: and the welfare system

Wesak Festival, I:32, 34, 39, 276, 278, 283, III:6, 14, 29, 131, 196, 249, 266, V:93, 95–96, VI:19, 28–29, 123, 125, 149–54, 226, 242, VII:116, 149, VIII:131, 138–39, 181, IX:7, 52, 93–94, 200–201,

X:152–53, XI:30, 48, 115, 142, 173–75, 225–26, 228, 262, XII:14, 16, 77–81, 83–85
~ functions and purposes of, V:95–96, VI:153, XI:174, XII:79
~ Huna prayer for, IX:214–16
~ and mass ascension, XI:173, 177
~ Wesak Ceremony Meditation, XI:284–86, 299–302, XII:81–83
Western society, IV:132, VIII:99
~ mantras of, I:257, XII:22
We, the Arcturians, III:78, IV:63, 68, VI:80
wheel of rebirth, I:80, 101, 170, 276, V:13, 15, 50, 88, 163, 170, X:52, 236, XIII:84
~ liberation from, I:24, 64, 80, 138, 198, 200, 268, III:2–3, 5, IV:188, 219, 222, 232, 269, V:12, 94, 109, 136, 209, VI:1, 59, 61, 67, 123, 160, 163, 208, 222, 244, VII:12, 140–41, VIII:xxi, IX:265, XI:11, 74, 173, 186, 267 (*See also* enlightenment; nirvana; samadhi (enlightenment))
When Daylight Comes, V:205. *See also* Murphet, Howard
White Eagle, VIII:99, 166
White Lodge, I:217
The White Sands Incident, IV:51
White Sands, New Mexico, IV:4
Whitewater, IX:147
Whitman, Walt, I:118
Whole Life Expo, V:100, VIII:162
Wiley, Dr., IX:59
will, I:17, 40, 45, 48, 61, 76, **I:96,** I:109, 115–16, 118, III:10, 170–71, 173, 175, 179, IV:161, 163, 207, 226, 233, 243, 256–58, 291, V:50, 109, 128, VI:47–48, 50–51, 56, **VI:57,** VI:155, 168, 175, 213, VII:13, 49–50, 53–55, 162, VIII:99, IX:1, 249, 253, X:22, 27–29, 84, 94, 109, 112, 123, 137, 140–41, 143, 153, 179, 181, XII:88, XIII:64, 170–71
~ divine, I:111, 172, IV:301, 310, IX:38, X:70, 198
~ of God, IV:120, 129, 284, 325, V:53, 84, 120, 155, 160, 172, VI:49, 72, 86, 117, 138, 155, 223, VII:13, 49, 53, 113, 130, 133, 135, VIII:9, 100, IX:39, 184, 275–76, X:22, 56, 71, 212, 239, XII:87, XIII:117
~ and the rays, I:119, VI:188, 191
~ of the Solar Logos, III:174–75, IV:129
~ spiritual, I:17, 43, 47, 109–10, 223, III:63, 81, 175, IV:300, **VI:17,** VI:18, 181, VII:35, 84, VIII:133
~ and the spiritual triad, I:43, 109–10
will energy, I:47, 119, 143, VII:162
Williams-Heller, Ann, IV:302, 311

Williamson, Marianne, IX:230

The Will of Apollonius, V:176. *See also* Apollonius of Tyana

Winfrey, Oprah, IX:76

Winged Pharaoh, IV:167. *See also* Grant, Joan

Wingo, Dr. E. Otha, IV:158

wisdom, I:18, 24, 44, 92, 108, 268, III:55, 188, 220, 224, 246,
   IV:206, 225–28, 234, 243, 256, 300, V:48, 75, 108, 110, 112, 121,
   140, 153, VI:76, 150, 155, 197, VII:53–54, 79–80, 139–41, VIII:9,
   62, IX:241, 245, X:16, 18, 21, 23, 26, 33, 44, 55, 91–94, 116,
   140–41, 159, 177, 206, 213, 218, 225–26, 240, XI:40, XII:88,
   XIII:102–3, 106
      ~ of animals, VIII:94–95

wisdom principle, I:143, 208, V:95

The Wise Ones and Attractive Energies of Shamballa, III:10

Wolf 424, IV:43

Women Who Love Too Much, XIII:169

wood sprites, VII:7, 109, 111, 121. *See also* devas; nature spirits

words of power, I:48–50, 82, 249–62, IV:189, 205, 245, 262, 269,
   V:136, XII:19, 22, 99. *See also* chanting; mantras; sound

Wordsworth, William, VII:97, X:235

A World Before, VIII:167. *See also* Montgomery, Ruth

A World Beyond, I:95, VIII:167. *See also* Montgomery, Ruth

World Health Organization, IV:8

World Invocation Day, VI:155. *See also* Festival of Humanity

World Peace Meditation, III:29

World War I, V:180, VI:191. *See also* war

World War II, IV:14, V:65, 181, 247, VI:126, IX:99, 245–46. *See also*
   Germany: Nazi; Hitler, Adolf; war

Wright, Machaelle Small, IV:142–45, 148–49, VII:119

Y

Yahweh, VIII:58
    ~ covenant of, VIII:63
Yama (the lord of death), V:170
Yankee Beacon of Buddhist Light, V:214. *See also* Murphet, Howard
yantras, IV:247–48
    ~ Sri Yantra (Auspicious Wheel), IV:248, **IV:248**
yati (ascetic), V:16
Ye Are Gods, I:31. *See also* Skarin, Analee
Yeravda prison, V:73
YHWH (God), I:227, III:217–18, 220, 222–24, 228–32, IV:120, 278–79, 314, V:153, XI:30, 194
    ~ covenant of, III:223
    ~ flame of, III:230
    ~ names of, III:231
    ~ nogan shells of, III:220, VIII:63
    ~ Temple Sanctuary of Light of, III:220
yin and yang, I:127, IV:228, V:27, 116, 121, 130–31, VI:56, VIII:14–15, 104, IX:120, XIII:55, 65, 100, 104
    ~ and the Kabbalistic tree of life, IV:301
    ~ and relationships, XIII:2, 18
Yoda, X:246. *See also* Star Wars
Yod Hay Vod Hay. *See* Jehovah (Yod Hay Way Hay)
Yod spectrum, VI:43, 115, 194, VIII:50, 60, XI:182
    ~ anchoring of, III:219, 226
    ~ invocation of, VI:195–96
    ~ ten lost cosmic rays ascension seat of, VI:115
    ~ ten lost cosmic rays of, **VI:41,** VI:42–43, 193
Yod spectrum, cosmic, VI:43
yoga, IV:224–26, 239–51, 257, 262, 264, V:22, 42, 44, 48, 61, 65, VI:59, VII:33, 105, VIII:160, IX:83, X:89, XII:108. *See also* Hinduism; mantras; mudras; Patanjali
    ~ Agni yoga (Fire yoga), **I:5, 59,** I:125, IV:239, 249–50, **VI:78,** VII:151
    ~ asana (posture), IV:264–65

~ ashtagraha, V:83
~ Ashtanga yoga, **I:59,** IV:239, 249–50, 257, VII:151
~ Asparsha yoga, IV:239, 245–46
~ Bhakti yoga, **I:5,** I:58, **I:59, 133,** IV:239–41, 257, 260, V:67, **VI:78,** VII:151
~ charana (attention), IV:264
~ chitta, IV:254, 258–60, 266
~ Deity, V:109, 111
~ dharana, IV:266
~ dhyana (meditation), IV:264
~ Eco yoga, IV:239, 250
~ Hatha yoga, **I:5,** I:58, **I:59,** IV:239–41, 265, V:67, **VI:78,** VII:151, VIII:146
~ and Hinduism, IV:220
~ Integral yoga, IV:239, 250–51
~ Japa yoga, IV:244, 249
~ Jnana yoga, IV:225, 239, 243–44
~ Kaivalya (absoluteness), IV:254, 264
~ Karma yoga, IV:225, 239, 242–43, 260, V:67
~ Kriya Kundalini Pranayama, I:159–60
~ Kriya yoga, I:159–66, IV:239, 249, V:39, 41, 44, 46, 56, VI:161, VIII:164, XIII:132
~ Kundalini yoga, IV:239, 245–46
~ Lama, I:166
~ Lambika yoga, IV:239
~ Laya yoga, **I:59,** IV:239, 245–46
~ Mandala yoga, IV:247
~ Mansa yoga, IV:239
~ Mantra yoga, IV:239, 244–45, 249
~ Nada yoga, IV:239, 249
~ niyama (rules), IV:264
~ and pranayama, IV:264
~ pratyahara (abstraction), IV:264–65
~ Raja yoga, **I:5,** I:58, **I:59, 132,** IV:239–42, 253, 257, 260, 270, V:67, **VI:78,** VII:151
~ and the rays, I:132–33
~ and the root races, **VI:78**
~ Sabda yoga, IV:239, 249, V:163–64
~ samadhi (contemplation), IV:264, 266
~ Sankirtan yoga, IV:239, 249
~ sanyama, IV:266
~ and the seven root races, I:4, **I:5,** I:58, **I:59,** IV:239–42, 249, 257
~ Shiva yoga, IV:239, 250
~ Siddha yoga, IV:239, V:85–91
~ Tantra yoga, IV:239, 246–47, XIII:44
~ Taraka yoga, IV:239, 247

~ yama (commandments), IV:264
~ Yantra yoga, IV:239, 247–48
~ Yoga of Synthesis, IV:239–40, 251, V:64
Yoga: Mastering the Secrets of Matter and the Universe, IV:240, 251
Yogananda, Paramahansa, I:34, 121, 156, 159, 162–63, 167, 256,
    IV:196–97, 241, 256, V:23, 39–47, 55–56, 88, VI:7, **VI:112,**
    VI:247–48, VIII:9, 158, 160, 165–66, IX:2, 54, 93, 143, 206,
    XI:36, 162, XII:110, XIII:109, 132
        ~ affirmations of, VIII:82
        ~ ashram of, V:44
        ~ and conscious death (mahasamadhi), I:76, IV:198
        ~ and Kriya yoga, I:160–63, 165–66, IV:249, V:41, 44, 46
        ~ mantras of, I:219–20, VIII:101, XII:21
        ~ miracles of, V:44–45
        ~ quotations from, I:76, 87, 159, 163, III:88, VI:14, 141, 162,
            214, VII:33, 72, 90, VIII:21, X:81, 153, XI:77, 118, 155,
            XIII:85, 134
        ~ and the Self-Realization Fellowship, V:46, VII:16, 23, 143,
            148, VIII:164, X:139
        ~ and the Yogoda Satsanga Brahmacharya Vidyalaya, V:42
Yogananda, Swami, V:30
Yoga of the Inward Path, IV:251. *See also* Beasley, Ronald
The Yoga Sutras of Patanjali, IV:253, VIII:164. *See also* Patanjali
Yoga Vaistha, V:9
Yoga-Vedanta Forest University, V:65
Yogeswari, V:24
Yucatan, IV:23
        ~ entrance to the inner Earth in, IV:24–25
Yucca, California
        ~ extraterrestrial bases at, IV:6
Yukteswar, Sri, I:159, 162, IV:256, V:41–46, IX:2, XIII:55

Y

Z

Zadkiel (archangel), **I:199,** III:199, X:44
~ and the seventh ray, **I:204, IV:121, 124, VII:115,** X:95

Zarathustra. *See* Zoroaster (Persian avatar)

Zar (teacher of Jesus), I:173

Zebedee, IV:288

Zechariah (prophet), IV:288

Zend (father of Zoroaster)
~ as an incarnation of Jesus, I:169, 236, V:151, 153, VI:147

Zeneperin, I:83. *See also* death, physical

Zephaniah (prophet), IV:288

Zeroana Akerne, V:153

Zerubbabel, I:170

Zeta Reticulum, III:178, **IV:33,** IV:73–75, 85, 97–98. *See also* extraterrestrials; Grays
~ and the Grays, IV:5–6, 17, 73–75, VI:71

Zeus, XI:227

zodiac. *See* astrology

zohar body, III:218–19, 222, **III:238, VI:3,** VI:25, 194, 206,
VIII:51, 60, XI:154, 182, 194–95
~ anchoring of, III:220, 250, VI:54, **VI:62,** VI:194, VIII:59,
XI:194, 266, 268

Zohar, the Book of Splendor, III:217, IV:286

Zoroaster (Persian avatar), I:169, IV:327, V:151–53
~ as an incarnation of Gautama Buddha, I:236–37, IV:198,
VI:148
~ other lives of, I:217, V:133–34, 151

Zoroastrianism, I:236–37, V:151–54. *See also* Avesta; Parsi religion

Zoser (Egyptian pharaoh), IV:174–75

Zoser pyramid, IV:169

Zu, I:173, IV:171

THE ENCYCLOPEDIA OF THE SPIRITUAL PATH

DR. JOSHUA DAVID STONE

Dr. Stone has a Ph.D. in Transpersonal Psychology and is a licensed marriage, family and child counselor in Los Angeles, California. On a spiritual level, he anchors the Melchizedek Synthesis Light Academy & Ashram.

The Encyclopedia of the Spiritual Path consists of thirteen books and an index in this ongoing series on the subject of **ascension, self-realization** and **a further deepening of the ascended-master teachings.**

These books collectively explore the **deepest levels** and understanding of ascension through the personal, planetary and cosmic levels, offering the reader tools to work with that span the spectrum of all of the bodies and ultimately bring them into the subtle realms of cosmic ascension.

These tools are practical gems for the **purification, healing, cleansing, acceleration** and **ascension process** that covers the individual incarnated soul and extends into the vast monadic and cosmic realms.

✦ THE COMPLETE ASCENSION MANUAL
How to Achieve Ascension in This Lifetime

A synthesis of the past and guidance for ascension. An extraordinary compendium of practical techniques and spiritual history. Compiled from research and channeled information. SOFTCOVER 297P.

$14^{95} ISBN 0-929385-55-1

✦ Contents

	Introduction	ix
1	The Story of Creation	1
2	The Monad, the Soul and the Personality	13
3	The Path of Probation and the First Five Initiations	21
4	Ascension—the Sixth Initiation	27
5	The Building of the Antakarana	43
6	Glamour, Illusion, Maya	57
7	Death, Dying, and the Science of the Bardo	73
8	Between Lifetimes	87
9	The Soul	105
10	Esoteric Psychology and the Science of the Twelve Rays	115
11	The Reappearance of the Christ and the Externalization of the Hierarchy	137
12	The Cosmic Christ: the Advent of Sathya Sai Baba	147
13	Babaji, the Yogi Christ	159
14	The Untold Story of Jesus the Christ	169
15	Sanat Kumara's Training	177
16	Sanat Kumara and the Planetary Hierarchy	185
17	God and the Cosmic Hierarchy	197
18	The Galactic Core and the Cosmic Masters	205
19	Teachings of Vywamus on the Avatar of Synthesis, the Mahatma	211
20	The Inbreath and Outbreath of Brahma	219
21	the Melchizedek Priesthood	227
22	The Universality of Religion	235
23	Prophecies of Things to Come	239
24	Mantras, Names of God, and Words of Power	249
25	Golden Keys to Achieving Ascension in this Lifetime	263
26	The Cutting Edge of Ascension: Information and Techniques	275
27	Ascension Meditation and Treatment	287
	Bibliography	295
	About the Author	297

SOUL PSYCHOLOGY
Keys to Ascension

Modern psychology deals exclusively with personality, ignoring the dimensions of spirit and soul. This book provides ground-breaking theories and techniques for healing and self-realization. SOFTCOVER 256P.

$14^{95} ISBN 0-929385-56-X

Contents

1   The Development of Personal Power and the Functioning of the Conscious and Subconscious Minds 1
2   Unconditional Self-Love and the Inner Child 13
3   Integrating the Three Minds and the Four Bodies 25
4   The Christ Consciousness and How to Achieve It.......................35
5   Soul Psychology as Compared to Traditional Psychology 63
6   Pitfalls and Traps on the Path of Ascension 77
7   Romantic Relationships from the Soul's Perspective 83
8   The White Brotherhood Medical Assistance Program 95
9   Tools for Healing the Emotions 101
10 How to Reprogram the Subconscious Mind.................................121
11 Hypnosis and Self-Hypnosis 135
12 Physical Immortality..149
13 An Esoteric Understanding of Sexuality.....................................157
14 Psychic Self-Defense 173
15 The Human Aura and the Seven Bodies 199
16 The Twenty-Two Chakras 207
17 The Raising of the Kundalini 215
18 Channeling 221
19 A Spiritual Perspective on Dreams and Sleep.............................227
20 The Laws of Manifestation 239
21 The Laws of Karma...253
22 Children in the World Today 263
    Bibliography 273

◆ BEYOND ASCENSION

How to Complete the Seven Levels of Initiation

Brings forth new channeled material that demystifies the 7 levels of initiation and how to attain them. It contains new information on how to open and anchor our 36 chakras. SOFTCOVER 280P.

$14⁹⁵ ISBN 0-929385-73-X

◆ Contents

1	The Seven Levels of Initiation	1
2	How to Open, Anchor, and Activate the Fifty Chakras	13
3	How to Build Your Light Quotient	23
4	New Ascension Techniques	37
5	The Core Fear Matrix Removal Program	69
6	The Advanced Light Technologies of the Arcturians	75
7	The Golden Key to Accelerating Your Spiritual Evolution	85
8	More Ascension Tools and Information	91
9	The Ultimate Ascension Meditation	135
10	The Twenty-Four Dimensions of Reality	139
11	Huna Prayers	155
12	The Seven Paths to Higher Evolution	167
13	Ascension Meditations, Techniques, and Insights	187
14	Kabbalistic Ascension Techniques	217
15	Cosmic Ascension	237
	Conclusion	263
	Afterword: What's Next?	265
	Bibliography	270
	Subject Guide	271

✦ HIDDEN MYSTERIES

ETs, Ancient Mystery Schools and Ascension

Explores the unknown and suppressed aspects of Earth's past; reveals new information on the ET movement and secret teachings of the ancient mystery schools. SOFTCOVER 330P.

$14⁹⁵ ISBN 0-929385-57-8

✦ Contents

Introduction ix

Part One: EXTRATERRESTRIAL ACTIVITY IN THIS UNIVERSE
1   Extraterrestrials and Other Government Cover-ups 1
2   Agartha in the Hollow Earth 19
3   Walk-ins 29
4   Extraterrestrial Activity 33
5   The Pleiades 35
6   Orion 41
7   Ummo 43
8   Iarga 45
9   Mars 47
10 Venus 51
11 The Ashtar Command 55
12 Arcturus 63
13 Sirius 69
14 Hydra 71
15 The Grays 73
16 The Reptilian Race 77
17 Procyon 79
18 Cessna 81
19 Alpha Centauri 83
20 Lyra 85
21 Antares 87
22 Andromeda 89
23 Proxima Centauri 91
24 Ra 93
25 Alabram 95

(continued on page 6)

ENCYCLOPEDIA—DR. JOSHUA DAVID STONE

(*Hidden Mysteries* continued from page 5)

26   Zeta Reticulum 97
27   Vega...99
28   The Ataien...101
29   The Essassani 103
30   Implants 105
31   The Association of Worlds 107
32   Star People 109
33   The Organization of the Physical Universe 113
34   Summary 115

Part Two: THE ANCIENT MYSTERY SCHOOLS
35   The Angelic Hierarchy 119
36   Pan and the Nature Spirits 131
37   Evolution and Ecology 147
38   The Huna Teachings 157
39   The Egyptian Mysteries 167
40   Initiation in the Great Pyramid 179
41   The Science of Soul Travel 193
42   Healing with Color and Sound 205
43   Brama, Vishnu, and Shiva..217
44   The Bhagavad-Gita 223
45   The Vedas: Gods Revelation 231
46   The Sacred Paths of Yoga 239
47   The Yoga Sutras of Patanjali 253
48   The Church's Contamination by Ego 271
49   An Esoteric Understanding of Judaism 277
50   The Essene Brotherhood...287
51   The Kabbalistic Tree of Life 297
52   The Keys of Enoch 313
53   The Mighty I Am Presence 317
54   Sufism 323
55   Shinto: the Way of the Gods...325
56   Baha'i: the Worlds Newest Religion 327
     Bibliography

✦ THE ASCENDED MASTERS LIGHT THE WAY
Beacons of Ascension

Lives and teachings of forty of the world's greatest saints and spiritual beacons provide a blueprint for total self-realization. Guidance from masters. SOFTCOVER 258P.

$14⁹⁵ ISBN 0-929385-58-6

✦ Contents

1   Shirdi Sai Baba 1
2   Sri Rama and the Ramayana 9
3   Mahavira and Jainism..15
4   The Life and Teachings of Sri Sankara 19
5   Sri Ramakrishna: His Life and Teachings 23
6   The Holy Mother, Sri Saradamani Devi 27
7   The Life and Teachings of Swami Vivekananda 33
8   Paramahansa Yogananda and the Self-Realization Fellowship 39
9   Sri Anandamayi Ma, the Joy-Permeated Mother 47
10 Giri Bala, the Woman Who Never Ate 55
11 The Life and Teachings of Ramana Maharshi.......................................57
12 Swami Sivananda and the Divine Life Society 63
13 The Life and Teachings of Mahatma Gandhi 69
14 Swami Nityananda, Guru of Muktananda 77
15 Baba Muktananda and the Path of Siddha Yoga 85
16 The Life and Teachings of Buddha 93
17 Quan Yin, Bodhisattva of Compassion and Mercy 99
18 Tibetan Buddhism and the Dalai Lama...105
19 Lao-tzu and the Taoist Religion 115
20 Confucius and Confucianism 119
21 Hermes — Thoth and the Seven Great Universal Laws......................123
22 Akhenaton, the Egyptian Pharaoh 133
23 Orpheus, Founder of the Greek Mystery School 135
24 Pythagoras and Biosophy 139
25 Plato 147
26 Zoroaster, the Avatar of Persia 151
27 Mohammed and Islam 155
28 Kabir, Sublime Poet...163
29 Apollonius of Tyana 173
30 Appearances and Teachings of the Virgin Mary 179
31 Mother Teresa, Modern-Day Saint 191
32 Joseph Smith and the Mormon Religion 197

(continued on page 8)

(The Ascended Masters Light the Way continued from page 7)

33	Madam Blavatsky and the Theosophical Society	201
34	Colonel Henry S. Olcott and the Theosophical Society	213
35	C.W. Leadbeater and the Theosophical Society	223
36	Krishnamurti and the Theosophical Society	231
37	Count Saint Germain — the "Wonder Man" of Europe	239
38	The Sleeping Prophet: Edgar Cayce	245
39	Peace Pilgrim	249

◆ COSMIC ASCENSION
Your Cosmic Map Home

Almost all the books on the planet on the subject of ascension are written about planetary ascension. Now, because of the extraordinary times in which we live, cosmic ascension is available here on Earth! Learn about self-realization, evolvement of nations and more. SOFTCOVER 263P.

$14⁹⁵ ISBN 0-929385-99-3

◆ Contents

	Channeled introduction from Melchizedek, the Universal	xi
1	What Is Cosmic Ascension?	1
	The Initiations	1
	Cosmic Initiations	2
	Planetary Light-Quotient Ascension Process	2
	The Cosmic Light-Quotient Ascension Process	5
	The Soul and the Monad in the Ascension Process	8
	The Cosmic Monad and the Cosmic Soul	8
	Planetary and Cosmic Trinity	9
	Cosmic Monads	10
	Planetary Chakras	10
	Installation, Activation and Actualization	11
	Cosmic Chakras and the Ascension Process	12
	Planetary Bodies and the Ascension Process	17
	The Cosmic Bodies and Cosmic Ascension	19
	More Advanced Cosmic Bodies in the Ascension Process	24
	Cosmic Bodies and the Keys of Enoch	25
	The Twelve Strands of DNA and the Ascension Process	26
	Cosmic Light-Quotient Building Scale	27
	How to Make Progress on Your Cosmic Ascension	28

Dr. Joshua David Stone—Encyclopedia

2   Instructions for Utilizing the Planetary and Cosmic Ascension Seats 31
    Cosmic Ladder of Ascension Seats 31
    The Synthesis Ashram of Djwhal Khu..35
    The Love Seat of Sai Baba 36
    How to Use the Ascension Seats 36
    The Atomic Accelerator 37
    Anchoring of Ascension Seats 37
3   The Cosmic Rays 39
    Summation and a Few Shortcuts..45
4   Cosmic Evolution and the Organization of the Higher Mind 47
    Solar Activation 51
    Galactic Activation...53
    Universal Activation...54
    A Mind Map of Consciousness 56
    Dimensions of Consciousness 61
    Dimensional Spectrum of Consciousness 62
    The Eighth- and Ninth-Dimensional Levels 63
5   A Cosmic Day and a Cosmic Night 67
    More on Universal Evolution..74
    The Sacred Planets 82
    Sacred Planets and Their Rays 82
    The Nonsacred Planets and Their Rays 83
    A Footnote from Melchizedek 83
6   Ultimate Monadic Ascension: The Next Step...85
    Unification with Your Soul Extensions 85
    Ultimate Monadic Merger Prayer Request 88
    Walk-in Soul Extensions 89
    A Higher Level of the Ascension Process 89
7   The Importance of Integrating One's 144 Soul Extensions................................91
8   Self-Realization and the Issue of Accountability 99
9   Spiritual Leadership and World Service: The Next Step 107
10 Cosmic Golden Nuggets 111
    Cosmology of Ascended Teachers 111
    Communicating with the Masters 113
    Interviews with the Masters...114
    Cosmic Light-Quotient Building 115
    Cosmic and Planetary Light-Quotient Building 115
    The Great Central Sun Cosmology 116
    The Cosmic Council of Twelve Cosmology..116
    Activation of the Solar, Galactic and Universal Sun 117
    The Importance of Sending Light 117
    Becoming a Mystical Traveler 118
    Lightworkers and Physical Health Lessons 118
    Why Don't We Have Superhuman Abilities after Ascension? 122

(continued on page 10)

(*Cosmic Ascension* continued from page 9)

Loneliness and the Spiritual Path 123
Ganesha Ceremony 124
Our New Planetary Logos 125
Clearing the Seven Veils and the Twelve Veils 125
Cancer-Removal Activation 125
The Etheric Webbing 126
Atomic Bomb Testing 126
All Christed-Universes Activation 127
Strange Humming Sound in New Mexico 127
The Bermuda Triangle 127
Initiation Process for Fundamentalist Christians 129
The 64 Sacred Letter Grid of the DNA and RNA Activation 130
The Ban of Noninterference 130
An Expanded View of Projection 131
Misconceptions About Initiations and Ascension 132
The Six Types of Soul Incarnations 134
Spiritual Artery-Connection Activation 135
Soul-Braid Activation 136
Monadic Braid 136
The Issue of False Godliness 136
The Issue of Good and Bad 137
The Issue of Spiritual vs Egotistical Ambition 140
The Issue of Integrity and Your Word 142
Twilight Masters 143
Evolution Beyond the Seven Levels of Initiation 143
The Emerald Tablets 145

11 Past Lives of Some of the Well-known Ascended Masters 147
12 The Twelve Planetary Festivals 149
The Festival of the Christ (Easter) 150
The Festival of Wesak 150
The Festival of Humanity and Good Will 155
Summation 155
13 Comparative Overview of Eastern and Western Stages of Initiation 157
Step One: Waking Consciousness 158
Step Two: Sense Withdrawal 158
Step Three: Concentration 158
Step Four: Meditation 158
Step Five: Enstasis 158
The Nine Stages of Samadhi 159
Other Ideas on Samadhi 162
Summation 163
14 Planetary and Cosmic Discipleship 165
Little Chelaship 165
The Chela in the Light 166

DR. JOSHUA DAVID STONE—ENCYCLOPEDIA

	Accepted Discipleship	168
	The Chela on the Thread	169
	The Chela Within the Aura	170
	The Chela Within the Master's Heart	172
	Discipleship	172
15	Evolvement of Nations	177
	The Five Major Ideas Manifesting in the World Today	178
	First-Ray Influence in the World I	178
	Second-Ray Influence in the World Today	178
	Third-Ray's Affect on Humanity	179
	The Sixth and Seventh Rays' Influence in the World Today	180
	The Nations and Their Rays	182
	The Effect of the Incoming Rays	184
	Rays In and Out of Manifestation	184
	Major Cities and Their Rays	185
	Seventh-Ray's Effects on the Four Kingdoms	186
	What Causes the Differences among Disciples?	187
	The First Initiation and the Seventh Ray	187
	The Second Initiation and the Sixth Ray	188
	The Third Initiation and the Fifth Ray	188
	The Fourth Initiation and the Fourth Ray	189
	The Fifth Initiation and the First Ray	191
16	Cosmic Ascension Training	193
	Spiritual Training	193
	Ascension Activation Number One	194
	Ascension Activation Number Two	194
	Ascension Activation Number Three	194
	Ascension Activation Number Four	194
	The Christ/Buddha-Archetype-irnprinting Activation	194
	The Christ/Bucldha, Melchizedek Imprinting	195
	Christ/Buddha/Lord of Sirius/Melchizedek Imprint	195
	The Lord of Arcturus Wake-up Call	195
	Invocation of the Yod Spectrum	195
	Spiritual Mudra Exercise	196
	The Alchemical Marriage	197
	Cosmic-Cleansing Triangulation	198
	The Nine Levels of the Soul Mantra	199
	Paradigms of Body Systems	203
	The Planetary and Cosmic Ashrams and the Dimensions of Reality	204
	God's Ashrams and Dimensions of Reality	204
	Bodies and Dimensional Levels	204
	Chart of Our Bodies and Their Dimensional Levels	204
	Second Model for Cosmic Bodies and Dimensions	205
	Cosmic Bodies and Dimensions Chart	205

(continued on page 12)

(*Cosmic Ascension* continued from page 11)

Dimensions, Bodies, Chakras, Initiations and Light Quotient 205
Second Cosmic Model Breakdown of Dimensions, Bodies, Chakras,
    Initiations and Cosmic Light Quotient..206
Why Advanced Ascended-Master Abilities Are Slow to Develop 208
The Seamless Body of Golden Light 210
The Arcturian Light Chamber 212
Lord Michael's Sword of Clarity and Vision 212
Prana Wind-Clearing Device 212
Misconceptions about Ascension.....................................214
Command and Vow to Live in Harmony...............................223
The Externalization of the Hierarchy 223
The Issue of Using External Channels.................................226
Helios and Vesta's Solar Chamber 230
Atomic Structure Increase 230
My Favorite Clearing Tools 231
Cosmic Ascension Battleplan..233

17   Eighteen Great Cosmic Clearings.................................237
    1. Genetic-Line Clearing 237
    2. Past-Life Clearing...238
    3. Soul-Extension Clearing 238
    4. Archetypal Clearing 239
    5. Cosmic-Cellular Clearing 239
    6. Generalized Karma Clearing 239
    7. PhysicaWody Clearing.......................................240
    8. Emotional Desire and Astral-Body Clearing 240
    9. Mental-Body Clearing 240
    10. Etheric-Body Cleansing 240
    11. Core Fear Clearing..240
    12. Implants and Elementals 241
    13. Twelve-Body Clearing 241
    14. Fifty-Chakras Clearing....................................241
    15. Clearing Negative-Ray Influences 241
    16. Clearing Negative Astrological Influences................241
    17. Monadic Clearing..242
    18. Super Cosmic-Clearing Invocation 242
The Ultimate Divine Dispensation.................................243
Conclusion and Summation 244
Personal Summation of Cosmic Ascension Process 246
A Channeled Message from the Mahatma.........................250
A Message from Archangel Michael................................254
Channeled Concluding Message from Archangel Metatron 257

◆ A Beginner's Guide to the Path of Ascension

with Rev. Janna Shelly Parker

This volume covers the basics of ascension clearly and completely, from the spiritual hierarchy to the angels and star beings. Softcover 166p.

$14⁹⁵ ISBN 1-891824-02-3

Contents

1 Humanity As Spiritual Beings 1
  The Physical Body 1
  The Etheric Body 2
  The Astral Body 2
  The Mental Body 3
  Synopsis 3
  More on Our Spiritual Selves—the Higher Bodies 4
  The Monadic Body 4
  The Soul Body 5
  Reincarnation of the Bodies 5
  The Spiritual Realms or Planes 6
  The Etheric Realm 7
  The Astral Realm 8
  The Mental Realm 10
  The Buddhic Realm 11
  The Atmic Plane...12
  The Logoic Plane 13
  Conclusion...13
2 The Spiritual Hierarchy..15
  The Masters of the Hierarchy..15
  Younger Masters...17
  The Form of the Hierarchy 19
3 The Path of Initiation 21
  The Probationary Path..22
  The Accepted Disciple 23
  The First Initiation...24
  The Second Initiation..25

(continued on page 14)

ENCYCLOPEDIA—DR. JOSHUA DAVID STONE

(*A Beginner's Guide to the Path of Ascension* continued from page 13)

The Third Initiation 27
The Fourth Initiation 30
The Fifth Initiation 31
The Sixth Initiation 32
The Seventh Initiation 34
4   The Psychology of Ascension 39
Loving Self 40
Reprogramming Self to Self-Love...41
Self-Love Meditation 41
No Comparing or Competing 43
Chart of Comparisons 43
Chart of Competitions 44
Asking the Masters to Aid in the Self-Love Process 45
Technique for Healing Faulty Thinking..45
Owning Your Own Personal Power 46
Diffusing Others' Negativity...48
Conscious Control over the Subconscious Mind 50
Meditation for Reprogramming the Subconscious 51
The Marriage of Love and Will 53
The Divine Triad of Light, Love and Power (Will) 54
Conclusion 55
5   The Question of Karma 57
Karma as Motive 57
Karma as Lessons...58
Positive Karma 59
Judge Not, Lest You Judge in Error 60
An Esoteric Look at Karma 61
The Permanent Atoms 62
Devachan and the Buddhic Realms 63
The Lords of Karma and Other Karmic Overseers 65
Reincarnation and Karma 66
Group Karma 68
Impersonal Collective Karma...68
6   Opening to the Higher Senses 71
Sensing Unity with All Things..71
The Development of Intuition 73
Intuition's Place in Dreams 74
Developing Psychic Abilities 75
Channeling and Higher Telepathy 77
The Call to Channel..80
Energy Rushes 81
Sensing a Master 83
Hearing a Master 83
Seeing a Master 83

	The Sense of Pre-Vision	84
	Conclusion	87
7	The Practicality of the Ascension Process	89
	The Ascension Process Is in the Moment	89
	Relating to People through Spiritual Consciousness	92
	In the Corporate World	93
	Ascension and Relationships	94
	Ascension and the Family Unit	95
	Ascension in the World of the Artist	96
	The Artist As Cocreator with God	97
	Ascension and the Political Arena	98
	Summary	99
8	Thought and the Power of the Spoken Word	101
	Healing Words versus Harmful Words	101
	Gossip	102
	Other Negative Talk	103
	Being Vigilant	104
	Negative Thinking	104
	Healing Thoughts, Words and Sounds	105
	Om Meditation	105
	The Prayer of St. Francis	106
	Elohim/Yod He Vau He	106
	Holy Prayers of Various Religions	107
9	The Devic Line of Evolution	109
	Overview of the Angelic Hierarchy	110
	Tools for Protection from Negative Thought Forms	111
	Eliminating Negative Thought Forms	112
	Devas, Nature Spirits, Elementals and the Growing of a Flower	113
	The Elohim	113
	The Archangels	114
	The Angels	117
	Pan: The Overlighting Deva of the Nature Kingdom	118
	The Practicality of the Devic and Angelic Beings	119
	In Your Own Garden	120
	The Angelic/Human Interblending	120
10	Our Animal Brothers and Sisters	123
	The Wild Animals	123
	Our Pets and Domesticated Animals	124
	Emotions and Animals	124
	The Evolution of the Animal Kingdom	125
	Factors Determining Individualization	126
	The Psychological/Mind Connection Between Humans and Pets	126
	Final Comment on Our Animal Brothers	127
11	Our Brothers and Sisters of the Stars	129

(continued on page 16)

Encyclopedia—Dr. Joshua David Stone

(*A Beginner's Guide to the Path of Ascension* continued from page 15)

     The Evolution of Humanity and Our Space Brethren 130

     Why We Don't Often See the ETs 131

     The Arcturians 132

     The Pleiadians 132

     The Sirians 133

     The Hollow Earth...133

     The Negative Extraterrestrials 134

     Preventive Protection from Negative ETs 134

     The Ashtar Command 135

     Conclusion...136

12 The Many Lenses of Ascension...137

     The Lens of Light..137

     The Lens of Love 138

     Psychological Wisdom and Service 139

     Transcendence from Negative Ego to Christ Consciousness............................140

     Synthesis/Mahatma Consciousness 140

13 Synthesis and Integration 143

     The Fear-Matrix-Removal Program 144

     More on the Synthesis Ashram 145

     The Unity of Spiritual Paths and Religions 145

     Across the Great Divide of World Religions 146

     The Various Spiritual Paths 147

     Across the Great Divide of the Races..149

     Root Races 151

     The Healing and Integration within the Family Unit 152

     The Pulling-Away Period 153

     Inner- and Outer-Plane Forgiveness 153

     Journal-Processing for Forgiveness 154

     The Healing 155

     Affirmations 155

     Integrating Our Individual Rays and Astrological Signs 156

     The Rays..156

     Personal Integration..158

     Tools for Self-Integration and Creating Your Physical Body 158

     Understanding and Application of Journal and List 159

     Emotional-Body Integration...160

     Journal Affirmation List for the Emotional Self. 160

     Mental-Body Integration 162

     Total-Body Alignment and Integration Meditation 163

     Concluding Thoughts on Self-Integration..164

  About the Author 166

  About the Author 166

  Books Published by Light Technology 173

✦ Golden Keys to Ascension and Healing

Revelations of Sai Baba and the Ascended Masters

This book represents the wisdom of the ascended masters condensed into concise keys that serve as a spiritual guide. These 420 golden keys present the multitude of insights Dr. Stone has gleaned from his own background and his path to God realization. SOFTCOVER 205P.

14^{95} ISBN 1-891824-03-1

✦ Contents

Dedication to Sai Baba		vii
Preface		xi
Foreword		xiii
Introduction: My Personal Experiences with Sai Baba		xvii
1	Core Spiritual Principles	1
	Keys 1-53	
	Unconditional Love	2
	View All with the Christ Mind	4
	The Heart of Compassion: Recognize the Oneness of All Life	5
	Power	6
	Seek Only God	8
	Surrender and Detachment	9
	Self-Inquiry and Getting Right with Yourself	10
	Balance	14
	Service	16
	Live Life As a Spiritual Warrior	20
	Spiritual Vows	23
2	Healing from the Higher Dimensions	27
	Keys 54-76	
	Arcturian Technologies	28
Higher-Dimensional Healing Teams and Temples		31
Healing on All Levels		32
3	Evolution and Integration on All Levels	37
	Keys 77-118	
	Ascension	38
	Ascension Seats	41

(continued on page 18)

ENCYCLOPEDIA—DR. JOSHUA DAVID STONE

(*Golden Keys to Ascension and Healing* continued from page 17)

	The Chakras	42
	Evolving the Four-Body System	44
	Soul and Monad Evolution	47
	The Rays	49
	Higher Evolution	50
4	Inner-Plane Activations and Energies	53
	Keys 119-176	
	Light Packets	54
	The Tree of Life	55
	Language of Light, Sacred Geometry and Fire Codes	55
	Advanced Evolution of Your Bodies	56
	Metatron and the Evolution of Your Bodies	58
	Higher Bodies	59
	Cosmic Purification and Upgrading	60
	The Holy Spirit	61
	The Elohim	62
	Merging with Cosmic Beings and God	62
	Increasing the Power of Your Service	64
	Galaxies and Universes	65
	Advanced Ascension Seats	65
	Anchoring These Higher Energies	66
5	Manifestation: Principles and Practices	67
	Keys 177-221	
	Manifestation Prayers and Activations	68
	Working with the Subconscious Mind	69
	Guidelines for Prayer, Affirmation and Visualization	70
	Some Tools for Manifestation	73
	Special Help from the Masters	74
	From the Vantage Point of God	75
	Principles and Laws of Manifestation	78
	Attitudes for Manifestation	82
	Giving and Gratitude	85
	Karma	86
	Manifestation Stories	87
	The Power of Visualization	90
6	Anchoring Spirituality into Our Daily Lives	91
	Keys 222-267	
	Guidelines	92
	Love for the Earth and Her Creatures	94
	Mantras, Sound and Light	95
	Prayers of Protection and Clearing	96
	Meditation and Silence	97
	Specific Meditations	100
	Anchoring Higher Energies into Your Environment	101

(continued on page 20)

ENCYCLOPEDIA—DR. JOSHUA DAVID STONE

(*Golden Keys to Ascension and Healing* continued from page 19)

Keys 390-420
    Special Blessings and Energy Penetrations 176
    Light Infusions...176
    Love Infusions and Expansion of the Heart 177
    Energies from the Divine Mother 179
    Cosmic Activations 179
    Further Ascension Acceleration.......................................181
    Inner-Plane Healing 182
    Elevated Living...182
  Blessing and Benediction from the Ascended Masters 187
  Index to the Keys 195

◆ MANUAL FOR PLANETARY LEADERSHIP

Here at last is an indispensible book that has been urgently needed in these uncertain times. It lays out the guidelines for leadership in the world and in one's life. It serves as a reference manual for moral and spiritual living.
SOFTCOVER 283P.

$14⁹⁵ ISBN 1-891824-05-8

◆ Contents

  Introduction by Melchizedek xiii
1 Spiritual Leadership in the New Age 1
    Self-Leadership..1
    The Second Key Leadership Quality 2
    Spiritual vs. Egotistical Leadership 3
    Psychological Clarity 4
    Techniques for Owning Your Power 4
    One's Ego Structure 6
    Transcendence 6
    Three Classic Leadership Styles..7
    Our New Planetary Logos 7
    The Nature of Leadership in the Spiritual Hierarchy 9
    Knowing Your Proper Puzzle Piece 10
    Autocratic vs. Consensus Leadership 13
    Constructive Criticism...13

Impersonality 14
Boundaries 14
The Know-It-All..16
Mystics, Occultists and Manifesters...16
A Universal, Eclectic Focus 17
Sexuality..18
Projection 18
Personal Reflections and Colin Powell on Leadership 18
Leadership by Example 20
The Cancer of Ego 20
Cooperation 21
Soul Extensions 21
Initiation Level...22
The Pursuit of Excellence 22
Charisma 22
Intuition and Common Sense 23
Social Skills 23
The Ability to Sell Self 23
Money..24
Fame...25
Rewarding Team Members...26
Vision 26
Organization...26
Friendship 27
Feedback 27
The Ability to Change 27
Communication 27
Process and Goal Orientation 28
Creativity 28
Humor 28
Loyalty 29
Dealing with Egos 29
2   Laying the Foundation 31
Tools for Handling Political Issues 32
Tools for Handling the Business World 33
Tools for Handling the Arts 34
Tools for Handling the Scientific and Medical World 34
Tools for Handling the Judicial and Prison Systems 36
Self-Forgiveness 37
Conclusion..38
3   The Political, Social and Philosophical Issues of Our Time....................43
Leadership As It Manifests through the Seven Rays 43
Politics 44
Campaign Advertising 46

(continued on page 22)

ENCYCLOPEDIA—DR. JOSHUA DAVID STONE

(*Manual for Planetary Leadership* continued from page 21)

Political Spin 47
Voter Apathy 47
Free Elections...47
Reform of the Primaries...48
Polls 48
Push Polling 49
Entitlement Programs 49
Republicans vs. Democrats 49
Spiritual Education 49
Business, Finance, Trade and Economics 50
The Arts and Sociology 51
Religion 53
The Sciences...54
Traditional Western Medicine 55
Flu Vaccinations...58
Self-Leadership As a Patient...61
Scientific Research 61
Center for Disease Control 62
Our Judicial System 63
Our Criminal Justice System 68
Police Departments 69
The Prison System 71
Mass Media...73
The Education System 77
Government Workers...78
Care for the Elderly 79
The Welfare System 80
The Health-Care System 81
Medicare...89
Care for Veterans 90
The Homeless..91
Unemployment..92
Community 92
Hunger 95
Abortion...96
Euthanasia 96
The Space Program 97
The Death Penalty 98
War..98
Gun Control..101
Nuclear Bombs and Nuclear Energy 104
Extraterrestrials 105
Foreign Aid 106
The United Nations 106

DR. JOSHUA DAVID STONE—ENCYCLOPEDIA

Immigration 107
Environment and the World's Economy 107
Plastic Surgery 107
Isolationism vs. Internationalism...............108
Surrogate Mothers 109
The Fundamentalist Right 109
Ecological Concerns...............109
NAFTA 112
Voting 112
IQ Tests 116
AIDS Awareness 117
Recreational Drugs...............117
The Tobacco Industry 118
Cremation vs. Burials...............118
Halloween...............119
Taxes 119
Patriotism...............120
Feminism 120
Animal, Human and Godly Identification 120
Technology...............121
Pornography...............122
Sexual Harassment 122
Sports 123
Sport Hunting...............124
Earthly Law vs. Spiritual Law 126
Open Marriages 126
Affairs 127
Mixed-Race Marriages 127
The Political Independents 128
Child Abusers...............128
Advanced Ascended-Master Abilities...............128
The Government and Militia Groups 129
Death 133
The Superheroes of Our Children and Adults...............134
Our Credit-Card Society 135
Term Limits 135
Evolution vs. Creationism 136
Science and Religion 136
The Christian Right 137
Sex in the Media 138
Cults...............140
The Flat Tax...............143
Three Strikes and You're Out...............144
Campaign-Finance Reform 144

(continued on page 24)

(*Manual for Planetary Leadership* continued from page 23)

Legalized Drugs 145
Using Marijuana for Medical Purposes 145
Assignments 146
Flexibility 146
Circus Animals...146
Frog Dissection in Public Schools 147
Lobster Rights 147
Electroshock Therapy 147
The Minimum Wage 147
Gays in the Military 147
Politics and Perception 147
Divorce 148
Child and Spousal Abuse...149
Crime 150
Gangs 151
Veterans 153
Prostitution 154
The O.J. Simpson Trial and Verdict 156
Chain Letters 161
Pyramid Moneymaking Schemes..161
Governmental Cover-up of ETs' Existence 161
J.F.K. Assassination and Other Cover-ups 162
The Destruction of All Nuclear Weapons 163
China: Most Favored-Nation Status....................................164
Cloning/Genetic Engineering...165
CIA: Drug Sales to Finance Nicaraguan Rebels..................166
Social Commentary on the Word "Christmas" 166
Wearing Furs 167
Nuclear-Waste Disposal 167
The National Debt 168
Conclusion...169
4   The Ascended Masters' Perspective on Leadership 173
The Pressures of Leadership 174
Views on the Hierarchy 175
Stages of Leadership...183
The Ascension Buddy System 186
An Open-Ended Question 189
5   The Pursuit of Excellence..191
Praise 191
Listening...191
Goals 191
Visionaries and Manifesters 192
Being Attacked 193
Large Groups 194

DR. JOSHUA DAVID STONE—ENCYCLOPEDIA

(continued on page 26)

(*Manual for Planetary Leadership* continued from page 25)
Good Judgment 226
Saying No 227
Fostering a Sense of Accomplishment 228
Self-Knowledge...228
Leadership Must Be Earned 228
Building Relationships 229
Self-Motivation...229
How to Deal with Ego-Sensitive Personalities................................230
The Ability to Motivate 231
Conflict Resolution 231
Considerate Supervision 232
Benefits...232
Negative Manipulation vs. Clear Communication 233
Hard Work 233
Leadership Can Be Learned 234
Consistency 235
Task and Relationship Orientation 236
Leadership Dreams..236
Invocation and Prayer for Leadership 237

6   Leadership Gems...239
Bridging Traditional Religion and the Ascension Movement 239
The Leadership Role of the United States in the Global Community.............241
A Look at Russia and Other Aspects of Nations 242
The Bombing of Hiroshima and Nagasaki......................................245
Terrorism 247
The Olympics...248
Affirmative Action 251
Superstition 252
The Mayan Calendar 254
No Leader Is an Island unto Him/Herself 255
Another Look at Leadership within the New Age.............................256
Gossip..259
The Glamour of Words 260
The Glamour of the Ascended Master...262
The Glamour of Initiation 264

7   God's Law vs. Man's Law...269
Civil Laws and the Negative Ego 270
Freedom of Speech..271
Discernment..273
Challenging Authority 274
Time and the Shifting of Spiritual Law 275
Civil Law and the Awakened Soul/Spirit 278
Summation 278
Conclusion by the Mahatma 279

⑩ YOUR ASCENSION MISSION
Embracing Your Puzzle Piece
with REV. JANNA SHELLEY PARKER

This book shows how each person's puzzle piece is just as vital and necessary as any other. All aspects of living the fullest expression of your individuality. SOFTCOVER 249P.

$14⁹⁵ ISBN 1-891824-09-0

⑩ Contents

Introduction	ix
1 The Search for Your Puzzle Piece	1
A Purpose for Every Person under Heaven	1
Obstacles to the Search for Meaning	2
Be Wholistic in Your Approach	3
Being Willing	6
Clearing the Blocks between You and Your Mission	6
Meditating Your Way to Your Ascension Mission	7
Bigger Is Not Always Better	8
2 Using the Rays to Find and Embrace Your Ascension Mission	11
The Various Ray Colorings	12
Basic Ray Coloring and Tendencies	12
The Higher Rays	13
The Rays and Their Corresponding Professions	14
The Chohans of the Rays	14
The Glamour Trappings of the Rays	15
Ray Strengths	22
The Harmony of the Rays	25
3 The Planetary Ascended Masters and Their Divine Puzzle Pieces	27
Ray 1	27
Ray 2	30
The Reappearance of the Christ	30
Kuthumi and Djwhal Khul	32
Ray 3	33
Ray 4	35
Ray 5	38
Ray 6	40
Ray 7	42
4 The Spiritualization of All Puzzle Pieces	47

(continued on page 28)

ENCYCLOPEDIA—DR. JOSHUA DAVID STONE

(*Your Ascension Mission* continued from page 27)

    God Can Be Expressed in Any Career 47
    Seeing with the Eyes of the Negative Ego 47
    Seeing through the Christ Mind 48
    Connecting and Serving through Your God Attunement 48
    You Are Your Puzzle Piece 49
    The Little Things That Mean So Much 49
    Maintaining Your Spiritual Center...51
    You Don't Have to Be Perfect to Do Your Part 52
    Spiritualizing Your Puzzle Piece While Moving On 53
    Passing the Torch 54
    Your Puzzle Piece and Spiritual Peer Pressure............................55
5   Relationships, Puzzle Pieces and Ascension Missions 59
    Mates and Mission Mates...60
        Mission Mates 61
        Romantic Mates..63
        Romantic Relationships That Are Also Mission Mates.............64
        Mission Mate Marriages 66
    Group Relationships 67
    Spiritual Group Relationships 68
    Relationships That Push the Rules 70
    Relationships on the Soul and Monadic Levels 71
    The Relationship with Your Ascended-Master Lineage 74
    Your Relationship with God..76
6   Living Your Joy, Drifting with the River 79
    Joy 80
    Eliminating Misconceptions 82
    The Precious Moment 83
    Doing "Things" or Participating in Life Freely 85
    Integrating Joy into the Four Lower Bodies 86
    The Mental Body 86
    The Emotional Body 87
    The Etheric/Physical Vehicles 88
7   Blending the Puzzle Pieces of the Whole 91
    The Interrelating Roles of Our Solar System and Planet................92
    The Mission of the Angels 94
    The Nature Kingdom 96
    Dovetailing Earthly Puzzle Pieces 98
    Dovetailing in Spiritual Work 98
    The Expanding Puzzle Piece 101
8   The Glory and Glamour of Ascension 107
    The Dangers of Knowing Your Initiation Level...........................109
    Using Initiation Levels to Control Others 112
    Ascension Doesn't Make You Better Than, Just More Equal 113
    The Glamour of the Highest, Best, the Twin Flame etc. 116

DR. JOSHUA DAVID STONE—ENCYCLOPEDIA

	Using Ascension As a Means of Escape	118
	The Channeling Process and How Best to Avoid Its Glamours	121
	The Glamour of the Lightworker	123
9	Puzzle Pieces, Past Lives, Karma and Other Influences	127
	Karma and the Rays	127
	The Influence of Past Lives	128
	Intuiting Our Past to Help with the Present	129
	Trusting the Past Helps You with the Now	130
	Karma and Unfinished Business	131
	Unfinished Business with Self	131
	Unfinished Business with Family	133
	Unfinished Business with People You Work With	135
	Unfinished Business with Soul Mates and Romantic Relationships	138
	Our Special Past Life-Connection with the Masters	139
10	The 352 Levels of the Mahatma That Synthesize the Puzzle Pieces	145
	The Puzzle Piece of the Mahatma	145
	Calling on His Presence or Becoming a Walk-In	147
	Djwhal Khul and the Synthesis Ashram	149
	My Personal Mission of Synthesis	151
	The Harmony of Varying Puzzle Pieces	153
	Synthesis and Integration	155
	Tolerance versus Forgiveness	157
	Mahatma, Melchizedek and Metatron	159
11	Spiritual Etiquette	163
	Respecting Other Lightworkers' Puzzle Pieces and Boundaries	164
	Common Courtesy	166
	If You're Not Going to Do It, Don't Say You Will!	167
	Telepathy Is Not the Answer to Spiritual Etiquette	170
	Don't Bulldoze Your Way into Someone Else's Puzzle Piece	171
	Spiritual Competition versus Spiritual Cooperation	174
	Code of Ethics	177
	Spiritual Etiquette among the Hierarchy of the New Group of World Servers	178
12	Puzzle Pieces in Group Bodies	185
	Achieving the Maximum Potential of Group Consciousness	185
	Staying Aligned with Your Own Puzzle Piece	187
	Subtle Adjustments Help Keep Perfect Balance	189
	False Expectations of Another Person	193
	The Importance of Total Self-Love and Self-Acceptance	196
	Loving the Physical Body	198
	Loving the Emotional Body	199
	Loving the Lower Mental Bodies	201
	The Group Consciousness within the Ashrams of God	201
13	The Puzzle Piece of Being Human	205
	Personality	206

(continued on page 30)

(*Your Ascension Mission* continued from page 29)

What the Masters Mean by "You Are Only Human" 209
Love and Light Radiance 211
   Responsibilities to the Animal Kingdom 212
   The Devic Evolution 213
"Give Us This Day Our Daily Bread" 215
Human Intimacy 219
Representing the Divine in Manifestation 221
14 Puzzle Pieces in the Next Millennium 225
The Release of Ancient Wisdom 226
Downloading Information 227
In Service of the Golden Age 228
The True Purpose of Prophecy: To Change the Future 229
Positive Prophecy, a Tool for Divine Manifestation 231
Puzzle Pieces across the Board 234
We, the Masters 234
The Grace of the Violet Transmuting Flame 240
Conclusion 244

REVELATIONS OF A MELCHIZEDEK INITIATE

Dr. Stone's spiritual autobiography, beginning with his ascension initiation and progression into the 12th initiation. Filled with insights, tools and information. SOFTCOVER 306P.

14^{95} ISBN 1-891824-10-4

Contents

Foreword iii
Introduction by Melchizedek, the Universal Logos ..ix
1 The Order of Melchizedek 1
   The Order of Melchizedek and the Mahatma 3
   Unity 4
   The Age of Melchizedek 5
   Conclusion 7
2 My Actual Ascension 9
   Misconceptions about Ascension 12
3 Some Reflections on My Path of Ascension 15
4 My Experience of the Initiation Process 19
   Djwhal's Clarification about Initiations 22
5 Ascension and the Importance of Meditation 25
   Ascension Meditation Experiences 26
6 Golden Nuggets of Ascension 35
   My Inner-Plane Work 40

DR. JOSHUA DAVID STONE—ENCYCLOPEDIA

September 6 through September 12...41
The Comet Fragments Hitting Jupiter in July 1994 41
New Inner Spiritual Guidance Hot off the Press 42

7 My Meditations with the Core Group 47
The Sixth- and Seventh-Dimensional Chakra Grids 47
Our Next Session 50
The Following Week 52
Our Following Session..53
The Seventh-Dimensional Chakra Grid..54
Lenduce's Ashram 54
Our Next Meditation 57
Meditation Session, June 24, 1994 58
Meditation Session, July 2, 1994 58
Meditation Session, July 11, 1994 59
Meditation Session, July 13, 1994 60
Meditation Session, July 19, 1994 60
Meditation Session, July 29, 1994 61

8 The Completion of My Sixth Initiation and Ascension 63
Reflections on Completing My Ascension..65
More Reflections 67
Standing before Sanat Kumara...68
Meditation on August 5, 1994 71
Realizing and Completing My Sixth Initiation and Ascension 72
Meditation on August 8, 1994 74
Meditation on August 15, 1994 76
Meditation on August 19, 1994 77
My (Former) Wife's Dream on August 20 78
Saturday Night Meditation..79
Sunday Morning, August 21, 1994 80
Another Valuable Meditation 81
Meditation on August 21, 1994 81
Reflections 82
August 22, 1994 83

9 Taking My Seventh Initiation 85
A Second Meditation on August 23, 1994.......................................88
Meditation on August 24, 1994 91

10 The Process of Completing My Seventh Initiation...........................93
Meditation on August 31, 1994 93
Meditation on September 3, 1994 93
Meditation on September 4, 1994 94
Meditation on September 7, 1994 96
Wednesday Night Class, September 7, 1994 97
Meditation on September 11, 1994 97
Meditation on September 18, 1994 98

(continued on page 32)

ENCYCLOPEDIA—DR. JOSHUA DAVID STONE

(*Revelations of a Melchizedek Initiate* continued from page 31)

Meditation on September 18, 1994 99
Meditation on September 25, 1994 100
Meditation on October 1, 1994 101
Meditation on October 12, 1994 102
Meditation on October 16, 1994 102
Meditation on October 23, 1994 103
Meditation on October 30, 1994 105
Sai Baba Dreams 105
Meditation on November 13, 1994 106
Meditation on November 20, 1994 107
Meditation on November 27, 1994 109
Some Reflections on the Path 113
Meditation on December 11, 1994 114
Elohim-Scripture Meditation 114
The 12:12 Planetary-Ascension Activation 115
Meditation on December 20, 1994 117
Meditation on December 24, 1994 118
Meditation on December 30, 1994 119
Meditation on January 1, 1995 120
Meditation on January 2, 1995 120
Meditation on January 22, 1995 121
Ultimate Huna Prayer and Meditation...121
More Meditations..126
Learning to Live on Light Instead of Physical Food 127
The Next Installment 130
A Meditation on This Subject 131
Meditation on February 5, 1995 132
Meditation on March 3, 1995 134
A Meditation with Friends...136
A Meditation by Fax 137
Fax Letter...138
Huna Prayer 141
Meditation on March 8, 1995 141
Meditation on March 10, 1995 141
Meditation on March 16, 1995 143
Meditation on March 18, 1995 145
Meditation on March 22, 1995 149
Meditation on March 24, 1995 151

11 My Dream Process in Relation to Ascension 157
Sports Dreams 164
School Dreams 165
Dreams about Sanat Kumara 168
Dreams about Sai Baba..169

12 Wesak and the First Ascension Wave...173

Clarion Call to Lightworkers 173
Meditation before Wesak 176
The Wesak Festival, May 12–14, 1995 177
Mount Shasta Meditation..180
Meditation on May 21, 1995 182
Cosmic Meditation...183
May 23, 1995—Humanity's Mass Vote 185
Meditation on May 28, 1995 185
Meditation on June 1, 1995 188
Meditation on June 10, 1995 192
A Huna Prayer 193
The Zohar Body 194
The Cosmic Overself Body...194
Gematrian Body 195
The Adam Kadmon Body...195
The Epi-kinetic Body 195
The Eka Body 196
Meditation on June 15, 1995 196
Meditation on June 18, 1995 198
Meditation on June 24, 1995 203
A Huna Prayer 204
The Ascension Rosary 206
Global Healing Meditation and Training 206
Meditation on July 2, 1995 207
Ascension Tapes...212
Energy Evaluations 213
Meditation on July 8, 1995 213
My Melchizedek Dream 215
Meditation on July 12, 1995 216
Djwhal Khul Dream 217
Meditation on July 22, 1995 217
The Synthesis Ashram 218
The Four-Day Pow-Wow 219
Our Group-Bonding Ceremony 220
The Atomic Accelerator 224
Our Cosmic Ascension-Seat Journey..225
Visiting the Great White Lodge on Sirius 228
Our Subsequent Dreams 229
Our Journey to the Multiuniversal Ascension Seat 230
Going to the Source Ascension Seat 231
Group Consciousness and the Ascension Buddy System 233
Ascension-Activation Meditation...235
Our Arcturian Starship Meditation 236
Concluding Dream and Meditation 239
Lord Metatron Meditation 241

Encyclopedia—Dr. Joshua David Stone

(continued on page 34)
(*Revelations of a Melchizedek Initiate* continued from page 33)

Afterword of 1996-1997 245
  Wesak 1996 245
  Sai Baba Meditation 249
  Between 1996 and 1997 Wesak 250
  The Melchizedek Synthesis Light Academy & Ashram 250
  My Thirty-Volume Series 251
  Taking My Eleventh Initiation..252
  My God Ascension-Seat Experience 253
  God Ascension-Seat Anchoring 255
  Health Activations 255
  A Constant Energy Circulation by the Three M's 256
  A Series of God Experiences 256
  Melchizedek Anchoring..258
  Living on Light...258
  Cosmic Love Quotient and the Light Rods of God.....................259
  Huna Prayers 259
  An Exercise in Psychological Archetypal Personages 260
  Two New Ascension Seats 262
  The 1997 Wesak Ceremony..262
  Wesak 1997 263
  Wesak 1998 and 1999 265
  My Twelfth Initiation 265
  The Completion of My Twelfth Initiation 268
  A Final Note...269

Epilogue from Melchizedek 271
Appendix A; the 1997 Wesak Meditations 273
  Ultimate Cosmic-Ray Meditation...273
  God Ascension-Seat Meditation...276
  The 1997 Wesak Ceremony..279
  Special Ascension Activation 281
  Final Wesak Meditation 284
  Fifty-Point Cosmic Cleansing Meditation 286
  Ascension-Activation Meditation in the Golden Chamber of Melchizedek 289

Appendix B; New Meditations of 1998..293
  The Seven Levels of Initiation within the Great Pyramid 293
  Cosmic Ascension Activations in the Temple of God 296
  Updated Wesak Ceremony Meditation 299
  Ascension-Activation Meditation in the Golden Chamber of Melchizedek 302

◆ HOW TO TEACH ASCENSION CLASSES

This book serves as an ideal foundation for teaching ascension classes and presenting workshops. It covers an entire one-to two-year program of classes.

SOFTCOVER 135P.

$**14**$⁹⁵ ISBN 1-891824-15-5

◆ Contents

A Request from the Spiritual and Cosmic Hierarchy x
Introduction...xii
1   Opening and Closing Your Classes 1
     Opening a Class Session.......................................1
        1. Clearing Negative Energies: The Burning Pot 1
        2. Unifying the Group Energy: Holding Hands 2
        3. Establishing the Ascension Column and Pillar of Light............2
        4. Clearing with the Platinum Net 2
        5. Axiatonal Alignment...2
        6. The Ascension Flame 2
        7. Invoking the Spiritual and Cosmic Hierarchy 2
        8. The Soul and Monad Mantras.......................................2
        9. Michael's Golden Dome of Protection 3
        10. The Great Invocation 3
             Short Version 3
             Long Version 4
        11. Three Oms..5
        12. Optional Prayers 5
             The Lord's Prayer...5
             Prayer of Saint Francis...5
             Traditional Rosary 6
             A New Age Rosary..7
             The Affirmation of the Disciple...................................8
     Closing a Class Session 9
        1. Clearing with the Platinum Net 10
        2. Axiatonal Alignment..10
        3. Removing the Core-Fear Matrix....................................10
        4. Infusing Core Love and the Christ/Buddha Qualities 11
        5. The Soul and Monad Mantras.......................................11
        6. Visiting the Golden Chamber of Melchizedek 11
        7. Invoking a Golden Cylinder 12

(continued on page 36)

(*How to Teach Ascension Classes* continued from page 35)

        8. Invoking Galactic Healers and Healing Angels 12
        9. The Great Invocation 12
        10. Three Oms..12
        11. Prayer of Thanksgiving 12
      Social and Networking Time 12
2   Logistical Considerations 13
3   Mantras and Power Names of God..19
      Mantras from the Mystical Jewish Tradition 19
      Hindu Mantras 20
      Islamic Mantras 22
      Western Mantras 22
      Egyptian Mantras 22
      Christian Mantras 22
      Word Mantras..23
      The Tibetan Foundation Chakra Mantras 23
      Buddhist Mantras 23
4   Structuring Your Classes..25
      The Opening 25
      The Lesson 26
      The Meditation or Exercise 26
      Sharing 27
      The Closing 27
      Social and Networking Time and After 27
5   Ascension-Activation Meditations 31
      Personal Growth Meditations 31
        1. Cosmic-Ray Meditation 31
        2. Meditation in the Golden Chamber of Melchizedek 34
        3. Specialized Ascension Activations 37
        4. God Ascension Seat Meditation 39
        5. Fifty-Point Cosmic Cleansing Meditation 42
        6. Ascension Meditation and Treatment 45
        7. Divine Mother and Lady Masters Meditation and Activation 52
      World Service Meditations..56
        1. Planetary Axiatonal Alignment..56
        2. Platinum Net Sweep 57
        3. Meditation for the Earth Mother 57
        4. Political Hot Spots 57
        5. Social Issues 58
        6. Child and Spousal Abuse 59
        7. Invocation to the Healing Angels 60
        8. Invocation for Transitioning Souls 61
        9. Invocation to Liberate Earthbound Souls and Those Trapped in the Astral....62
        10. Invocation for Harmony between the Earth Kingdoms 63
        11. Removing the Core Fear from the Earth and Humanity 64

12. Connecting the Consciousness of Humanity with the Extraterrestrials to Prepare for Open Dialogue...65
13. Invoking a Golden Cylinder 66
14. Preserving the Rainforests and All Other Forests....................................67
15. Protecting Endangered Species and Treating Animals with Love 68
16. Removing Implants and Negative Elementals 69
17. Clearing All Interfering Astral Entities and Energies 71
18. Healing the Four Bodies of Planet Earth 71
19. Clearing All Planetary Illusion 72
20. Clearing Atmospheric Pollution and Repairing the Ozone Layer 73
21. Anchoring Earth's Monadic Blueprint 74
22. Invoking a Shower of Core Love and Core Light......................................75

6   Celebrating the Holy Days 77
    Wesak 77
    Introduction to the Wesak Festival 77
    Your Wesak Ceremony..80
    How to Structure Your Wesak Ceremony 81
    The Wesak Ceremony Meditation 81
    Djwhal Khul on the Wesak Celebration 83
    The Festival of the Christ 85
    Introduction to the Festival of the Christ 85
    Meditation for the Festival of the Christ 86
    The Festival of Humanity 87
    Introduction to the Festival of Humanity 87
    A Christmas Ceremony 89
    Easter 89
    Celebrating Thanksgiving 89
    Sai Baba's Birthday 90
    Full Moon Celebrations 91

7   132 Class Outlines 93
    Class 1   Removing the Core Fear Matrix 93
    Class 2   Working with the Twelve Planetary Rays 94
    Class 3   The Seven Levels of Initiation..94
    Class 4   Achieving Christ Consciousness...94
    Class 5   Soul Psychology Compared to Traditional Psychology 95
    Class 6   Owning Your Personal Power 95
    Class 7   Integrating the Three Minds and Four Bodies 95
    Class 8   Ascension Activation Class 96
    Class 9   How to Reprogram the Subconscious Mind 96
    Class 10 Glamour, Illusion, Maya 96
    Class 11 The Soul, Higher Self or the Oversoul 97
    Class 12 Golden Keys to Achieving Ascension in This Lifetime 97
    Class 13 How to Build Your Light and Love Quotient 97
    Class 14 The Golden Keys to Effective Romantic Relationships 98

(continued on page 38)

ENCYCLOPEDIA—DR. JOSHUA DAVID STONE

(*How to Teach Ascension Classes* continued from page 37)

Class 15   Working with the Ascension Seats 98
Class 16   Channeling Practice 98
Class 17   Mantras, Names of God and Power Words....................................99
Class 18   God and the Cosmic Hierarchy..99
Class 19   Building the Antakarana 100
Class 20   Death, Dying and the Science of the Bardo 100
Class 21   Understanding and Working with your Dreams...........................100
Class 22   An Esoteric Understanding of Sexuality 101
Class 23   Psychic Self-Defense 101
Class 24   The Twenty-Two Chakras 101
Class 25   Laws of Manifestation 102
Class 26   Laws of Karma..102
Class 27   Romantic Relationships from the Soul's Perspective 102
Class 28   Parenting the Inner Child 103
Class 29   Hypnosis and Self-Hypnosis 103
Class 30   The World's Religions 103
Class 31   The Story of Creation 103
Class 32   Between Lifetimes 104
Class 33   Lord Buddha and the Planetary Hierarchy 104
Class 34   The Mahatma 104
Class 35   The Melchizedek Priesthood...105
Class 36   Prophecies of Things to Come 105
Class 37   Hermes-Thoth and the Seven Great Universal Laws 105
Class 38   How to Open, Anchor and Activate the Fifty Chakras................105
Class 39   The Seven Paths to Higher Evolution...106
Class 40   Cosmic Ascension 106
Class 41   Extraterrestrials and Governmental Cover-ups 106
Class 42   The Hollow Earth 106
Class 43   The Angelic Hierarchy 107
Class 44   Pan and the Nature Spirits 107
Class 45   Initiation in the Great Pyramid..107
Class 46   Healing with Color and Sound 107
Class 47   The Twenty-Two Sacred Paths of Yoga 108
Class 48   Fundamentalist Christianity and Contamination of Negative Ego ..108
Class 49   The Kabbalistic Tree of Life 108
Class 50   Working with the Huna Prayers 108
Class 51   Working with the Arcturians 109
Class 52   Life and Teachings of Mahatma Gandhi 109
Class 53   Paramahansa Yogananda's Life and Teachings 110
Class 54   The Life and Teachings of Baba Muktananda 110
Class 55   A Course in Miracles...110
Class 56   The I AM Discourses of Saint Germain 111
Class 57   The Keys of Enoch 114
Class 58   The Urantia Book 114

DR. JOSHUA DAVID STONE—ENCYCLOPEDIA

Class 59   Babaji, the Yogi Christ..114
Class 60   The Galactic Core and the Cosmic Masters 115
Class 61   The Inbreath and Outbreath of Brahma 115
Class 62   The Life and Teachings of Buddha 115
Class 63   Shirdi Sai Baba...116
Class 64   Quan Yin, Bodhisattva of Compassion and Mercy 116
Class 65   The Virgin Mary 116
Class 66   Madam Blavatsky and the Theosophical Society 117
Class 67   The Sleeping Prophet: Edgar Cayce 117
Class 68   Saint Germain 117
Class 69   The Golden Key to Accelerating Your Spiritual Evolution.............118
Class 70   The Twenty-Four Dimensions of Reality 118
Class 71   The Ashtar Command...118
Class 72   The Huna Teachings 118
Class 73   The Science of Soul Travel 119
Class 74   Brahma, Vishnu and Shiva 119
Class 75   The Egyptian Mysteries..119
Class 76   The Bhagavad-Gita 119
Class 77   The Yoga Sutras of Patanjali 120
Class 78   The Vedas: God's Revelation 120
Class 79   The Essene Brotherhood 120
Class 80   Clearing Negative Implants and Negative Elementals 121
Class 81   Clearing Negative Ego through the Archetypes 121
Class 82   Clearing Negative Ego through Developing a Healthy
Psychoepistemology 121
Class 83   The Fifteen Major Tests of the Spiritual Path 121
Class 84   The Planetary Ascended Masters and Their Divine Puzzle Pieces 122
Class 85   What Is Cosmic Ascension?...122
Class 86   The Cosmic Rays...122
Class 87   How to Use Planetary and Cosmic Ascension Seats.......................123
Class 88   Self-Realization and the Issue of Accountability...............................123
Class 89   Spiritual Leadership and Planetary World Service 123
Class 90   Eighteen Great Cosmic Clearings 123
Class 91   Integrated Ascension...124
Class 92   Transcending Negative-Ego Archetypal Dualities.............................124
Class 93   Dr. Lorphan's Healing Academy on Sirius 124
Class 94   Developing an Optimal Physical, Psychological and Spiritual
Immune System...124
Class 95   Developing a Proper Relationship to the Inner Senses.....................125
Class 96   An Overview on Nonintegrated Ascension....................................125
Class 97   Twilight Masters, Cults and Nonintegrated Ascension Groups 125
Class 98   Ascension in the Many Kingdoms of God 126
Class 99   Deeper Explanation of the Eight Quotients and How to Use Them 126
Class 100   Seeing Life through a Single Lens Rather Than a Full-Spectrum

ENCYCLOPEDIA—DR. JOSHUA DAVID STONE

(*How to Teach Ascension Classes* continued from page 39)

Perspective 126
Class 101   Integrating the Seven Rays and Ray Types 127
Class 102   Channeling Your Subquotient Scores 127
Class 103   Clearing Negative Ego through the Rays 127
Class 104   Clearing Specific Diseases 127
Class 105   Psychological Causation of Disease 128
Class 106   The Search for Your Puzzle Piece 128
Class 107   Clearing Negative Ego through the Tree of Life 128
Class 108   The Transcendence of Negative Ego and the Science of the Bardo 129
Class 109   The Glamour of Ascension 129
Class 110   Cosmic Evolution and the Mapping of the Higher Mind 129
Class 111   A Cosmic Day and a Cosmic Night 129
Class 112   Ultimate Monadic Ascension: The Next Step 130
Class 113   Integrating and Cleansing One's 144 Soul Extensions 130
Class 114   Comparative Overview of Eastern and Western Stages of Initiation
and Meditation 130
Class 115   Planetary and Cosmic Discipleship 131
Class 116   Evolvement of Nations 131
Class 117   Past Lives of Some Well-Known Ascended Masters 131
Class 118   Cosmic Ascension Training 131
Class 119   Synthesis and Integration 132
Class 120   The Practicality of the Ascension Process 132
Class 121   Our Animal Brothers and Sisters 132
Class 122   The True Meaning of Marriage 132
Class 123   Our Brothers and Sisters of the Stars 133
Class 124   The Many Lenses of Ascension 133
Class 125   Finding Your Spiritual Mate 133
Class 126   God, the Consummate Union 133
Class 127   Living Your Joy 134
Class 128   Puzzle Pieces and the 352 Levels of the Mahatma 134
Class 129   Spiritual Etiquette 134
Class 130   The Spiritualization of All Puzzle Pieces 134
Class 131   Relationships, Puzzle Pieces and Ascension Missions 135
Class 132   Blending the Puzzle Pieces 135

◆ 13 ASCENSION AND ROMANTIC RELATIONSHIPS

with Rev. Janna Shelley Parker

Inspired by Djwhal Khul, Dr. Stone has written a unique book about relationships from the perspective of the soul and monad rather than just the personality. This presents a broader picture of the problems and common traps of romantic relationships and offers much deeper advice. SOFTCOVER 184P.

$14⁹⁵ ISBN 1-891824-16-3

◆ 13 Contents

Preface..xii
Introduction..xiii
1 Finding Your Mate 1
   "Seek and Ye Shall Find" 1
   The Four Lower Bodies 4
   Your Physical Appearance 5
   Your Emotional Appearance 7
   Your Mental Appearance 7
   Summary 8
2 Bonding Patterns...9
   The Balance within Self 9
   The Balance within the Relationship 9
   The Controller and the Controlled 10
   The Artist and Caretaker Trap 11
   The Occultist and the Mystic...13
   The Businesswoman and the House Husband.........................16
   Relationships with the Same Sex 18
   The Interracial Partnership 19
   Summary 19
3 Unconditional Love and Commitment.......................................21
   Unconditional Love of Self 21
   Never Use Love as a Weapon..22
   Remaining Unconditionally Loving During Severe Testing....24
   Unconditional Daily Living 25
   Commitment 27

(continued on page 42)

Encyclopedia—Dr. Joshua David Stone

(*Ascension and Romantic Relationships* continued from page 41)

	Forgiveness through Acceptance	27
	When Forgiveness is Truly Necessary	29
4	Competition and the Path of Ascension	31
	Doing Our Personal Best	31
	Spiritual Support vs. Spiritual Competition	31
	Fame and Recognition in the Spiritual Arena	32
	Success in the Marketplace	34
	Competition between Couples in the Same Line of Work	36
5	Our Sexual Selves	39
	The Emotional Level	41
	The Mental Level	41
	The Spiritual Level	44
	Pleasing Your Partner	44
	Sex and Fun	45
	Soul Passion and the Lightworker	46
6	The Differing Elevator Syndrome:	49
	Being on the Path of Ascension When Your Partner Is Not	49
	"Judge Not, Lest Ye Be Judged"	50
	When Your Elevators Are at Opposite Ends of the Spectrum	51
	Choosing to Stay Together	52
7	In Search of Your Soulmate: The Deeper Meaning	55
	Soulmates and Twin Flames	56
	Mission Mates	58
	Monadic Mates	59
	Group Monadic Mates	60
	Sex on the Inner Planes	60
	The Astral Realm	61
	The Mental Realm	62
	The Causal (Buddhic) Realm	63
	The Atmic and Monadic Realms	64
	The Logoic Realm	65
	Merging with the Master	66
	Bodies of the Masters	67
	The Unique Accounts of Saint Germain	67
	Splitting of Souls and Oversouls	68
	Your Pet Mate	69
8	Spiritual Parenting	71
	Choosing Your Parents	71
	The Power of Parental Programming	72
	The Importance of Self-Parenting	73
	Parenting Our Children	74
	Parenting the Infant	76
	Parenting Your Unborn Child	76
	Abortion	77

Late-Term Abortion 78
Prebirth Environment and Communication 79
Birthing in Water and Welcoming with Love 81
An Esoteric View of the Birth Process 82
Birth Bardo 82
Past-Life Effect on Infant and Parents 83
The Permanent Atoms 84
The Blank-Slate Theory 85
It Takes a Village 85
The Hierarchy's View on Spanking 86
Letting Go of Parenting Roles 86
The Mother/Son or Father/Daughter Relationship in Couples 88
God, the Ultimate Parent 88

9   The True Meaning of Marriage 91
Making a Commitment 91
Gay Marriages 91
"For Better or for Worse" 92
When a Relationship Ends 94
When Divorce is the Best Option 94
Recommitting to the Commitment 95
The Sexual Bond 97

10   God, the Consummate Union..99
Ecstasy 99
Lost in Love, Found in Love 101
The Marriage of Minds 102
Taking Time Alone 103
Your Alone Time Together 105
Experiences That Accompany Your Changing Frequencies 105
Other Symptoms of Spiritual Acceleration 107
Safe in God's Love and Light 108

11   Living the Spiritual Life Together 111
Maintaining Your Balance 111
Balance within the Relationship 112
Balancing the Extremes 115
Affairs vs. Communication 117
Stopping an Affair at the Mental Level 119
Affairs and Soul/Monadic Connections 121
Affairs of the Lower Nature 122
Living Together 123
The Traditional Way..126
Prenuptial Agreements..127
The Hierarchy's View of Multiple Spouses..128
The Effect of AIDS and other Sexually Transmitted Diseases 129
Celibacy and Marriage 132

(continued on page 44)

(continued on page 46)